FOREIGNERS IN MIKADOLAND

FOREIGNERS IN MIKADOLAND

by

HAROLD S. WILLIAMS

Decorations by
Jean Williams

CHARLES E. TUTTLE COMPANY
Rutland, Vermont & Tokyo, Japan

Representatives
Continental Europe: BOXERBOOKS, INC., *Zurich*
British Isles: PRENTICE-HALL INTERNATIONAL, INC., *London*
Australasia: PAUL FLESCH & CO., PTY. LTD., *Melbourne*
Canada: M. G. HURTIG LTD., *Edmonton*

Published by the Charles E. Tuttle Company, Inc.
of Rutland, Vermont & Tokyo, Japan
with editorial offices at
Suido 1-chome, 2-6, Bunkyo-ku, Tokyo, Japan

© *1963 by Charles E. Tuttle Co., Inc.*

Library of Congress Catalog Card No. 63-19394

International Standard Book No. 0-8048-1049-4

First edition, 1963
First paperback edition, 1972

0221-000296-4615
PRINTED IN JAPAN

"I cannot cease from praising these Japanese. They are truly the delight of my heart."

St. Francis Xavier, 1549.

"The people are all white, courteous and highly civilized, so much so that they surpass all the other known races of the world .... On the other hand they are the most false and treacherous people of any known in the world, for from childhood they are taught never to reveal their hearts .... They are likewise so poor that it is amazing thing to see with how little even kings and lords can sustain themselves."

From letter written by Jesuit Alessandro Valignano, 1580.

"Japonia may be said to be, as it were a bodye of many and sundry Ilandes, of all sorts and bignesse; which Iles, as they are separated in situation from the rest of the whole worlde, so are they, in like manner, inhabited by people most different from all others, both for manners and customes."

The Kingdom of Japonia
(From the Hakluyt Collection, 1616).

"Bold ... heroic ... revengeful ... desirous of fame ... very industrious and enured to hardship ... great lovers of civility and good manners, and very nice in keeping themselves, their cloaths and houses, clean and neat ..."

Dr. Engelbert Kaempfer, 1692.

"Japan is the England of Asia, because of their strength of will, independence of spirit and dogged attachment to existing institutions."

Histoire du Christianisme dans l'Empire du Japon,
by Father Charlevoix, 1715.

"It is lamentable that so much ignorance should prevail as to the evidence of the two fundamental doctrines that Japan is the country of the gods and her inhabitants the descendants of the gods."

Summary of the Ancient Way—Hirata Atsutane, 1811.

7

"The gentlemen of Japan were most polite and courteous, conducting themselves with refined and polished urbanity; and exhibiting in their actions a dignified and respectful demeanour that put to shame the ill-breeding of the seamen who ventured to laugh at them."

> *Voyage of H.M.S. "Samarang",*
> by Captain Sir Edward Belcher, 1848.

"What a country of verdure and shade is Japan; what an unlooked for Eden."

> *Madame Chrysanthème,* Pierre Loti, 1887.

"It has been said with reason that in no country of the world do 'les petits cadeaux qui entretiennent l'amitié' play a more charming part than in Japan. On the other hand the Japanese, no less than the Greeks of old, are often most to be dreaded when bearing gifts."

> James Murdoch, *History of Japan,* 1922.

"At times the Japanese show themselves the most aesthetic people in the world; at others they emerge as the least aesthetic."

> *The World of Dew,* D. J. Enright, 1956.

PREFACE

This is an account of life in the foreign communities and former Foreign Settlements or Concessions in Japan, and of the social contacts of the foreigners (*gaijin*) with the Japanese among whom they lived. It is written in the form of a series of chapters, each woven around some of the happenings and personalities of those times.

It tells of the impostors, the eccentrics, and the scandals, no less than the achievements of the scholars, the merchants, and the diplomats who contributed so much to the development of modern Japan. It is believed to be historically accurate in every detail.

It is hoped that no dreadful mistakes have passed unnoticed—none such as that made by Mrs. Julia D. Carrothers in her book—now a costly rarity—*The Sunrise Kingdom* published by the Presbyterian Board of Publication, Philadelphia, 1879, wherein she described seven years of missionary life in Japan from her arrival there in 1869. Included among many innocent illustrations depicting *"life and scenes in Japan and woman's work for woman there"* is one of a scene of jollity, described as a "Japanese hotel." By some dreadful mistake it is in fact an interesting

9

picture of *oiran* entertaining their male guests in the Shinagawa licenced quarters!

An explanation of the title *Foreigners in Mikado-land,* or *gaijin* as we are known to the Japanese, may be necessary for those not familiar with Japan.

Fosco Maraini in his book *Meeting with Japan* wrote: *"Before the war 'gaijin' was a term highly charged with feeling for the Japanese, inspiring on the one hand admiration, envy, curiosity, even servility, and on the other hatred, suspicion and contempt."*

That was true enough, but in post-war Japan, *gaijin,* literally "a person from outside," is now freely used in the latter sense only by Japanese when referring to us, and is frequently used by we foreigners when referring to ourselves. It is not normally used by the Japanese when alluding to the Chinese or Koreans, where special words are mostly used, and so it now normally has the meaning of "Occidentals," rather than "non-Japanese."

For simplicity in story-telling when speaking of Chinese (who have always comprised a large, if not the largest, group in the foreign communities) I have generally referred to them as such, although logically they are *gaijin* or "foreigners."

The word "Mikado" was used by the Japanese officials, when speaking to the early foreign arrivals about their sovereign, and so the word came to be generally accepted during the latter half of the last century in foreign circles, in and outside of Japan.

The Japanese, however, developed the habit, especially after the Restoration of 1868, of using the Chinese titles *Tenshi* (Son of Heaven) or *Tenno*

Preface

(Heavenly Emperor), the designation of which titles, according to the official translations of public documents into English, is "Emperor." The latter word then gradually took the place of "Mikado" in foreign circles.

The old term "Mikado," although one of high respect and distinctly Japanese, has fallen into disuse, both among foreigners and Japanese. It is now even omitted from concise Japanese dictionaries, although the word is firmly established in English and American dictionaries.

"Mikadoland," a fanciful term, meaning Japan, although a common enough expression in some circles half a century ago, and during the period covered by this book, is never used, and rarely seen, nowadays.

Japanese words have been avoided as much as possible. Even the word *jinrikisha* has been used sparingly; instead I have generally used "rickshaw," or one other of the Anglicised forms which seemed to fit best the time and case. Most foreigners in the Settlements used the word "rickshaw."

Although Japanese nouns have no plural form, I have for the convenience of non-Japanese readers and for clarity of meaning, in some instances such as *Shogun* and *Tokugawa*, treated them as subject to English laws of grammar, and used a plural form of *Shoguns* and *Tokugawas*.

Japanese words have been reproduced according to the Hepburn System, the form familiar to most foreigners, such for example as *jujutsu* and *Fuji*. Few foreigners recognize the same words when reproduced according to the Japanese official system as *Zyuzyutu* and *Huzi*.

11

Preface

The chapters are arranged as nearly as possible in chronological order. As each deals with some separate personality or incident, during the period since foreigners first came to Japan, some of the same ground has of necessity to be travelled over in several of the stories.

Grateful acknowledgements are made to my wife for the decorations, and to numerous friends who have made available to me records concerning various Shades of the Past.

H. S. WILLIAMS

Shioya, Japan

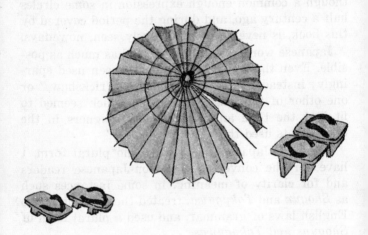

CONTENTS

Contents

ILLUSTRATIONS

(Following page 144)

PLATE I. Charles Longfellow (on left) son of the American poet, Henry Wadsworth Longfellow, riding in a *kago* whilst touring Japan in the early 1870's. Note the *kago* bearers are clad only in loin cloths; some have towels wound around their heads. See chapter, "Those Very Queer Japanese."

PLATE II. A street scene in a Japanese town in the 1870's. Children playing hop-scotch. See Note 1 re "The Disappointed Rev. Wilton Hack."

PLATE III. View of Yokohama Foreign Settlement, looking along Water Street. Drawn by C. B. Bernard in 1882. The two-storied building on the right was the office of the Pacific Mail Steamship Co. at No. 4, followed by No. 3; then Walsh Hall & Co. at No. 2, later the site of the Hongkong & Shanghai Banking Corp. At the end, on the right, was Ichiban (No. 1) Jardine Matheson & Co. In the foreground on the left, chests of tea, destined for Chicago, are being loaded onto a hand cart. A *taipan* can be seen riding in a *jinrikisha*.

PLATE IV. Main Street (Honcho-dori) in the

former Foreign Settlement of Yokohama, in the 1890's, showing the Bluff in the background.

PLATE V. Grand Hotel, Yokohama, in early 1890's. See chapter, "Those Very Queer Japanese."

PLATE VI. Nagasaki harbour about 80 years ago. Inasa, or Russian Village, is across the harbour, left of centre. See chapter, "The Wild Oats of the Grand Duke Alexander."

PLATE VII. One of the streets in the Yoshiwara licenced quarters in Tokyo, in the 1890's. This section of Tokyo at that time contained some of the most costly private dwellings in Japan, and was a small town in itself, occupied entirely by the demimonde. The quarters were completely destroyed in the earthquake of 1923. Licenced prostitution was abolished throughout Japan in 1957.

PLATE VIII. View of Ueno Park, Tokyo, during cherry blossom season, from drawing by C. B. Bernard in 1895.

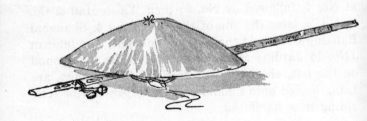

FOREIGNERS IN MIKADOLAND

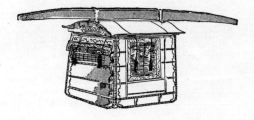

HISTORICAL FOREWORD

> *About the month of April, 1547,
> I fell in with a Portuguese mer-
> chant, a man of exceeding piety
> and veracity, who talked to me
> unceasingly of the great islands of
> Japan, lately discovered. It seems
> that the Christian religion might
> prosper better there than in any
> other region of the Indies, since
> the people are of inquiring minds
> eager for enlightenment beyond
> any upon earth.*
>
> Letter of Francis Xavier, 1549.

Although Japan's commercial and cultural contacts
with China and Korea went back to ancient times,
the story of Westerners in Japan, commenced with
the arrival of the Portuguese in 1542 and the con-
sequent introduction of Christianity. The new religion at first gained many converts, until it came to be
regarded by the authorities as a disruptive element
in Japan's social system. It was then forced under-
ground with persecution and merciless massacres.

The Spanish, many of whom were priests and missionaries, followed the Portuguese. Then came the
Dutch in 1600, but nine years were to elapse before
they set up a branch of their East India Company.
In 1613, the English East India House established a
trading post in Hirado, a small island off Kyushu in

19

southern Japan. However, after ten years of unprofitable trading they closed down and departed.

Persecution of Christians increased in violence. Families were wiped out, or divided, and the surviving members sent into exile. Christianity was crushed, and in the years that followed was driven almost out of remembrance. Only in a comparatively few families and in a few isolated hamlets, where for over two centuries the people succeeded in clinging to their faith and worshipping in secret, despite the unceasing effort of the authorities to stamp it out, did any vestige of Christianity remain.

The Spaniards were the first to be deported, followed by the Portuguese who were expelled in 1639. Shortly afterwards Japan decided to isolate herself from the Western World, by closing all her ports, except Nagasaki, to the entry of foreigners, and by forbidding her own nationals, under penalty of death, to leave Japan.

The Dutch alone of all the Europeans were allowed to remain, but were compelled to move from Hirado to Deshima, a small island in Nagasaki harbour, where they were given a monopoly of Japan's overseas trade—other than that carried on with China through the Chinese merchants—although under restrictions that were not much different from imprisonment.

Then, with the exception of that Chinese and Dutch trade, on a limited and controlled scale, and apart from the trickle of knowledge which entered through Nagasaki in a clandestine manner, Japan remained more or less isolated from the rest of the world for more than two centuries.

This was the period when the Tokugawa Shogunate controlled Japan from their strongholds in Yedo (now Tokyo) and Osaka, whilst the emperors were kept cooped up in Kyoto, without political power, and often short of funds, leading aimless lives in a setting of petty Court intrigues, love-making, and endless trivialities.

The Shogun was a military dictator, or, as was more usually the case, the hereditary and nominal head of the dictatorship which his family, or clan, maintained over the whole country. The Tokugawa Shogunate was more powerful than any of its predecessors had been, and held the country in subjection for over two hundred and fifty years.

However, those centuries, known as the Tokugawa era, were mostly years of peace for Japan, years during which the civilization and culture of Japan stood still at its then high level, years when European philosophers and scholars were making great progress in scientific discoveries, but years also when the countries of Europe were racked with constant wars.

During those decades, when Japan held the Christian world at bay, only Dutchmen and Chinese traded in Nagasaki, formerly the centre of Christianity in Japan—a place where friars had preached and martyrs, both Japanese and foreigners, had died for their faith. Those years of peace cost Japan dearly, because during that period of isolation she turned more and more to China. She continued to steep herself in Chinese philosophy, culture, and science, from which crushing handicap she had to unlearn herself when she finally was compelled to open her doors and

21

when she decided, with characteristic enthusiasm, to throw over the past and imitate the ways of the West.

Whether Japan paid too high a price for those years of isolation and peace is a subject which scholars will continue to argue about.

Although years of peace for Japan, during which she was spared the losses arising from wars, nevertheless the economy of the country had grown steadily worse. Having cut herself off from most foreign trade, production was at a low ebb and she was yearly becoming poorer. Retainers and clansmen, that is to say the samurai class, could only be paid in rice for their services, although they were seldom worth even that. As a class they were doing little and producing nothing. The commoners were mostly living close to poverty, which inured them to hardship. Only the usurers and the merchants were unobtrusively growing wealthier, and laying the foundations upon which would be built some of the great trading companies of modern Japan.

Towards the end of the period of isolation the country was almost in a state of collapse.

In 1854, Commodore Perry succeeded, where others had failed, in forcing Japan to abandon her isolation and open her doors to the Western World. A number of Occidental Powers thereupon concluded treaties with Japan, in consequence of which the ports of Nagasaki, Yokohama, and Hakodate were opened to foreign trade in 1859. Kobe, Osaka, Tokyo, and Niigata were opened later.

The foreigners resided in those ports—known as treaty ports — under extra-territorial conditions, whereby they were subject to the laws of their own

country, and not those of Japan. That condition was
written into the treaties because Japan then was still
a feudal country and the system of justice—with tor-
ture and summary executions—was still that of the
feudal ages. The foreigners lived and carried on trade
in special areas, known as the Foreign Concessions
or Foreign Settlements, and so began the Settlement
days of Japan, some phases of which are described
in this book.

The decade or so which followed Perry's arrival,
marked the awakening of Japan.

In 1868, a number of the powerful clans succeeded
in overthrowing the Tokugawa forces, whereupon the
Emperor was restored to his full authority, and took
up his residence in the castle of the Tokugawa Shoguns in Yedo, which from that time became known
as "Tokyo," or Eastern Capital. Then followed a period of development, the like of which has seldom
been seen.

By 1894 Japan had changed from a feudal country
into a nation impatient to take its place among the
great powers of the Western World. In that year
Great Britain, soon to be followed by other powers,
agreed to a revision of the old treaties, and to an
abolition of extraterritoriality to take effect five years
later in 1899, at which time foreigners living in
Japan became subject to Japanese jurisdiction.

Some of the stories of those colourful days of the
Foreign Settlements were told in my previous books
—*Tales of the Foreign Settlements in Japan* and
Shades of the Past. Others are related in the pages
which follow.

23

AN EARLY
ENVOY
FROM
RUSSIA

*Our countrymen wish to carry on
no commerce with foreign lands,
for we know no want of necessary
things . . .*

Japanese official warning to
Russians, 1813.

During the two and a half centuries or so when
Japan had shut herself off from the west, many Europeans from time to time had landed on her shores
either as castaways from shipwrecked vessels, as
evangelists hoping to propagate their faith, or as
adventurers attempting to establish trading or political contacts. Invariably they were soon apprehended
and were then often treated in a most outrageous
manner, as is only too well recorded, although not
more severely than was laid down by the laws of the
country at that time. But it is equally true that in
some cases the Japanese captors with strict regard
for their duty, carried out the law with all the severity and cruelty demanded of them, but, at the same
time whilst doing so, attempted to ameliorate the
suffering of their captives by acts of exceptional
kindness.

There was the strange case of the Russian naval
officer, Captain Golownin, who in 1811 was sent on a
mission to survey the Kurile Islands. When he ap-

proached the coast of Kunashiri, the island next to Hokkaido and the most southerly of the Kuriles, he saw the warning fires blazing on the mountain tops, a signal to the inhabitants that a foreign vessel was in the vicinity and to prepare to repel all who might attempt to land. Furthermore he was fired upon by shore batteries—clear evidence that he was not welcome.

Nevertheless he anchored off shore and attempted to communicate with the Japanese in the following novel manner:

"I imagined that by means of signs I might make myself understood by the Japanese. For this purpose I caused a cask to be sawed in two, and set both parts afloat in the water in front of the town. In the inside of one half of the cask were placed a glass containing fresh water, a piece of wood, and a handful of rice, to denote that we were in want of these articles; the other half contained a few piastres, a piece of yellow cloth, and some crystal beads and pearls, meaning thereby to intimate that we would give them either money or other articles in exchange for provisions."[1]

The reply which the Japanese sent back, in the same casks, consisted of a Japanese letter, which however the Russians could not read, and several sketches which indicated that the Russians would be fired on if they attempted to land. Despite this warning, Golownin insisted upon going ashore and making contact with them.

The Japanese then invited the Russians into their fort, an invitation which the credulous Golownin accepted. The conference which ensued carried on until such time as the tide had receded and left the Russians' shore-boat stranded in the mud. With all means of retreat thus cut off, the Russians, comprising Golownin and his seven companions, were thereupon made prisoners. Under the laws of Japan of those days they were criminals for having dared to land on her shores, and as such they had to be transported to the nearest castle town for examination and trial.

They were therefore trussed up in the manner of criminals. Their arms were tightly bound behind their backs, and the cords were then looped around their necks in such a way that by pulling on the cords their captors could tighten the noose about their necks to a point of strangulation.

Then commenced a long painful march of more than a month's duration. In all they tramped considerably over five hundred miles. At first down the length of Kunashiri, then across the straits by ferry, and then down the whole length of Hokkaido to Hakodate. At times their bindings were so tight that they cut into the flesh and their faces became swollen and discoloured. When they fainted they were revived and the march pressed on. Yet, on the other hand, when at times the gnats and flies tortured the bound men, their captors stood constantly near, and fanned them with boughs of shrubs to drive away the insects.

The Japanese did what they could to relieve their sufferings. When the bandages about their limbs became hard with blood and purulent matter, they massaged them and bathed their feet in warm water with salt. During the march the prisoners were given exactly the same food as their escort, but in addition they were allowed to accept gifts of extra food and refreshments from the villagers who took pity on their sad plight, all of which their guards permitted and indeed encouraged.

The severity of their bondage during the month's march was barbarous, yet, at the same time, was accompanied by so many acts of kindness and consideration that it became evident to Golownin their treatment was dictated by a strict interpretation of orders, that the prisoners should not be allowed to escape or commit suicide, rather than any desire to inflict cruelty. The fact that, after arrival at their journey's end, they did escape into the mountains for a period of seven days when their bonds had been untied, could be advanced as an argument that their cruel bondage was justified.

After their arrival at Hakodate and later at Matsumae (now known as Fukuyama) their bonds were removed. Although then confined in prison, life became more bearable. For weeks on end they were visited daily by officials whose duty it was to interrogate them. However, as the interrogators had little real knowledge of the Russian language, their questionings were often farcical. But there were more welcome visitors. Japanese men of learning, who were anxious to further their knowledge of foreign languages and the sciences, were permitted to visit them. Then there was a most agreeable young Japanese linguist whom they were required to instruct in the Russian language. He proved a most adept pupil, and with their aid translated into Japanese a Russian treatise on vaccination.[2]

Another visitor was a man of science who possessed an English sextant, a compass, and a case of mathematical instruments. He was anxious to make lunar observations, but was disappointed to find that the Russian officers did not have in their baggage the necessary mathematical tables to enable them to instruct him, and to his disgust he found that the Russian sailors were of no help because they could neither read nor write. With the assistance of the officers, he did however succeed in translating into Japanese a Russian schoolbook on arithmetic which had found its way into Japan at a much earlier date. A physician visited them daily ostensibly to attend to their ills, but also to further his knowledge of the world which lay beyond the closed doors of Japan.

Whilst the Russian prisoners were required to teach Russian to the Japanese, and whilst they picked up a fair amount of the Japanese spoken language in the process, they were not permitted to study the written characters.

One Russian book was found in the officers' baggage, but the paper was of such poor quality[3], as compared with Japanese paper, that the Japanese did not form much regard for Russian bookmaking.

Other visitors were Japanese artists who were required to execute full length portraits of every member of the party, for despatch to the capital as records of identification, but in Golownin's opinion the portraits resembled no one in particular. Said he:

"The artists drew them in India ink, but in such a style that each portrait would have passed for that of any other individual as well of him it was intended for. Except for a long beard we could trace no resemblance in them."

An Early Envoy From Russia

Actually the features of Westerners presented a difficulty to most Japanese painters of those days, who seemed unable to avoid giving them almond shaped eyes in the traditional Japanese style.

Another visitor was a tailor who measured each of them for a new suit. No doubt the tailor did his best, but when the suits were delivered they were found to be strangely shaped, bearing some resemblance to a cloak, a greatcoat, and nightgown, and yet differing from all three.

The Japanese, even at that early date, were acquainted with European styled playing cards, which knowledge they had picked up from the Dutch in Nagasaki, but the Russians taught them how to gamble with cards. Their Japanese gaolers then proved to be such reckless gamblers and lost so heavily, that such games had to be prohibited.

The Russians also taught their Japanese gaolers European draughts. Soon that popular game spread beyond the confines of their prison to the nearby town of Matsumae, where it became the rage.

Among the many kindnesses shown to the Russians was the gift from one of the goalers of three pictures of Japanese pin-up girls—all fully clothed and richly dressed.

Eventually after a confinement of more than two years and following upon protracted and complicated negotiations, they were released. In doing so the Japanese provided them with a document in which they made clear that the Russians had been detained for having broken the laws of Japan by landing:

"In our country the Christian religion is strictly prohibited, and European vessels are not suffered

*to enter any Japanese harbour except Nagasaki . . .
All that may henceforth present themselves will be
driven back by cannon balls.*

*Among us there exists this law: If any European
residing in Japan shall attempt to teach our people
the Christian faith, he shall undergo a severe
punishment, and shall not be restored to his native
country. As you however have not attempted to do
so, you will accordingly be permitted to return
home. Think well on this."*

In regard to foreign trade, they told the Russians
they wanted none of it:

*"Our countrymen wish to carry on no commerce
with foreign lands for we know no want of necessary things. Though foreigners are permitted to
trade in Nagasaki, even to that harbour only those
are admitted with whom we have for a long period
maintained relations, and we do not trade with
them for the sake of gain, but for other important
objects. From the repeated solicitations which you
have hitherto made to us, you evidently imagine
that the customs of our country resemble those of
your own; but you are very wrong in thinking so.
In future, therefore, it will be better to say no more
about commerical relations."*

And so there came to an end a strange story of
captivity in which the Russian prisoners were at
times treated with a curious mixture of harshness
and consideration. Their Japanese captors probably
profited more than did the Russians, who with the
exception of the officers, were culturally much the
inferiors of the Japanese, and were unable to under-

stand or record much of what they saw and experienced.

Later when Golownin wrote an account of their captivity, which had lasted for more than two years, he rather confounded his countrymen by his acknowledgement of the goodwill that was shown to his party by the Japanese on innumerable occasions during their long captivity.

Golownin's record is rich in detail of Japanese life and customs of that time, and despite the severity of their experience is without bias or malice.

As is often found among prisoners of war, there was a renegade in the Russian ranks—Midshipman Moor—who sought to escape the trials of captivity by co-operating with his captors and winning their favours at the expense of his fellow countrymen. After release he committed suicide by hanging, whereupon his fellow officers generously erected a monument to the memory of one whom "Despair precipitated into error, but whose faults were expiated by bitter repentance and death."

And so ended one of the many strange episodes which occurred during the period when the Japanese authorities were striving to isolate their country from contact with the world outside.

THE FIRST
AMERICAN
TEACHER

*The people are king. Then are the
source of all authority.*
Ranald MacDonald, 1849.

It might come as a surprise to many people to
know that long before the time of Commodore Perry and Townsend Harris, an American Red Indian
half-breed deliberately slipped into Japan, and most
likely saw far more of the country than those distinguished men ever saw, and probably more than
some Americans and other foreign residents are
seeing to-day.

So much fiction has been woven into many stories
which are related about Perry and Townsend Harris that many Americans, and other people also,
believe they were the first Americans, and the first
foreigners for that matter, to visit Japan.

Actually quite apart from the Portuguese traders
who came to Japan over three centuries before Perry, and apart from the Dutch who had been living
in Japan continuously for over two hundred and
fifty years before Perry and Harris came, and apart
also from the Dutch vessels which had been visiting Japan for well over two centuries, there were
in addition several American vessels which had
been coming to Japan long before Perry arrived.
Those American vessels had been slipping into
Nagasaki harbour and getting safely out again de-

pite the laws which forbade non-Dutch vessels to call at Japanese ports under penalty of death for the crews.

The Dutch East India Company at one time and another made a great deal of money in the Japan trade, but much of the trade was carried on in the nature of private enterprise, the profits from which did not go into the Company's books. For a period of 16 years the Dutch East India Company had not paid any dividends, and so around 1798 was dissolved and its affairs taken over by Netherlands Government organizations.[1] Thereafter Dutch vessels were not always available in Batavia to carry on the trade which was still to be done with Japan. Furthermore during those years when Holland was at war with England, Dutch vessels en route to Japan were in danger of capture, and so the Dutch frequently chartered American and other vessels to sail to Nagasaki. The first such American vessel to arrive was the *Eliza* in 1798. She had an English captain, who had to pass himself off as an American, because, while the English were forbidden to come to Japan, the Japanese officials did not at that time have any clear idea of what an American was. The Japanese had noted that the crew spoke English but when it was explained that they were not English but of another nation and were only acting as carriers for the Dutch, the *Eliza* was treated as a Dutch ship. On the next voyage when she left Nagasaki laden with camphor and copper— then the principal exports—she struck a rock and sank. Her place was then taken by other American vessels and thereafter for about eight years or so

the annual vessel from Batavia was American.
Those ships laid up in Nagasaki harbour for many
weeks, in some cases, months. And so it was that
several hundred Americans saw something of Japan half a century before Perry, even if it was only
from the decks of their vessels, although knowing
seamen as we do, and knowing something of the
houses of entertainment which had been established
in Nagasaki for several hundred years, seeking the
patronage of visiting vessels, we should say that
more than likely many of them had a closer and
more agreeable view of Nagasaki life.

All the Japanese officials in Nagasaki were not
blind to those deceptions. However Nagasaki was
so far removed from the central government in
Yedo (Tokyo) that the local governor, who was
often interested in some form of private trading,
for culture and art's sake, if not for profit, could
risk shutting his eyes to the comings and goings of
American and other vessels under false colours, so
long as the deception was carried out with some
degree of care, and was not made too obvious.

Apart from such clandestine visitors to Japan,
there were a number of other foreigners, Americans
and Russians and others, who had spent varying
periods in Japan in confinement, and who had probably seen as much or more of the country than Perry or Harris ever saw.

Certainly some of them saw it under unusual conditions, such, for example, through the bars of prison cages, which contraptions were not unlike the
circus cages in which wild animals are now confined,
except that they were made of bamboo and were not

nearly so commodious and far less comfortable. Some saw the country when marching through it trussed together like gangs of convicts. These unfortunate travellers were mostly shipwrecked sailors who had managed to scramble ashore from whalers which had foundered along her rocky shores. Others saw it under more enlightened circumstances.

From about 1847 or so, by which time there was a growing feeling in some quarters of Japan towards the re-opening of the country, shipwrecked crews landing on Japanese shores were not always treated as harshly as in earlier years. Castaways, instead of being imprisoned under most severe conditions, were then frequently sent to Nagasaki, there to be delivered to the Dutch for transportation back to their home countries. Such men had an unusual opportunity of seeing a great deal of what was then, to the world at large, a strange and unknown feudal country, and of observing the customs and life during their travels either overland or by junk through the Inland Sea. Some travelled overland in a leisurely fashion from Hokkaido to Nagasaki, yet their adventures have passed unrecorded, because, most of them being men of little education, they were unable to record their unusual experiences. Other less fortunate shipwrecked sailors were transported all the way to Nagasaki in closed palanquins and so saw nothing of the country through which they passed.

There were still other foreigners who came to Japan long before Perry and Harris. So much has been heard of adventurous young Japanese, in the days of a century ago, risking the penalty of death, by smuggling themselves out of Japan in order to learn something about the Western World, that it might come as a surprise to many to know that, at a still earlier date, some foreigners were attempting to smuggle themselves into Japan, risking the same penalty of death, in order to learn something about the strange land which was then striving to remain aloof from the rest of the world.

Those unusual persons should not be confused with the crew members of whalers who occasionally landed at secluded spots in order to refill their water casks and in the hope of bartering for fresh vegetables. Some mariners may have landed for more lawless reasons, or in the hope of replenishing their larders by slaughtering a few cattle. But there were some, inspired by the spirit of adventure, who seized every opportunity to enter forbidden Japan and see what lay within. Several Russians landed in northern ports of Japan.

And there was the young man from Oregon—the Red Indian half-breed—who risked death by landing in Japan for no greater reason than a desire to satisfy his curiosity about that strange land.

Among the minor mysteries concerning our hero is that while some historians refer to his Christian name as Ronald, it appears to have been Ranald. Another is that although his father seems to have been a McDonald, he called himself MacDonald.

Anyhow he was born in 1824 at the old Hudson Bay Company's trading post at Fort George (Astoria) of an Indian squaw, named Princess Sunday,

and a trader in the Company's service, named Mc-
Donald.

From the age of ten to fifteen years he attended a
missionary school at Fort Garry (now Winnipeg,
Canada) and then became a clerk in a small bank.
After two years, at the age of seventeen, he was so
weary of working perched high on a bank stool, that
he ran away to sea. He sought adventures in every
part of the globe where his ship happened to be
sailing—mostly whalers on the Pacific. He saw the
coast line of Japan. At times he saw the beacon fires
flaming on the hilltops, warning that a foreign ship
was close by. Looking through the spyglass he had
seen the *torii*, which are to be found at the ap-
proaches to all shrines, and perhaps he also believed
the story, common among the sailors of those days,
that such structures were gallows ready for the
hanging of any foreigners who landed. He heard
stories of the fate of those who had defied the laws
of Japan and landed on her shores. Nevertheless he
decided to enter the country. He reached the Japan
Sea in the American whaler *Plymouth*. Then leaving the ship in a small boat, which he had prepared
for the purpose, he paddled towards shore.

When close to land, he capsized his boat and landed on shore under the guise of a shipwrecked sailor.

He was promptly captured and imprisoned, and
then began a remarkable adventure, during which
he travelled overland and by sea practically the
whole length of Japan under unusually favourable
conditions. Although a prisoner, he seems to have
been given exceptionally good treatment. Perhaps

his captors realised that he was of much superior intelligence to most of the shipwrecked seamen whom they had been capturing. At any rate they determined to use him as a teacher of English to those Japanese who were studying to become government interpreters. Whilst at that time there were a number of Japanese interpreters with a knowledge of Dutch, there were very few with any knowledge of English. As a teacher, he appears to have been quite successful, and it must have been some satisfaction to him, a few years later, to hear that some of his pupils figured as the Japanese interpreters in negotiations with both Commodore Perry and Consul General Townsend Harris.

In 1849, after about a year in Japan he was rescued by Commodore Glynn of the U.S.S. "Preble." Later after further wanderings and adventures, including a period on the Australian goldfields, he returned to the United States where the remaining years of his life were comparatively uneventful. He died poor and unknown. His remains were buried in an unmarked grave in an old Indian cemetery.

Such was the end of one of the most adventurous spirits of the last century, and one who has since been honoured by inclusion among those U.S. citizens who have made contributions to the development of Japan during the last hundred years.[2] Ranald MacDonald's contribution is said to have been in the educational field where, as already related, he proved to be an effective teacher.

But we feel he doubly earned a place in those ranks, because he was probably the first foreigner, and certainly the first American, who attempted to teach the Japanese the meaning of democracy.

When the U.S.S. "Preble" arrived to take him away, the Japanese were curious to know the relative rank of the commander of that vessel, and asked MacDonald to describe it by counting down in the order of succession from the highest in the United States.

MacDonald began with "the people," and followed with "the President," but the Japanese could make nothing of that, nor of his explanation—*"The people are king. They are the source of all authority."*[3]

THE TOWNSEND HARRIS CALUMNY*

> *I hope I may so conduct myself that I may have honorable mention in the histories which will be written on Japan and its future destiny.*
>
> Townsend Harris' Journal, 19 Aug., 1856.

> *He so conducted himself that his virtues are even now profoundly esteemed by the people of the country to which he was accredited. Truly can we say of him that he was a veritable model for diplomats of all nations and all ages.*
>
> Viscount Eiichi Shibusawa— *The Record of Townsend Harris in Japan*, 1927.

During the American Revolutionary War when the English "redcoats" set fire to the house of Thankful Townsend in Massachusetts, they did something which, it could be argued, had some effect ultimately on the history of Japan.

---

* This article, in an abbreviated form, appeared in the *Mainichi* in May, 1959.

The Townsend Harris Calumny

Because of that, and other actions between the English soldiers and the American colonists, Thankful Townsend taught her grandson, Townsend Harris, to tell the truth, fear God, and hate the British. Whilst it is believed that he did the first two, it is not certain that he succeeded in the third, although some of his contemporaries thought he tried. For example, one of his biographers[1] tells us that because of his antipathy to the English, he would never use a Sheffield knife or wear English cloth. Considering what American cloth was like in those days, this, if true, would show the strength of his character. However, later in life we know he bought some of his clothes in Paris. The blue pantaloons in which he appeared at the Shogun's Court, as told later in this chapter, came from Paris. We have sometimes thought his biographer hated the British more than he did.

Although Harris had launched upon a commercial career, and was without diplomatic training or a university education, he was the man whom President Pierce appointed in 1855 for the post of the first U.S. Consul General in Japan[2]—and it is doubtful whether, had all political considerations been set aside, he could have made a better choice. Even if Harris' selection did smack of a political appointment, his mission was carried out in a manner which was a triumph over immense difficulties, and his name has come to be written for all time into the histories of Japan and his own country.

Good Townsend Harris was a great American who achieved great things for his country, some in fact while en route to take up his appointment, and

before he was put on his country's pay roll.[3] He was
an unfortunate man in that the rewards due to him
did not come in his own lifetime. Had he been a
career diplomat, not unlikely many rewards and
honours from a grateful country would have been
showered on him. Unluckily by the time he had ful-
filled his difficult mission with outstanding success,
his patron was dead and a new president from the
opposite political camp was in the White House.

Even if Thankful Townsend's memory of the
American Revolutionary War did inspire in Harris
a hatred of the British, most likely it was only when
as a young man he was conducting a chinaware
shop in New York. Probably much of it wore off
later when he went abroad. Certainly some British
who later met him in Japan were charmed by his
courtesies and old world politeness, even if they,
and the other foreign diplomats in Yedo and Yokohama, were a little irked at his outstanding success
in his lonely negotiations with the Japanese, un-
backed as they were by any display of military or
naval forces—no warships with which to enforce
his demands, only patience, persistence, and courage from his lonely consulate in remote Shimoda.

Anyhow, not unlikely the strength of character
and determination, which he displayed in the face
of untold difficulties and ill health, were inherited
from Thankful Townsend.

Harris, under the terms of his appointment, had
to establish his consulate at Shimoda, because that
had been provided for in Commodore Perry's treaty.
Harris, no less than many others also, was surprised that Perry should have concluded an agreement

with the Japanese which provided for only two ports—Shimoda and Nagasaki—being made available as ports of call for American shipping. The U.S. Government had spent no less than $30,000 on the purchase of charts for the expedition, and had interviewed many American sea captains regarding the most suitable ports in Japan, and yet, such was the lack of reliable information regarding the secluded country of Japan, that the two ports selected were in Harris' words, "the worst in Japan."

He had proceeded to Japan via Hongkong, where he had learnt that the British were planning to send a plenipotentiary to Japan[4] to negotiate a commercial treaty. Therefore upon arrival at Shimoda in August, 1856, he realised that he was embarked upon a race against time, if he was to conclude a treaty before the British were able to do so. Although a man of great patience and tact, he met such a barrage of opposition during his negotiations with the Japanese that he soon fell ill.

Finally after nearly two years of negotiations he overcame Japanese opposition by picturing to them the terrors to be apprehended from an English fleet about to bear down on the country. He remembered the stories heard from his grandmother about the English "redcoats," and he passed them on to the Japanese, embroidered and coloured, as some indication of what was in store for them. He pictured to them that Japanese honour, which then would be lost, could be saved by meeting his peaceful demands. His efforts were successful, and so the United States became the first to conclude a commercial treaty with Japan.[5]

The Townsend Harris Calumny

Later, when the English envoy and suite did arrive, it came as a surprise to the Japanese diplomats to discover that they did not at all resemble the picture which Harris had painted, nor did they act as marauders. On the contrary, negotiations were carried out in a spirit of almost gay conviviality, amidst a surfeit of champagne and pâté de foie gras,[6] so different to the austere spirit in which negotiations with teetotaller Townsend Harris had been carried on.

Despite the many hard things which he said about the Japanese in his diary, some of which were hasty generalizations, it probably is correct to say that until the last decade or so, he was more honoured in official Japanese circles than in his own country, where, for eighteen years after his retirement from Japan, he lived modestly and unhonored, but in the fashion of a gentleman of old New York.

When he died in 1878, he was even more of a forgotten man than when living at Shimoda—the turmoil of the advancing times, following the Civil War, had surplanted in the minds of his countrymen memory of his name. That which he had accomplished in Japan was largely forgotten. So much was he a forgotten man that there was a picture on the walls of the old American Embassy in Tokyo which for many years was pointed out to visitors as his portrait. Ironically enough it was subsequently found to be that of Secretary of State Lewis Cass under whom he had served![7]

Sadly enough it has only been during the last decade, following the Occupation of Japan, that the name of Townsend Harris has become known to the majority of Americans and others also, and then largely through the medium of a soft-backed sensational novel[8] which purported to be straight history, and a screen version[9] of that book which presented in gorgeous colours and stage settings the scandalous fabrications which grew out of the gutter talk of Shimoda of three quarters of a century ago. When the calumnies were first dramatized in Japan around 1928, it was the British owned newspaper— *The Japan Chronicle* which defended with almost irritating persistency his good name, while the American newspaper of that time was more inclined to keep to straight news, rather than become involved in anything of a critical nature, even although the good name of a great American was involved.

But the idea that an American diplomat should have kept house with a second-rate prostitute— euphemistically described as a geisha—had such a popular appeal in Japan that it started a veritable flood of newspaper articles, operas, songs, *naniwa-bushi*[10] ballads and *kabuki* dramas. The legend of Okichi caught on, and over the years grows worse and worse; what started off as fiction has now become history in the minds of millions.

During the last decade the commercially minded city fathers of the backward port of Shimoda were not slow to seize upon the calumny in order to lift the finances of Shimoda by boosting its tourist trade. The fictional romance of Townsend Harris and Okichi was recited by the bus girls on the tourist buses to Shimoda, whilst the temple authorities, the souvenir vendors, and the Municipal councillors all combined to commercialize the calumy. In 1961, the *Asahi Evening News,* one of the leading English language newspapers in Japan, exposed the falsity of the story and the sordid exploitation of the whole slanderous lie.

When Harris arrived in Japan in 1856 to take up his appointment as Consul General, the two Chinese male servants whom he brought with him soon proved to be scallawags. Speaking in the name of the United States of America they demanded squeeze and tribute from the local Japanese shopkeepers and opium from the apothecary shops in Shimoda. When that came to the notice of Harris, he did everything possible to bring their plundering to an end, but he had to retain them in his service because of the absence of any means of shipping them out of the country. He did, however, turn more to Japanese servants for whom he had the same high regard as have the many foreigners who have followed him. But it is to be imagined that he would have stuck to his Chinese male-servants, with all their wiles, could he have known that by engaging a female Japanese servant he was giving the fiction writers and movie producers of the future the opportunity of robbing him of his honour and his good name, of which he was so justly proud.

Had he depended more upon his two rascally Chinese man-servants, had he neglected the affairs of his country to do his own washing and mending, to cook his own meals, and to manage his own housekeeping, he may have escaped the slurs and the scandals that have been embroidered about his name, but almost certainly he would then have gone

down in history as the worst of the U.S. envoys to
Japan, instead of one of the best.

If in his illness he had dispensed with the assistance of a female nurse, he would have robbed the
fishwives of Shimoda—who were in those days as
lascivious as the times in which they lived—of the
opportunity of gossip, but he may have succumbed
to his illness.

The myth of Okichi San as Harris' mistress
would not then have been born, nor would there
have been any Shimoda legend of how poor Okichi
had drowned herself to escape the shame of having
become the mistress of a *Tojin* (barbarian).[11] Instead, Okichi would long since have passed out of
everyone's memory as have almost all the other inhabitants of sleepy little Kakizaki, the Oyster Point
of Shimoda of more than a hundred years ago. Certainly then the fame of Shimoda would not have
been as great as it is, and there would have been
fewer of the money-making devices that have been
invented in Shimoda of recent times to extract a
few yen from credulous tourists.

Among the relics of Harris' residence which are
still preserved at Shimoda at the Gyokusenji Temple, wherein his consulate was located, are a few
shabby exhibits including a chipped glass, a black-
ened pipe, and two mouldy cigars, and also several
combs and bed-pillows which they foist off as once
belonging to Okichi San.

But even rival temples, which can claim no connection with the mythical Harris-Okichi love story,
are striving to share in the tourist traffic which has

been whipped up by that bogus romance. The Ryosenji Temple, the site where Commodore Perry signed the first U.S.-Japan treaty of peace and amity has been the most successful. With the skill of showmen at an old-time fair, and a full appreciation of the appeal of the old fashioned naughty peepshows, the priests of that temple have gathered together a collection of erotic images and phallic symbols which far outdo anything which their rivals across the bay at Gyokusenji can show—an exhibition which in fact has no connection whatsoever with Japanese-American history or the temple. Indeed we would say that the exhibits at Ryosenji are not unlike some of the shows which the *entrepreneurs* of Asakusa put on, or some of the dirty postcards vendors of Port Said.

But let us return to Okichi.

It is a fact that the Japanese officials of the time did attempt to foist a mistress on Townsend Harris, so that he might dally longer in Shimoda and forget the purpose of his appointment, and so that they might be informed daily of his activities. The idea was in line with the times and not as far fetched as it might sound to-day. It is also a fact that when Harris spurned their offers, they sought to place a serving woman in the Consulate who at least could be relied to spy upon that lonely man.

Even Harris, patient, persistent, and conscientious though he was, almost despaired at times at the manner in which his own country had seemingly forgotten him.

Said he, in his diary, under date of 25 April, 1857:
"My last letters from the Department of State were

dated in October, 1855, more than eighteen months ago. It is too long a period to leave me here alone, and some order should be given to ensure more frequent communication with me.

In consequence of his isolation and lack of means of communication with his own country, he was at times without funds sufficient to pay for his daily needs and was even in debt to his servants. Finally he was *"reduced to the mortifying necessity of asking credit from the Japanese for necessary daily supplies."*

He was left short of suitable provisions and had to live largely on the country, except on those occasions when a Russian warship entered Shimoda harbour and there was an opportunity of securing needed foodstuffs.

It is pleasing to record that in those days United States' relations with the Russians were so cordial that Harris loaned his Chinese laundryman to the Russian commander to launder his soiled linen; the commander, in return, sent his carpenter to do some much needed repairs to the U.S. Consulate and the flagstaff. Unfortunately the Russians put on such a banquet for Harris, that his stomach suffered an upset and for some weeks he was off colour.

Surrounded by spies, plagued by annoyances, and worn out by the procrastination of the officials, poor Townsend Harris struggled against illness and despair. Suffering from ills which would in all probability be diagnosed today as due to nutritional deficiencies and stomach ulcers, he continued to carry out his duties by sheer force of character.

The real Okichi, who was planted in the home of

this lonely diplomat, was not a geisha, nor was she particularly attractive. Just another wayward girl, not over-particular, who had been in and out of many jobs and experiences, and who, for want of something better, agreed to the proposition of the local official that she should work at the consulate. But it is well established that she was discharged after a few days because she was suffering from a skin ailment. Thereafter, we can assume, as has been the similar experience of many other Japanese servants who worked for foreigners, she became a butt for the coarse jests of the Shimoda fishwives who dubbed her "Tojin Okichi" (the barbarian's Okichi). Anyhow after she left Harris' employ, she married a carpenter, later worked for awhile as a serving maid in a restaurant where she drank more than did the guests, led a loose life, and eventually drowned herself.

Such was Okichi San, but the fanciful legend which has been fabricated of recent times is that she was a beautiful geisha who sacrificed herself for her country by meeting the demands of the U.S. Consul that the Japanese authorities supply him with a mistress. We are asked to believe—and some do—that Okichi, at the cost of her own honour and life, thereby averted a crisis in diplomatic relations between the United States and Japan!

Then after that myth had been fabricated and publicised in Japan, it remained (as already mentioned) for an American moving picture organization in 1958, to produce the film *"The Barbarian and the Geisha,"* and at the cost of a considerable sum of money to present it in gorgeous colours to the whole world as real history, and with (so we were told in the advertising blurbs) "a delicate and sympathetic understanding"—delicate to the extent that the so-called geisha was represented as being kept in a back room rather than in the front bedroom.

Audiences, to the tune of millions of people the world over, watched the skilful action of the full-blooded well-nourished American actor, who played the part of Townsend Harris, living on the screen an ardent life and giving to his country's affairs such time as remained when he was not pursuing in the back room the charms of the delectable Okichi San (and her screen counterpart was delectable) or discussing with her U.S. affairs of state.

So different in fact to the life which poor Townsend Harris was actually living at the time, as recorded in his personal diary:

Jan. 15, 1857: *Ill, ill, ill, I am constantly wasting away in flesh. I am most careful in my diet, but all is of no avail. What is it that ails me, I cannot say.*

April 18, 1857: *My health is not good. I wish the frigate would arrive, that I could have some medical advice.*

June 23, 1857: *My health is miserable. My appetite is gone, and I am so shrunk away . . . .*

July 4, 1857: *I never felt more miserable and wretched than this day. Ill in health and in want of everything but low spirits, of which I have an abundant supply.*

For awhile he was living in such fear of death that he took the precaution of appointing his secretary and interpreter, Heusken, as vice-consul,[12] so that should he not survive, the consulate would not be left without an official to carry on.

The producers of the movie having set out to depict the imaginary love life of an American diplomat, did not hesitate to present a lover who bore as little resemblance to Harris as did the luscious Okichi San on the screen resemble one of Townsend Harris' female servants.

In line with the fiction that Harris' life was wrapped around Okichi, the producers of the film would have us believe that Harris could not separate himself from the woman in the back room even during the course of his visit to the Shogun in Yedo, where he hoped to fulfil the whole purpose of his mission. And so Okichi, all decked out in her gorgeous brocades, is put on a horse for the long dirty dusty ride to Yedo. In what seat-sore condition she would have arrived is not shown on the screen, but at any rate we next see her established in a luxurious apartment conveniently close to Harris' bedroom.[13]

However, the scenes depicting the U.S. cavalcade about to start off from Shimoda with Harris carrying a rucksack were sheer burlesque, but would have been suitable enough if this picture had been presented as comic opera, and not history—so different to the manner in which Harris actually travelled to Yedo. Throughout that journey and on entry into Yedo, Harris, as always, was meticulously careful to uphold the honour of his country, and surrendered no particle of the dignity of his official position as representative of the United States of America.

Another departure from history which we lament—although it is unimportant—was where Harris is shown attending the audience with the Shogun in a dress which although colorful, was not as startling as the outfit of the real Harris on that occasion.

Actually the ceremony took place in 1857 a full ten years before the U.S. Congressional Resolution of 1867 defined the ceremonial dress American diplomats thenceforth should wear. Harris was attending the Tycoon's Court[14] where there was a display of Oriental splendour and colour in dress, the equal of which could only be seen these days on the *kabuki* stage. Evidently the good Townsend Harris decided to deck himself out in a style no less striking than that of the Japanese court dignitaries. It has been described as "finery almost Oriental in its lavishness." Harris described it in his diary as follows:

"My dress was a coat embroidered with gold . . . blue pantaloons with a broad gold band running down each leg, cocked hat with gold tassels and a pearl handled dress sword."

In this dazzling outfit which had been especially made for him in Paris, Harris had already made such a hit with the King of Siam and his numerous concubines that he correctly concluded it would prove no less impressive at the Court of Yedo.

We do not doubt that Harris achieved more at the Tycoon's Court in that startling outfit, un-American though it may have been, than had be selected some colour other than blue for his pantaloons.

Actually Harris' attendance at the Court of Yedo all decked out like an Oriental potentate, was in fact one of the incidents which led to the U.S. Congressional Resolution where U.S. diplomats were never again to have much personal latitude in the choice of dress. After the passing of that Resolution no diplomat of the Land of the Free was at liberty to wear blue pantaloons!

However we are not afraid to say that we prefer the blue pantaloons and other finery, and also the moustache and beard of the real Townsend Harris to the make-up of the smooth-chinned actor who had to spend so much time on the screen dallying with his geisha.

Townsend Harris was a great and a good man, even although he may have disliked our compatriots, even to a greater degree than the irritation which they at times felt for him. Fortunately he was not to know of the slurs on his good name which would be broadcast throughout the whole world. Nor was he to know that about fifty years after his death a sexy and mushy dramatization would be made of the gutter talk of Shimoda that Okichi was his mistress, and after gaining much publicity in Japan, would then with variations and trimmings be re-written by an American for the films, and so would be carried to every corner of the world. It was bad enough that American diplomatic prestige plummeted in the eyes of many, but what did Townsend Harris do to deserve such treatment from his own nationals?

It has been of no avail that the foremost scholars—Japanese and foreign—of that period of Japanese history have discredited the whole story and shown it to be a fabrication. It has been of no avail that the *Asahi Evening News* in 1961 courageously challeng-

ed the Mayor of Shimoda[15] to cease commercializ-
ing on the slander, which his city had been en-
couraging, in order to boost the tourist trade of
Shimoda, or alternatively to produce proof of the
Harris-Okichi story — a challenge which was at
first accepted. Later the Mayor and his council
backed out of the discussion with a long statement
that although the romance is based on rumour,
nevertheless they imagine where there is smoke
there must be fire. However, stated the Mayor, nothing can be gained by debating the truth or otherwise of the story at this date, and therefore *"I am
now filled to the brim with the desire to drop this
issue."*[16]

And so the bus girls and tourist guides continue
to blare forth the sordid details as if they are
straight history, the shopkeepers to sell their Okichi
picture postcards and souvenirs, and the City authorities to build up their tourist trade on a fabricated scandal. The legend grows stronger with
each re-telling, and not many people now seem
interested in defending Harris' honour.

We can at least hope that American history will
come to the defence of the real Townsend Harris
and correct so much of the mischievous nonsense
spread by that empty but beautiful film. But who,
we ask, will defend the reputation of Harris' interpreter, the gay young Dutchman, Henry C. J. Heusken, who was murdered by two-sworded *ronin*
some years later? It is possible that nobody had
fluttered so many female hearts and been such a
success with the girls of the tea-houses as had
young Heusken. Yet seemingly it was necessary in

this movie that his charms should not compete with
those of the lusty American who portrayed Townsend Harris, and so the gay young Heusken was cast
as a wizened old shell, with as much sex appeal as
a desiccated crab!

But enough. All that need be said for the Townsend Harris film, apart from the gorgeous coloured
settings which are magnificent, is that it has presented the name of Townsend Harris to millions of
people who had never previously heard of him, and
in the cause of Yen, Dollars and Cents has departed
from history and vilified the good name of one of
America's most conscientious public servants.

THE FIRST
BRITISH
MINISTER
TO JAPAN

*. . . the Japanese rulers under the pressure of a
sudden danger and emergency . . . negotiated and
treated, because they felt unprepared to fight.
They smiled and dissimulated, employing their
utmost skill to give as little as possible; and re-
serving to themselves the full right hereafter of
nullifying all they might feel compelled for the
time to surrender. The Foreign negotiators went
away well pleased with their easy victories. The
Japanese Plenipotentiaries retired in disgrace. . .*
Sir Rutherford Alcock—Preface to *The Capital
of the Tycoon*, London, 1863.

Mr. Rutherford Alcock arrived in the capital of
the Tycoon of Japan on 26th June, 1859,[1] as the
first British Consul-General accredited to *"The most
High, Mighty, and Glorious Prince, His Imperial
and Royal Majesty at the Court of Yeddo."*[2] Later
he was knighted and appointed Minister, or to give
him his full title, he became "Her Majesty's Envoy
Extraordinary and Minister Plenipotentiary in
Japan."

He was disappointed to find on arrival[3] that
Japan, or rather Japanese officials, were not quite
what he had been led to believe they would be. Lord
Elgin who came to Japan before him had negotiated

a treaty in an atmosphere of "sweet harmony" interspersed with ham and champagne luncheons.[4]

By the time Alcock arrived a year later the "sweet harmony" had evaporated, and the Japanese officials had made a re-appraisal of the situation.

Alcock's task in establishing the first British Legation in Japan was therefore beset with unexpected difficulties, or as he expressed it:

". . . although the original negotiators were received with smiles, and their path strewn with flowers, their successors had only the poisoned chalice held to their lips, thorns in their path, and the scowl of the two-sworded samurai to welcome them, whenever they ventured to leave their gates, while the assassin haunted their steps, and broke their rest in the still hours of the night with fell intent to massacre the whole Legation."

He ended up by writing a book[5] in two volumes about *"the singular people among whom my lot has been cast."*

Unlike Townsend Harris, Alcock, although a man of patience and perseverance, as was his American counterpart, did not contract ulcers as a result of his dealings with the Japanese officials of the time. Perhaps it was that Alcock's long experience as a diplomat in the Far East had fortified him, or maybe Harris' ulcers first developed when he was a merchant and long before he became a diplomat. Anyhow Alcock's health survived the experience, whereas Harris barely did.[6]

Alcock's first official business was to request that a suitable residence be assigned to him by the Japanese authorities. After inspecting several places, all of which were without plumbing and in a cold and draughty style, he finally fixed upon a temple named Tozenji,[7] or Tozengee as he spelt it. It was a delightful place, and Alcock wrote:

"I felt doubtful whether a retreat so perfect in every respect, could possibly have fallen to my lot without some terrible drawback."

The drawback was discovered two years later, when he and his staff came close to being massacred when a gang of *samurai* attacked the place.[8]

Understandably enough the owners of the temple showed little enthusiasm for making the premises available as a diplomatic residence, and nothing short of a sharp order from the Shogun would have persuaded them to do so. Whilst they watched the four-poster bedsteads being moved in, and the carpenters altering the rooms to meet the requirements of a European mode of life, their feelings must have been similar to those of the Japanese who, in the recent Occupation days, had the painful experience of seeing the beautiful woodwork[9] in their homes painted over to fit the notions of interior decoration of the Occupationaires, who had been allotted those houses as residences.

The quiet of the old Tozenji temple-ground[10] was transformed into turmoil with the arrival of about two hundred packing-cases containing the furniture and personal effects of the new occupants. In the bustle and excitement of unpacking that immense array of cases, conversations and orders in English, French, Dutch, Japanese, and Chinese were resounding in the temple, where for centuries nothing but Japanese had been heard.

There was a rush to locate and unpack the cases containing the beds and sufficient crockery so that about twenty people could be fed and bedded down before dark.

In time all the confusion sorted itself out, all except the case containing the entire cutlery for the Legation, which was lost and did not turn up for three weeks! Just how the Englishmen met that crisis is not related, whether they temporarily adopted the customs of the Esquimaux and ate with their fingers, or whether they borrowed some Japanese chop-sticks is not now known. Alcock confessed that it tried their patience, but was reticent about the details. That they did survive the experience is sufficient proof that they were equal to the emergency.

Alcock described Tozenji, the delightful old world Buddhist retreat which had become his legation, as follows:

"On turning off the Tocado[11] (as the great high road through the island is called, and which skirts the bay here) we passed through a gate giving entrance to a long avenue of cryptomerias and pines; then through a second more imposing gateway of two stories, across an open square with lotus ponds, and trees on each side, and finally, by an entrance to the right, through another courtyard, and gained a fine suite of apartments looking on to as beautiful a specimen of Japanese garden and grounds as can well be conceived. A lawn was immediately in front,—beyond a little lake, across which was a rustic bridge . . . and beyond this again, palm trees, and azaleas, large

*bushes trimly cropped into the semblance of
round hillocks, while the background was filled up
with a noble screen of timber composed of the
finest of all Japanese trees, the evergreen oak
and maple. Palms and bamboos were interspersed,
and a drooping plum tree was trained over one
end of the rustic bridge giving passage across the
lake. To the right, a steep bank shut in the view,
covered equally with a great variety of flowering
shrubs and the ground bamboo; and crowned with
more of the same timber. Through this a path led
upwards by a zig-zag flight of steps to a fine avenue of trees, the end of which widened into a
platform, whence a wide view of the bay and part
of the city below could be obtained, with a per-
fectly scenic effect. The distant view was set in a
frame-work of foliage, formed by the branches
and trunks of pine trees, towering from fifty to
a hundred feet high . . . a more beautiful hermitage could not have been chosen. . . "*

Alcock unfurled the Union Jack in Tokio, or Yedo
as it was then known, for the first time on 6th July,
1859. Thereafter one of his first duties was to arrange the preliminaries with the Japanese authorities for the exchange of ratifications of the treaty
which had been signed by Lord Elgin in the previous year.[12]

Days were consumed in discussions on protocol.
Then after every detail had been settled, Alcock discovered that the Japanese planned "to palm off" on
him (the expression is Alcock's) a ratification of a
Japanese version of the treaty. As the original
treaty had been executed in English, Dutch,[13] and

Japanese, Alcock was not willing to accept a ratification on an alleged copy of the Japanese version only, particularly since no one on his staff could read the document. Finally, after much argument, the Shogun gave way and set his seal to the original treaty.

Such ratifications nowadays are usually carried in a portfolio by a gentleman in a top-hat riding in a limousine, and accompanied by a secretary and a chauffeur (in or out of livery). But not so in those more colorful days. The treaty was carried through the streets of Yedo under a canopy ornamented with flags and evergreens, surrounded by a British guard of marines and followed by fifty naval bluejackets. The procession headed by the flag of Great Britain, surrounded by a guard of honour and a large escort of mounted officers, made a great impression as it marched in the mud and wound its way through the tortuous streets of old Yedo, across the moats to the gates of the palace of the Tycoon[14]—the present Imperial Palace of Tokyo.

Then, after the ceremony was completed, the news was signalled by waving of fans from street to street back to the British warship in Yedo Bay— a distance of six miles in a minute and a half. The warship thereupon fired a royal salute of twenty guns (much to the alarm of the local fishermen) and the British and Japanese flags were raised at the main mast in celebration of the occasion.

Just as President Pierce of the United States of America some four years earlier had charged Townsend Harris with the responsibility of personally delivering a letter to the Emperor of Japan, so also

62

had Queen Victoria furnished Alcock with a letter to be delivered in person to the Tycoon, who was then thought to be the Emperor.

In a sense Townsend Harris had been the pace-maker. The efforts he made to deliver the President's letter consumed his energy for fifteen months, and cost him his health. When he finally did hand the letter over to the wrong person,[15] namely the Shogun or Tycoon, President Pierce had long since been dead and a new president was in the White House.

Except that Harris had finally got rid of the letter, the ceremony had not been to his liking. No steps had been taken by the authorities to keep his passage to the palace open. The progress of his palanquin had been interrupted, and he had been hustled in an unseemly manner by the retainers, grooms, and servants hanging about the outer courts of the palace. As an *amende honorable,* Harris had therefore demanded another audience, under more fitting conditions and ceremonial.

The second audience went through smoothly. Harris thus having established a precedent, as it were, for the manner in which foreign diplomats should be received by the Shogun, Alcock sought an audience in order that he might deliver the Queen's letter which he had already been holding for several months.

The day finally fixed was in broiling August. The procession composed of the Japanese Governor of Yedo, accompanied by his suite, standard-bearers, umbrella-holders, the British Minister, members of the British Legation guards, and others, moved through four miles of streets, sweating profusely, until finally they arrived at the entrance to the palace. Every detail had been arranged in advance even to camp-stools upon which Alcock and his staff sat whilst changing into clean shoes, prior to entering the Palace and stepping onto the *tatami* or mats.

They first gathered in an anteroom to cool off and to be presented to various Court officials. Although conversation on such occasions was always a problem, the heat of the day provided a topic. The conversation was largely confined to the Court equivalent of *"Atsui-na."*

When the master of ceremonies announced "Inglesa Minister," Alcock moved forward between rows of Japanese dignitaries seated on the floor on either side of the corridors and assembly rooms through which he advanced. As he did so, he became conscious of a faint hiss, which grew in volume as he proceeded down between the rows of court nobles, until it seemed to circulate throughout all the courts and corridors of the palace, growing in intensity the further he proceeded.

It was explained to Alcock later that the sound was the manner of bespeaking profound reverence. The explanation was of course correct, but we venture to believe that the shock to the courtiers of seeing a foreigner walking on the court *tatami* with shoes,[16] could have been such that something more than profound reverence was subconsciously introduced into the sound, and that, in a sense, diplomat Alcock was hissed at Court without being aware of it!

The problem of diplomats walking into Japanese buildings with their shoes on[17] had arisen previously, but no one could suggest a solution. Foreign diplomats could hardly be expected to shuffle about in their stockinged feet, even when in the presence of a "High, Mighty and Glorious Prince." It has been said, by some who profess to know, that even Japanese males, in national costume, find it difficult to stand on their dignity on *tatami,* and so hasten to assume a kneeling or sitting position with the least possible delay.

An effort had been made earlier to persuade Alcock to rehearse the ceremony with someone standing in for the Shogun. However he refused to go through any such mummery, but did compromise to the extent that he agreed a Japanese official should shuffle along the floor behind him, ready to tug at his trouser leg should he advance too far.

Everything at first went swimmingly. However Alcock was a bit slow in backing out of the Presence after handing over the Queen's letter, and when he did retire it was with the definite impression that the Shogun had shortchanged him. Alcock had been provided in advance with a translation in Dutch of the gracious speech which the Shogun would make upon receiving the Queen's letter. According to the translation it consisted of several long involved sentences, yet the Shogun had only mumbled what seemed to be about four words. Alcock continued to stand in front of the Shogun trying to figure out how so many gracious ideas could possibly be condensed into what seemed to be four grunts. It was then he felt a tug at his trouser leg.

That was his cue to move off. He concluded that the audience was at an end and he commenced to back out of the Presence. Although he had been informed that he might turn around, he was determined to show the Shogun the same degree of respect as to any other sovereign. In walking backwards he unfortunately trod upon the long trailing court garment of the official who had been shuffling about on the floor behind him, but who had by then regained his feet and was moving off. For a moment it appeared that the unfortunate official would either be stripped of his garment or would topple backwards.

It was in fact such misadventures as these, which were bound to occur at such receptions, that decided the Japanese court authorities to adopt Western dress and customs without delay. And so it was that at a very early date the Shogun placed a subscription for the *Illustrated London News* to enable the court ladies and gentlemen to begin a study of European manners and costumes.[18]

Although under the treaties, Foreign Representatives had been granted unrestricted right of travelling throughout Japan, Alcock found that right was *"like so many other stipulations to be regarded as a dead letter to all practical purposes."* In 1860 he therefore determined to exercise his right of travel by climbing Fuji, the far famed sacred mountain and the highest point in the country.[19] By the time he had overcome most of the obstacles *"August was already past and the first days of September were gliding on"*—a time normally considered too late for the climb.

The Japanese officials had already explained to

Alcock that although a great number of Japanese
did climb Fuji every summer, they were mostly pilgrims or of the poorer class, consequently such an
expedition would not be consistent with the dignity
of a great man. Then in dismay at his insistence
upon going, they correctly pointed out that usually
only during July[20] and August is the mountain sufficiently free from snow to permit of the ascent being made in safety.

Sir Rutherford was not however to be deterred,
and on 4th Sept., the party of eight foreigners
started out on horseback from the British Consulate
at Kanagawa. He had especially stipulated the ex-
cursion should be without escort or parade. That
however was not to be. By the time the Vice-Governor
and his staff with their attendants, umbrella and
spear bearers, had joined in, the cortège comprised
over a hundred persons and more than thirty horses.

The Japanese officials rode in palanquins[21] as
befitted their rank, whereas the foreigners sacrificed dignity for comfort by travelling on horseback.
They travelled down the Tokaido to Odawara, but
even that was an adventure then, because of the
rivers which had to be forded. At the wide Sakawa
river the horses were led across but the riders had
to dismount and were carried on the backs of the
river porters who had a monopoly of such work at
each crossing. At some rivers the porters had a reputation of holding up travellers with extortionate
demands for payment. Alcock however was as pleased with their service as that which he met everywhere from the ordinary people during the trip:

"... *stout porters carried us without demur across,*

though the water was surging round their hips in many places; but they seemed to know where to pick their steps, and taking us in a zig-zag line up the stream made their way without much difficulty. Our whole party was carried over for eleven itziboos—about 15s.—a large sum in Japan to be divided among some thirty men for a half hour's work; but it is by no means certain this sum was paid to them. That was the amount charged to us; whether it ever reached their hands could not be ascertained, as the payment was necessarily made through the attendant officers—and there was at least a great probability of diminution on the way."

After Odawara, they turned into the mountains, passed through Miyanoshita,[22] and crossed the Hakone mountains.

Townsend Harris, the American envoy to Japan, had crossed the Hakone mountains along the same road three years before. Apparently he had no desire to climb Fuji, even had his health been sufficiently robust to enable him to do so, because under date of 25 Nov., 1857, he wrote in his diary, with some truth, *"I have had Fusi Yama in view all day, but alas! like many other things in this world, the nearer approach does not add to its beauty or grandeur."*[23]

When Alcock's party arrived at the base of Fuji, most of the Japanese officials stayed at a Japanese inn and spent a pleasant two days, whilst the eight foreigners, accompanied by a few minor officials, porters, and guides made the ascent.

Before starting off they each bought a pilgrim's

staff "which the priests dispose of for the sum of
one penny each."[24]

*"The time actually spent in climbing up to the
summit[25] was about eight hours, but the descent
occupied little more than three. We slept two
nights on the mountain, and had greatly to con-
gratulate ourselves on the weather, having fallen
upon the only two fine days out of six that were
not bad, and escaped the typhoon while safely
housed at the foot. . . . We only found patches of
snow here and there near the summit, but on our
return to Yedo . . . we saw it completely covered.*

*We had thus succeeded in visiting the 'match-
less' mountain in the only interval of fine weather
—before the setting in of winter would have made
it impossible.[26] The prediction of the (Japanese)
Ministers, that we were too late was thus very
near indeed being verified."*

The only casualty on the trip was the death of
Alcock's favourite Scotch terrier, which was buried
according to Buddhist rites with a priest in attendance. Alcock was much attached to the dog and felt
the loss keenly. Following the kindly action of the
Japanese who had assisted at digging the grave,
erecting a tombstone, and burning incense, Alcock
wrote in his journal:

*"I had begun to forget I was in Japan, so much
goodwill was shown, and so few difficulties made
over the gratification of a whim".*

But he had reckoned without officialdom in the
capital. When he arrived back in Yedo, the officials
there began to reckon up the number of regulations
which he had broken, even the matter of erecting a

stone over the tiny grave was an action which according to the law of Japan of those days first required a permit from the governor of Yedo.

Six years were to elapse before any foreigners again climbed Fuji.[27] The experience gained during those early ascents by foreigners caused the compilers of the early foreign guide books to Japan to recommend that climbers should take with them a number of essentials including a bag of charcoal[28] and all the food they might require on the trip. In later editions the authors of those guide books deleted some items and added other such essentials as Keatings Flea Powder.[29] In these modern times flea powder is no longer a must when climbing Fuji. The fleas of Fuji have long since succumbed to modern insecticides.

Since those early times many thousands of foreigners and several millions of Japanese have made the ascent[30]—some under unusual circumstances. People have been pulled up, pushed up, and carried up. Some have run up and others crawled up.

Minister Alcock had more than the usual share of diplomatic difficulties to contend with. He was far from popular with the Japanese officials, and even less popular with the foreign residents.[31] The Yokohama Foreign Settlement in those early days was a rough place, not very different to a mushroom gold-rush town. The naval surgeon on one of the British war vessels in Yokohama in 1863, describing local conditions, made an entry in his diary[32] to the effect that the "Legation fellows were a very jolly crowd," whereas the residents were not at all desirable sort of people. He thought little of the social attractions of Yokohama, not even of Lady Alcock's "at homes" once a week, concerning which he rather ungenerously remarked that the guests were served with "bad tea[33] and worse sherry."

Incidentally after reading that British naval surgeon's diary we reached the conclusion that the U.S. military personnel who came to Japan with the Occupation in 1945 were not by any means the first to enter into temporary domestic liaison arrangements with Japanese girls, even although some people would have us believe it so. The English Tommies who were quartered in Yokohama about 80 years before the U.S. Army arrived in Japan, had done exactly the same. Said the naval surgeon in his diary:

"The fellows at the camp had very comfortable quarters and had nearly all entered into domestic relations of a temporary character."

Sir Rutherford Alcock has been described by an American journalist[34] as *"a messenger of wrath and vengeance"* in his dealings with the Japanese officials, although actually Commodore Perry and Townsend Harris had both adopted a far more "Vinegar Joe" attitude in their dealings with the Japanese and both had said far more harsh things about the Tokugawa officials than Alcock ever did. But if Alcock was critical of Japanese officialdom, he was just as critical of some aspects of life in the Foreign Settlements, and he thereupon proceeded to draw up *"Rules and Regulations for the Peace, Order and Good Government of British Subjects within the Dominions of the Tycoon of Japan."*[35]

He thereby goes down in history as being the first

in Japan to frame rules of the road and to impose speed limits. Traffic was required to keep to the left, furious driving and galloping along public roads and highways was forbidden. The speed limit was set at that of a walk—a limit no doubt only adhered to when Her Majesty's Consular constable was in sight. The discharge of firearms, in the manner which had become fashionable in Californian gold-mining towns, was prohibited.

Those rules at first gave rise to a riot of indignation among some of the British residents, but they had the effect of checking a tendency to lawlessness which was developing in those early Settlements.

It was a strange new land in which Alcock found himself. One of his staff in contrasting Tokugawa Japan with other countries wrote:—

"Women wearing no crinoline. Houses harbouring no bugs and the country no lawyers."[36]

The reference to bugs was to *nankin-mushi* or bed-bugs, but some came later. Fleas were not classified as bugs. Owing to the dampness of the weather in Japan the fleas sought the dryness of the inside of houses and so feudal Japan, in the absence of modern insecticides, had plenty—a hazard regarding which the early guide books duly warned intending travellers.

Visitors to Japan often comment upon the white gauze masks which so many Japanese men wear over their nose and mouth especially during the winter months, in order, it is said, to prevent infection. Whilst there may be no connection, it is interesting to note that nearly a hundred years ago, before germs were known, Alcock noted a similar tendency.

Describing the winter in Yedo, he wrote:

"The men in the streets seem, above all, careful of the ends of their noses, and on a cold day two-thirds of the population are to be seen with all the lower part of their faces concealed by the folds of a blue cotton muffler tied round the head, from under which nothing but a pair of eyes can be recognised."

Alcock, the trained diplomat, also had a keen interest in the industrial life of Japan and was ever mindful of the importance of developing trade, but he was not to find it easy to leave his legation in order to observe the commercial life of the great city that was to become Tokyo. The Japanese officials were not inclined to facilitate any journeyings outside his delightful hermitage. A month had passed since his arrival before an opportunity arose. It then being midsummer he asked the Japanese liaison officials to arrange a suitable boat with four to six rowers to convey him along the coast to the port area of Yedo.

"When the hour came and it was too late to make other arrangements, I found an open boat with no seat or awning, exposed to the blaze of the sun, and two rowers only, one a miserable old man of sixty or seventy. This was either a piece of deliberate impertinence, to punish me for objecting to their extortionate practices, or an official manoeuvre to deter me from going at all. On my sharply remonstrating, they uttered only a few nonchalant excuses, which were palpable lies: such as that 'no covered boat came out of the river' though we met several within an hour. I

*did not chose, however, to forego the expedition
and so we proceeded."*

Great crowds surged around them when they
landed and followed them with a boisterous hilarity,
*"nothing really offensive or hostile in appearance,
however . . . They offered no insult, but there was
a good deal of shouting and hooting, which was certainly not intended to be either respectful or com-
plimentary."*

Later as he travelled more extensively he recognised the immense possibilities of trade in tea and
silk,[37] in competition with China. In the first year
of trade, 3000 bales of silk were exported which was
thought by some to be about the limit available, but
then as always, Japan was able to quickly increase
production to meet a demand, with the result that
the following year over 18,000 bales were sent
abroad. The country was already well on the way to
becoming the world's principal source of supply for
silk.

He also saw possibilities of business in fishery
products, even although the age of refrigeration
ships and the canning of food had not commenced.
In speaking of the variety of fish and game, he
wrote:

*Almost every stall in the street was stocked with
fine salmon, weighing from fifteen to twenty
pounds, many of them still alive, at rates varying
from ninepence to one shilling and sixpence. Teal
. . . sixpence each, wild ducks somewhat dearer,
snipe, golden plover, all were there . . . Think of
that, ye epicures, and instead a shooting or a fishing season in Norway with its hackneyed fields*

*and fiords, come to Japan to catch salmon, hunt
the deer, the boar, and the bear, and if you like
it shoot pheasant, snipe, teal, and wild fowl without stint. It is rather far off, it is true—some sixty odd days—but then think of the game and the
novelty—to say nothing of the chance of being
carved up by two-sworded samurai in pursuit of
their game.*

He saw great possibilities also in the export of old
rags, of which there were plentiful supplies available in feudal Japan—a country where most of the
clothing was made of cotton, despite the erroneous
belief that the people of old Japan dressed in silk.
Except on special occasions the great majority of the
people wore cotton garments—and much of it home
spun and home woven. The labouring classes in winter had nothing warmer than cotton but they had
become so inured to the absence of clothing that for
the greater part of the year they wore nothing more
than loin cloths—a sight which impressed all visitors to Japan in those days, and upon which many
travellers wrote at great length. Actually the absence of clothing among the working classes, even
in seasons other than summer, is amply illustrated
in the woodcut pictures of those times.[38]

In Japan of those days where paper was then
made from the bark of trees and other vegetable
fibres, rags were worthless for home consumption
and were regarded as rubbish until some of the early foreign merchants began to buy up supplies. Over
a thousand tons of old rags were shipped to England and Europe during the first year for paper
making. Prices then began to advance. However dif-

ficulties were experienced in discharging the dark vegetable dyes which the Japanese used in those days. That, together with the rise in price, caused the trade to languish, and it was some years before old rags became an important export item.

Among the many complicated problems of protocol which fell to Alcock, was that of making final arrangements for the departure of the Japanese Mission nominated by the Tokugawa Tycoon to represent him at the courts of those nations in Europe with whom he had concluded treaties.

The object of the Mission was to obtain a postponement of the opening date of the ports of Hyogo and Osaka.[39]

The Japanese authorities of the time had no experience in the despatch of diplomatic missions abroad, other than that gained in the previous year when a mission was despatched to the United States, nor did they have any representatives abroad to arrange the details of travel and accommodation. Great Britain therefore agreed to provide a warship, H.M.S. "Odin," for their transportation, and it was for Mr. Alcock to arrange the details with the Japanese.

The Japanese preference for travelling about in large parties displayed itself when they presented a first list of nearly eighty members. To find accommodation for such a number on a frigate during the long voyage around the Cape of Good Hope to Europe, and then to convey them across Europe from one court to another, would have been a major travel problem at any time, quite apart from the expense.

Mr. Alcock, the diplomat, first had to convince the Japanese authorities that the dignity of their country would not be compromised if the number was reduced to less than half. Finally thirty-five were agreed upon, which number included secretaries, secret servicemen, doctors, servants, cooks and barbers. Even so in order to accommodate that number, as far as possible in Japanese style and with special bathing facilities, much of the inside of the frigate had to be ripped out and converted. Larger and larger pantries had to be constructed for the immense quantities of stores which began to arrive on board in more and more frightening quantities. In the end there were five hundred champagne bottles containing soy sauce, more than one complete tea service, including five cups, for every individual, and mountains of Japanese porcelain plates and bowls. Fifty *hibachi* (charcoal burning braziers) arrived on board, but the ship's officers quickly spirited them away and had them stowed "in utterly inaccessible places," but even so the entire ship—excepting the Japanese—lived in daily dread and constant peril of fire arising from their passengers who were found to be "reckless or utterly devoid of common care and prudence in regard to fire"[40] especially on a man-of-war.

Finally the day for departure arrived. The Japanese were due to come on board between one and two in the afternoon. The deck officers were all on duty, the whole ship dressed and waiting to receive the party. Two o'clock, three o'clock, four o'clock passed without their appearance,[41] but finally just before dusk the guns of H.M.S. "Odin" boomed out the signal that the party had come on board[42] and so the first Japanese diplomatic mission to the courts of Europe set sail from Japan.[43]

Alcock's appointment came to an end[44] whilst Japan was still a feudal country and before Kobe and Osaka had been opened to foreign trade, but he was a man of such foresight that he was able to visualize the great future which lay ahead for those cities. In 1861, which was seven years before Kobe and Osaka were opened to foreign trade, he wrote of Osaka as follows:—

> *"This great centre with its port of Hyogo (Kobe) must be worth more to foreign commerce than all the other ports put together."*

In parting company, as we must now do, with the forthright Sir Rutherford Alcock, we cannot help but regret that he could not have lived to see the truth of his prophecy and the greatness which has come to the cities of Kobe and Osaka.

"INSTANT"[1]
PROFESSORS

> . . . in the morning much raine,
> with wind encreasing all day and
> night, from the East to the South,
> and in the night happened such a
> storm or Tuffon (typhoon) that I
> never saw the like in all my life..
> Capt. Saris' diary, 1613.

From the time the fishermen along the Pacific
coast of Japan first put out to sea in search of fish,
they encountered the dreaded typhoons.[2] Frequently their tiny craft were engulfed, but over the centuries they gradually evolved more sturdy vessels,
which were capable of sailing beyond the China seas
and also far out into the Pacific. It was believed
that the gods in the shrines and temples of their
home ports protected them during those hazardous
voyages.

Their craft were capable of outriding most
storms. They were able to weather some typhoons,
and even when battered and disabled they did not
always founder. Some drifted on and on, into unknown seas and distant lands.

Following the suppression of Christianity and the
determination of the government of that time to isolate Japan from the rest of the world, orders were
issued in 1636 that all vessels of sea-going capacity
should be destroyed, and that no craft should thenceforth be built of sufficient size to venture beyond
home waters. Furthermore all vessels had then to

79

be constructed with open sterns and large square rudders. Such craft being unfit for ocean navigation, it was hoped thereby to keep the people isolated within their own islands.

Any such vessels plying along the coast of Japan, that were unfortunate enough to encounter great storms, soon had their rudders washed away, then, as the junks wallowed helplessly in the waves, the masts rolled out. With their sails blown away and their masts gone, the crews were powerless to control them. Frequently the battered hulks drifted helplessly into the Kuro-shio, or the warm "Black Current" which sweeps up from Indo-China, passes Japan and then spreads out into the Pacific, eventually curving around and moving south along the coast of California.

Once in that current the junks drifted on, and ever onwards out into the Pacific, at about ten miles or so a day, sometimes for months on end, until eventually they sank or ran aground on some far shore. Some even drifted right across the Pacific and stranded on the north-west coast of the American continent. It is known that some of the crews survived those long journeys. And so, over the centuries, there must have been a constant but limited infusion of Japanese blood into that of the tribes along the coastal area of the North American continent.

Often the crews starved to death. In some drifting ships it was found the living had moved the dead into the holds, and laid the bodies out for eventual disposal, rather than casting them overboard to the sharks. In other ships they had placed the bodies in casks to await burial. But a time came when on the drifting ships none survived to attend to the dead, and such vessels were borne along by the current as floating death ships.

When the Europeans eventually sailed into the Pacific they found wrecks of Japanese junks strewn about its northern shores, on the Aleutians, on the coast of Alaska, along the Canadian and Oregon coast, and on Hawaii and other islands.[3] With the increase of shipping in the Pacific, the chance of the crews being rescued from disabled craft improved.

Russian and American vessels and other whalers, picked up many Japanese castaways, but having saved them from a watery grave the problem of what to do with them immediately presented itself. All ports in Japan, except Nagasaki, were closed to foreign shipping, and even there the Japanese authorities were unwilling to accept the return of rescued Japanese seamen. The law was clear—any Japanese who left Japan, even if he had been blown away by storms, was forbidden to return, for the authorities rightly feared that if they did accept the return of such seamen, foreign vessels would make that the excuse for entering Japanese ports in defiance of the law, but on the excuse that they were repatriating shipwrecked Japanese nationals.

And so it came about that many of the Japanese who were rescued by the Russians in the northern seas, were landed on the coast of Asia, whence they were conveyed inland to Irkutsk, then the capital of Eastern Siberia. Some lived there many years, forlornly awaiting an opportunity of being received back in their own country. Some embraced the Russian Orthodox religion during their enforced stay and did not seek to return. Quite a number died in Siberia before their return ever became possible. Some, who showed an aptitude for learning, were given facilities for studying Russian, and were then used as teachers of the Japanese language.

In 1792, Catherine II of Russia had attempted to establish relations with her neighbour Japan, and to that end had selected Lieutenant Laxman as an envoy to escort back to Japan a shipwrecked Japanese crew who had been living in Irkutsk for ten years.

Laxman landed at Hakodate and then travelled overland to the Japanese settlement at Fukuyama, known then as Matsumae. There he was treated with courtesy, although restricted in liberty. In the meantime the Japanese authorities at Matsumae were in communication with Yedo, and in due course they were instructed to release Laxman with the warning:

"Although it is ordained by the laws of Japan, that any foreigners landing anywhere on the coast, except at Nagasaki, shall be seized and condemned to perpetual imprisonment, yet considering the ignorance of the Russians, and their having brought back the shipwrecked Japanese they will be permitted to depart on condition of never approaching, under any pretence, any part of the coast except Nagasaki. As to the Japanese brought back, the Russians are at liberty to leave them or take them away again, as they please, it being the law of Japan that such persons cease to be Japanese and become the subjects of that government into whose hand destiny had cast them . . ."[4]

Laxman was thereupon dismissed with presents,

given an ample supply of provisions and ordered to leave the country.

Catherine the Great's efforts to establish friendly relations with Japan had thus failed. However, with an eye to the future, she appointed several Japanese, selected from the shipwrecked crews then in Siberia, to serve as "professors" in Japanese at the navigation school in Irkutsk.[5]

Catherine's idea was they should teach the Japanese language to a selected number of Russians, who were being trained to accompany the Russian expeditions in their penetration into the Pacific.

It was under one such Japanese "professor" that Heinrich Klaproth, the German Orientalist and traveller, in 1806 studied Japanese. One of the treasures now in the British Museum in London is an elegantly written Japanese vocabulary which Klaproth compiled in Irkutsk, when studying under one of those Japanese "professors."

Whilst we may speculate with some amusement on the scholastic backgrounds of some of those unfortunate Japanese seamen who became "professors," it will nevertheless be with more tolerance than we look back upon some of the foreign charlatans who became "professors" in Japan shortly after the country was re-opened about a century ago.

Many distinguished scholars and many rank charlatans were to be found among the foreign residents of the treaty port days of nearly a hundred years ago. Most of the scholars arrived in Japan as members of the staff of the legations and consulates, or as missionaries, teachers, or employees in the service of the Japanese Government. Soon they were busi-

ly investigating and studying all phases of Japanese
life, culture, industry, and history. The results of
their work can be found in the transactions of the
Asiatic and other learned societies in Japan.

The charlatans drifted into Japan as beachcombers, adventurers, cranks, and impostors who saw
chances of picking up an easy living in this new-
found country. Some of them secured appointments
as advisers to the Japanese Government, as teachers,
or even as professors in universities. That we do not
exaggerate in this matter, we shall quote from what
F. V. Dickins of the British Legation had to say in
1894 in his authoritative book *The Life of Sir Harry
Parkes:*

*"It is an unalloyed truth to say that the majority
of the 'Professors' in the schools of Tokei (that
was the name by which Tokyo was first known)[6]
were graduates of the dry-goods counter, the fore-
castle, the camp, and the shambles, or belonged to
that vast array of unclassified humanity that floats
like waifs in every seaport. Coming directly from
the bar-room, the brothel, the gambling saloon, or
the resort of boon companions, they brought the
graces, the language and the manners of those
places into the school room ... Japanese pride re-
volted ... after a report had been circulated that
one of the professors was a butcher by trade."*

That was a short-lived phase of the early Settlement days which soon passed. The charlatans were
soon displaced, and over the past century many hundreds of foreign professors and teachers have made
an important contribution to the Japanese educational system.

YOKOHAMA: THE WILD WEST OF THE FAR EAST

> *"On the other side of the flat, where it was proposed to locate the Foreign Settlement, stood Honmura, an insignificant fishing village with the houses scattered about in an expanse of wheatfields and vegetable patches."*
> Joseph Heco—*The Narrative of a Japanese,* 1859.

About the middle of the last century, trade along the China coast had become so competitive for the Far Eastern merchants, that many were awaiting the opportunity of going still further east to what had once been called the *populos sylver islands of Japans,*[1] but which, for more than two hundred years, had been a hermit kingdom. Therefore as soon as the treaties providing for the eventual opening of Japan had been signed, many began planning to move into this market, which they hoped would prove to be a new found El Dorado.

The two great Far Eastern firms of Jardine Matheson & Co., and Dent & Co., were so determined to make a serious bid for whatever business might be offering in that new land, that their representatives, and several others also, moved in ahead of the appointed date and were even living on shore at Naga-

85

saki and doing business with the local Japanese authorities before the British Consular officials arrived for the formal opening of the port, and despite a Royal Proclamation by Queen Victoria that Her Majesty's Government would not protect them from any consequences of their action.[2]

The British merchants in question, argued that the Dutch, who were already on the spot in Deshima, would scoop the market unless they moved in quickly. Although this breach of the treaties was by no means to the liking of the Tokugawa Government in far off Yedo, there was nothing much it could do. The local authorities were well satisfied, because it gave them an opportunity to purchase ships and munitions of war, and so build up their fighting strength in preparation for the troublesome times ahead, and for the trial of strength which many of the clans were planning to make against the Tokugawa family.

In Yokohama, also, there were collisions with the Consular Authorities. Kanagawa was the place specified in the treaties for the establishment of a foreign settlement, and it was there that the foreign ministers insisted upon establishing themselves. They then endeavoured to persuade the incoming merchants to settle there also.

This did not by any means suit the Tokugawa officials. There were so many powerful clans in Japan who were opposed to the entry of the foreigners that they preferred to have the newcomers settle across the bay near the unimportant fishing village of Yokohama.[3] The treaties had been forced on Japan, and, while the officials could not prevent the entry of foreigners, they hoped that their presence should not be intruded too much upon the public's notice until the opposition had died down. Despite the terms of the treaties, they did not want them living in the flourishing old town of Kanagawa, athwart the main national highway, the Tokaido, where they would be seen by travellers, and could in turn observe the comings and goings to and from the capital stronghold of Yedo, now Tokyo. There were horses, troops, supplies, Imperial messengers, and couriers constantly moving along that great artery of Japan. Any variation in the tempo of that traffic could serve as a barometer of political happenings in Yedo.

And so it came about that when the Japanese Government found the foreign ministers were determined to resist all pressure and to establish themselves in Kanagawa, as provided for in the treaty, it decided to entice the foreign merchants away from bustling Kanagawa, where in any case accommodation was almost unobtainable, by providing a readymade town for them in the fishing village across the bay. Clapboard buildings and a Customs House were hurriedly constructed.

"... Here on a level sandy spot extending a few hundred yards in each direction, a foreign settlement of single-storied wooden houses and warehouses had speedily arisen ... There was a sense of negligence and discomfort throughout the whole place, and everything was in a state of transition towards something which it was hoped would be improvement ..."[4]

Such was the description by an early visitor of the modest beginning of Yokohama.

William Keswick, of Jardine Matheson & Co., was the first to oppose the British Consular Authorities by taking a house in Yokohama, rather than in Kanagawa. So great was their reputation that, where Jardines went, other merchants soon followed. Little wonder was it that British Consul-General Alcock found it altogether "too provoking" that the "ill advised proceedings" of his own nationals created for him "the greatest obstacles" in his negotiations with the Japanese.

Alcock was not the only Consul who was incensed at the action of the merchants in siding with the Japanese. Townsend Harris, the first U.S. Consul General, it is said, would never admit that Yokohama rightfully could be substituted for Kanagawa. Therefore he would not permit his Consul to reside there, and *"he even carried his opposition so far as to declare that he never would countenance the change of settlement. He carried out his vow by leaving Japan without having set foot in Yokohama."*[5]

Time however, was to prove that Keswick and the other merchants were right in fixing upon Yokohama, with its deep water harbour, as the site for a trading port, rather than Kanagawa.

With the inducement of a ready-made town, complete with accommodation, there is little wonder that the incoming merchants defied the advice of their consuls and settled down in Yokohama, although in doing so they created the first of many feuds, which drifted on for years between the foreign community and the diplomatic corps.

The Japanese authorities promised suitable buildings and other incentives for all who came to Yokohama; sea frontages and other desirable locations were made available to the merchants, and lots in the back streets for the shopkeepers and the tradesmen. For the saloon-keepers there were sites along the Creek. To all they offered the facilities of a Customs House—and what an establishment it was.[6] All the Japanese Government agencies with which the foreigners were likely to come into contact were congregated in one building. It served as a general information office, a travel bureau and a passport office, an employment agency, and a land registration office—even a matrimonial agency. It performed, for the foreigners of the time, the functions of a government bureau, a national bank, a tax office, and a customs house, in so far as the foreigners of those days were responsible to Japanese government establishments, which was not much, but the few matters in which they were concerned with officialdom would have been considerable hurdles for them to jump, if it had not been for the services of the so-called Customs House. And we must not forget the extra-curricular functions, so to speak, which the Customs House officials performed. But here I shall quote the words of an English bishop, lest my readers should think I am romancing:

" . . . The native officials contributed every facility for the perpetration of domestic vice and impurity. Young men were encouraged to negotiate through the custom house the terms of payment and the selection of a partner in their dissolute mode of living."[7]

As an additional attraction for their new town, the authorities had created a gay quarter across the

Swamp. It was a town in itself, approached by a causeway, and was centered around the fabulous Gankiro and Jinpuro, the wonders of which establishments are depicted in woodcut prints, now mostly costly rarities, generally to be found only in noted private collections or in art galleries here and abroad.

A visitor in 1862 provided the following description:

"I visited the 'Gankeroo' taking the precaution to go there in broad day, and, for my character's sake, in good company, and was a little startled at the systematic way in which the authorities conduct this establishment. Two officers showed us over the building, and pointed out its beauties with as much pride as if they were exhibiting an ancient temple sacred to their dearest gods. This was the courtyard; that was to be a fishpond with fountains; in this room refreshments might be procured; that was the theatre; those little nooks into which you entered by a sliding panel in the wall were dormitories, encumbered with no unnecessary furniture; there affixed to the walls, was the tariff of charges, which I leave to the imagination; and in that house across the court, seated in rows on the verandah, were the 'moosmes' themselves. Would we step over, for it was only under male escort that we might enter the main building? My curiosity had, however, been sufficiently gratified, and I departed . . . "8

News of those fabulous places soon spread throughout the world, and thereafter the crew members of many a vessel talked and dreamed of the times they would have, should their ship touch at Yokohama.

Yokohama: The Wild West Of The Far East

On several occasions in later years those notorious establishments were destroyed by fire and rebuilt in different locations, until eventually "Number Nine" came into existence—that name, although simply the house number, was a sufficient address. As such it came to be listed by Rudyard Kipling among the world's most notorious houses of ill fame.[9] However it had a Jekyll and Hyde character, which at least was understood by some members, both male and female, of the foreign community of Yokohama, who, when returning home in the early hours, recognized it as the place where one could get the best after-midnight ham and eggs in the town.

The house—and the girls—were efficiently presided over by a madam whom the foreigners of Yokohama profanely nicknamed *Mother Jesus*. She was said to have been related to one of the big hotel families in Miyanoshita, but her fame will survive in that she was the original *Mama San,* an odious word which came into popular use during the Occupation, and is now sometimes used by brazen upstarts in the Japanese community, when addressing elderly foreign women, particularly tourists, unless they are sufficiently well informed on history and the language to resent and suppress any such misplaced familiarity.

But let us return to Yokohama's opening year.

Although the foreigners of those days were loathe to give the Japanese credit for much, the fact is the officials had been preparing for several years for the time when they would be forced to associate with foreigners from the world outside their borders, distasteful though the thought was.

They had been studying foreign habits and cus-

91

toms, in so far as that was possible, from a perusal of such European books as were available. Those books had been trickling into Japan through the Dutch in Nagasaki, but unhappily by the time Yokohama was about to be opened much of the information was a century or more out of date. In addition they were studying current illustrated European periodicals for which subscriptions had been placed through the Dutch traders in Nagasaki.[10] From all those studies they were able to convey to their own carpenters an idea of the rudiments of a simple form of European building—an easy task for Japanese carpenters skilled in the building of such complexities as temples, pagodas, and palaces. The carpenters set about their new work without imagination or deviation from instructions. The result was a series of structures not unlike those in the mushroom gold mining towns of Australia and the Wild West of America—the type of architecture often depicted in American "Western" films, and so one with which some of us are familiar even to-day.

Many years were to elapse before Japanese carpenters and builders were able to unlearn the experience gained in the construction of those crude buildings. The insides were mostly barn-like, which feature, even if it did not make for comfort, at least had the advantage that the buildings could be adapted more or less to any purpose. Some served as godowns or warehouses. Merchants moved into others and converted them into hongs; publicans took over some and transformed them into saloons.

Sliding partitions in Japanese style were easily erected by way of dividing off a portion of the naked

and dreary interiors to form living rooms at one end,
separated from offices and storage space at the other.
A few folding screens in the corners, flowered Japanese paper on the walls, essential furniture such as
beds, dining tables, and long easy chairs—on which
the master could drift off into sleep after the midday
meal—some odd pieces of lacquered furniture, a pair
of paper lanterns hanging from the ceiling, and two
or three fans tacked on the walls, transformed a portion of the building into a place of residence.

A hundred years ago Japan was a dangerous place
for foreigners—a land of assassins—and even the
Yokohama Settlement was not a safe place of residence. On more than one occasion foreigners were cut
down in the streets of the Settlement[11]—happenings
which led, a few years later, to the garrisoning of
over 3,000 British troops and a lesser number of
French troops in the port.

The Wild West aspect of early Yokohama was described by Anna d'A, perhaps the first genuine female tourist to Japan, who arrived in 1862 and noted
that just as the pioneer outposts in America once
needed palisades as a protection against sudden at-
tacks from Red Indians, so also did those residing in
Yokohama Settlement need protection from assassins:

*"I was surprised to find that every European here
has wooden palisades round his compound, which
in case of any sudden attack, serves a temporary
defence."*[12]

The roads in the Settlement as with all roads in
Japan of that time—and many since—were quag-
mires in wet weather, but soft and pleasant enough

for horse riding on dry days. Furthermore, being
wide by Japanese standards, they offered better riding courses than did the roads in the Japanese areas
outside. As most of the foreigners of any substance
owned ponies, some of which had been brought with
them from China, a fair amount of dangerous riding
took place around the streets of the Settlement creat-
ing hazards for those on foot.

In feudal Japan only the samurai or military class
were permitted to ride on horseback, the merchants
had to walk. Hence it was that the Japanese officials
watched, at first with annoyance, the foreign merchants—the majority of whom were British then—
riding about on horseback, and in other ways also,
doing all those things which in Japan had been re-
served for the privileged military and governing
classes.   And so they commenced to wonder how
it could be that England, which they had been told
was described by Napoleon as a nation of shopkeepers, could have achieved greatness. Then they began
to speculate that perhaps the secret of a nation's
grandeur might be in its commerce, rather than in
the haughty bearing of its Great Ones.

The Chinese servants of foreigners also rode ponies
—some in a wild headlong manner—a circumstance
which the Japanese found particularly offensive because at that time, as already mentioned, all classes
below the level of two-sworded gentry were forbidden
to ride on horseback. They could proceed on foot,
travel in *kago*—a type of litter or palanquin—or be
carried on the backs of porters, but not on the backs
of horses. In these circumstances the Japanese naturally resented Chinese riding about on horses, espe-

cially as they had gained entry to Japan as servants of foreigners and not by virtue of any treaty, for at that time China had not signed a treaty of amity and commerce with Japan.

The clouds of dust which the galloping ponies kicked up, combined with the reckless firing of pistols, indulged in by a few, gave a Wild West atmosphere to the place, and it required warnings from the consuls before this rowdiness ceased. So far as the British nationals were concerned, it was soon brought to an end when Consul-General Alcock issued, as has already been mentioned, his famous proclamation[13] *"for the Peace, Order and Good Government of British Subjects within the Dominions of the Tycoon of Japan,"* which contained precisely ten commandments.

The third commandment in effect said QUIT DISCHARGING FIREARMS—OR ELSE.

After Consul-General Alcock came out with his ten commandments, or rather his proclamation, there was more restrained behaviour, no galloping through the Settlement as if in chase of Red Indians, and less dust raised; but his action was so resented that about half the community thereupon snubbed him. However Consul-General Alcock calmly survived that, as he did all other brushes with the foreign community.

The consul in those days had a great deal of authority over his own nationals. He was the only power in Japan—at least the only mortal power—who could sit in judgement over them. In those days of extraterritoriality, a foreign national could only be tried in his own consular court according to the laws of his own country. The consul was therefore a person of considerable importance in that he could, when necessary, summon his nationals for trial, fine, imprison or deport them. Also he could marry or bury them, or act as coroner over their mortal remains.

That his power did extend to all corners of the Settlement and nearby areas may be judged from the fact that no British subject could establish a boarding-house, an eating house or a drinking saloon, without the Consul's permission. We do not believe that the Consul was averse to people eating, drinking or sleeping, but, we rather imagine, to what at times might go with them.

In Kobe, a British subject could not open a butcher's shop or even keep pigs, cattle or sheep without the Consul's permission, and when it came to a British subject in Kobe, or his Chinese servants, wanting to slaughter a pig within the Settlement area, that required a special permit.

There was a reason for all that. In a country such as Japan around a hundred years ago, where there was little resembling sanitary or public health regulations, it was customary for the people to throw offal and most other things they did not want into the gutters, and so it fell to the Consul, on top of all his other duties, to perform, in a sense, those of a sanitation inspector and an inspector of nuisances, in order to maintain the Settlement in a more hygienic state than the native quarters over its borders.

In the early years of Yokohama, there were two odoriferous "cow-yards" within the Settlement. From letters of complaint in the local press, it seems they served the joint purposes of dairies and butcheries, much to the annoyance of the nearby residents, who appear to have disliked living next door to a slaughterhouse. It was to correct such conditions within the Settlement, that the Consuls had to exercise control over the activities of their nationals.

Cattle were regularly imported from Shanghai to provide meat for the foreigners. Beef from Japanese oxen did not find a ready sale among the foreigners, because in those times, before the days of modern dentures, they complained it was rather tough, a circumstance we can well imagine considering that the oxen were worked until they died from old age or disease. There was, however, even in those early days, a small but growing demand from Japanese for beef, despite the religious prejudices against eating meat. Photographs of Japanese towns a hundred years ago show the signboards of *niku-ya* (butcher shops) in the streets. Among the first Japanese to develop a taste and create a demand for meat, appear to have been the highway porters and others who did extremely arduous work.

If Japanese beef was tough in 1862, it may not have been so tough in 1872, because we have noted from the English-language newspapers around that time, that Kobe beef on the hoof was being shipped regularly from Kobe to Yokohama, forty or so head of cattle per steamer not being at all unusual.

Although the first foreigners in Yokohama were mostly well satisfied with their homes—strange though they were—and grateful to have a roof over their heads, the fire insurance companies looked sourly on those hazardous risks. A five percent premium against the risk of fire was required in some

97

cases, but generally speaking no fire insurance protection could be arranged during the first year or so in Yokohama.

It may have been that some insurance was written by Dutch or British companies during the first two years, although actually the first evidence of business in Yokohama by a British company appears to be in January, 1861, when The Imperial Fire Insurance Company—still in existence in amalgamation with another company—appointed agents to accept approved risks.

Within a few years, over fifteen companies were transacting business.[14] And then came the great fire of 1866,[15] which wiped out most of the town, its wild west appearance, and much that was typical of the first years of the settlement. As the fire swept through the town it destroyed most of the early weatherboard structures, and with them the hopes of many of the first arrivals, and the profits of the early foreign fire insurance companies in Japan.

The losses of the fire insurance companies are said to have exceeded Mex. $2,800,000 or about £700,000 Sterling,[16] which was a huge sum in those days.

Thereafter Yokohama was rebuilt on more permanent lines. Grander buildings were constructed to take the place of the clapboard offices, and palatial residences were constructed on the Bluff for the *taipans*. But it also had its Bloodtown, Creekside and Chinatown.

Thus Yokohama gradually came to be a place whose fame spread throughout the world. A town and an expanding port had sprung up where previously there had been ricefields and swamps. But the consuls were unwilling to recognise the existence of Yokohama as the treaty port, and for years continued to date their letters and reports from Kanagawa. Originally a small bay separated the two, and the quickest means of approach was by ferry across the water. Eventually as Yokohama expanded and following upon reclamation schemes, the two merged into one another.

But it was Yokohama that the world came to know and talk about. Of all Japanese place names, it rolled off the tongue easily; it was a name which Europeans had the least difficulty in remembering. Half a century ago the word was known to more people in the world abroad than was Tokyo, and the Yokohama Settlement lingered in the memories of all who visited the place. It was always too European to be Japanese, and too Japanese to be European.

In the years ahead the name came to breathe for the world outside, an air of Oriental romance, of silk, adventure, intrigue, and crime—it had started as a fishing village, grew overnight into a fabulous Wild West type of town, which in turn grew into the wondrous port of Yokohama—a place which captured the imagination of the West and attracted adventurers from all over the globe.

Immediately in the rear of the Settlement was a swampy area, ditched with broad shallow tidal channels filled with the concentrated essence of life and drainage, which the sea did its humble best twice a day, at the fall of the tide, to carry away.

Beyond "The Swamp," an area which was subsequently reclaimed by the construction of several canals, there were Chinese shanties and grogshops—

a place which came to be known as "Bloodtown." It was to the less respectable saloons, the cheap boardinghouses, and the gambling dens in that area, that the crews of the whalers and the sealers gravitated during their long stay in port, and it was there that occurred some of the hair-raising knife fights between seamen, to which gory episodes the place owed its name.

In later years when less blood was shed in Bloodtown, the Chinese restaurants in nearby Chinatown became popular feeding houses for the gay young foreigners who wished to dine in greater privacy than the dining rooms in the Settlement hotels offered. Often, after some of those gargantuan meals, they went rolling home, on foot or in rickshaws, through the Settlement, along the Bund (and off the Bund!) and over the bridge to the Bluff.[17]

More things happened in Yokohama, particularly in Chinatown and down Creekside, than the world, or the residents on the Bluff, ever imagined. But occasionally there was a happening which reverberated around the world.

It will be recalled that Henry M. Stanley, the travelling correspondent of the *New York Herald* set out on an expedition to find Doctor Livingstone who was lost in Central Africa, and after trials and adventures during which he met nothing but wild animals, dreadful insects, and jungle folk, he suddenly came upon a white man with a grey beard, whereupon he uttered that famous remark "Dr. Livingstone, I presume."

Now it is our theory—a preposterous theory you might say, but still it is our theory—that the inspiration for that famous remark was born thousands of miles away from Central Africa—in fact in Yokohama—and that, before going to Central Africa, Stanley must have been reading the Yokohama newspapers of 1869, describing the famous meeting between the Yokohama Foreign Municipal Director, Mr. Benson, and the editor of the *Japan Times*, Mr. Rickerby, when they met on the steps of the United Club.

"Mr. Rickerby, I presume," roared Mr. Benson, the Municipal Director, who thereupon commenced horse-whipping him. But Benson was not to have things all his own way, because Rickerby retaliated with a horsewhip, which it so happened he also was carrying.

Although H. M. Stanley's remark to Dr. Livingstone in Central Africa was quite appropriate, Benson's remark to Rickerby in the Yokohama Settlement was a rather silly one, because he knew Rickerby, just as well as Rickerby knew him. That, of course, was half the trouble in the early Settlements. The places were so small that you could hardly help rubbing shoulders with your worst enemy.

The clash of horsewhips arose out of nothing more serious than a disagreement over municipal affairs. But in early Yokohama even the matter of a municipal dust bin could become as important as a mountain of garbage.

It might seem strange that two important members of the Foreign Settlement should have been walking about armed with whips, but actually at that time most of the important members of the community—that is to say most of the members of the Yokohama United Club—when not sitting in their offices or in the club, were generally sitting on a horse or else carrying a horsewhip. Of course, when they entered the Club they left both outside. There were hitching posts in the street as in the manner of the Wild West.

Adding to the Wild West appearance were the coaching services and the pony expresses. The coaches were not to be compared to the stage coaches of England, as the English editor of the *Japan Weekly Mail* bluntly explained, when he described a trip in one of those *"partially covered wagons, which vehicle with humourous disregard of honorable associations was called a stage-coach . . . the driver winded a horn proclaiming our departure after the best English fashion . . . it held a dozen occupants . . . was drawn by a pitiful pair of bare boned ponies . . . We had to get out and walk on steep ascents . . . The Caucasians were civilly requested to descend while the Japanese were peremptorily ordered out. . . ."* Those stage coaches, poor affairs indeed as compared with those of Europe, were rough riding contraptions from the goldfields of pioneering countries. The first had been introduced from Australia, which in fact had adopted the type used in the Californian goldfields.[18]

The Japanese soon copied the first Australian coaches, but omitted some of the few nicer points, and so achieved a result believed to have been impossible, namely the construction of a vehicle more uncomfortable than the coaches of the goldfield days.

During its early days the port had the reputation of being a place of heavy drinking, second only to

Kobe. Perhaps, however, there was some improvement in its drinking habits, because we find in the *Japan Daily Herald* of February, 1873, a report that the room in the Yokohama Foreign General Hospital, which had been specially constructed for patients labouring under *delirium tremens*, had been unoccupied for several weeks. This cheering news was considered of sufficient interest for the Editor to give space to speculating whether individual excesses had diminished, or whether the quality of intoxicating liquors had become less pernicious.

In those times, as in these, often there were more happenings in foreign homes known to the servants than to the foreign master or mistress. Both the Chinese and the Japanese servants were inveterate gamblers and were able to conduct discreet gambling schools within their own quarters in comparative safety, because so long as they could "pull the wool over their mistress' eyes"—as simple and as frequent then as now—they had little to fear. As the foreign police in the Settlement were more interested in chasing drunken sailors or beachcombers out of the Settlement, than closing down games of chance, and as the Japanese police were not permitted to do any sleuthing in the Foreign Concession, servants quarters within the Settlement areas were comparatively safe from raids, especially if they were located within the compounds of a foreign consulate.

It is doubtful whether the foreigners gambled more in the colourful Settlement days than now.[19] Anyhow as they enjoyed the benefits of extraterritoriality they had nothing to fear from the Japanese police, and, unlike Japanese nationals, were able to purchase a sweepstake ticket without incurring penalties under the extremely strict anti-gambling laws of those days. But that was a long time ago. Gambling is now one of the main social activities of the nation.[20]

The purchasing of sweepstake tickets, issued by the racing clubs in China and India, was a peccadillo of which many of the early foreigners were guilty. An unusual number of big prizes came to the foreigners in Japan. One Englishman twice won a grand prize, but it mattered not at all, because he soon spent or lost the lot, and was back again in his original, and usual, impecunious condition.

All these things happened in Yokohama of a long time ago. The famed city was destroyed in the great earthquake and fires of Sept. 1st, 1923. Thereafter, when the rubble and ashes of the old town were dumped into the bay to form the sea-front park, all the romance and fame of old Yokohama seemingly disappeared for ever. Only the name remained.

In the place of the old Yokohama, which was so reminiscent of the Settlement days, a more or less modern city slowly grew up among the many empty lots, an unattractive place, which was mostly reduced to ashes for the second time during the air-raids of 1945. The Occupation did a great deal to improve Yokohama's lot. Once again vacant building sites are gradually being rebuilt on. An effort has been made by the municipal authorities to give the place a new look by the construction of a tall observation tower, and some new buildings of indifferent architectural design, although they seem only to add to its crude appearance. During the seventeen years or so which have elapsed since the city was destroyed by bombing, the trees which line some of the streets have grown in size and cover up much of its shabbiness. But, at the most, it is to-day an unimpressive city, with little to recommend it other than the memories hidden within its name.

YOKOHAMA
MUSUME

> *With a passion that's intense*
> *You worship and adore,*
> *But the laws of common sense*
> *You oughtn't to ignore.*
>
> Gilbert & Sullivan's opera, *The Mikado.*

It was related in the previous chapter that the Bishop of Hongkong, following a visit to Yokohama in 1861, wrote a book.[1] Actually it was sensational and proved to be a "best seller." He described therein the manner in which some of the officials at the Japanese Customs House acted as brokers to secure female partners for the early foreigners, much in the same way as the friendly laundryman so assisted Pierre Loti when he set up housekeeping in Nagasaki.[2]

Many of the foreign missionaries of the time wrote in the same vein as the Bishop, but most of those writings are now buried and forgotten in missionary literature, although at the time they also created a flurry in Yokohama and abroad.

To what extent the foreigners did actually avail themselves of the services offering at the Customs House is now very much a matter of personal conjecture and prejudice. Certainly about that time the word *musume*, spelled in a variety of forms—*muszme, museme, mouseme, mousme, moosme, moosmie,* etc—took its place among the jargon of the foreigners in the Far East, with such words as tiffin, chow, godown, bund, maskee, taipan, amah, etc.

The dictionary meaning of *musume* is "daughter," and it requires no effort, on the part of a person so disposed, to believe that same word would have been used frequently by the officials, in the negotiations which may have ensued, to describe the fictional family relationship and the virginal qualifications of the young ladies whom they introduced to the lonely Yokohama foreigners of one hundred or so years ago. Whether or not that did so occur, the fact is that within a short time the word in its wide variety of spellings had spread to the far corners of the earth, and began to appear in most of the travel books which came to be written about Japan during the next half century or so, as a designation for any Japanese female, old or young, good or bad. The prerequisite to its use was that she should not be too old.

W.S. Gilbert was one of the few who resisted the temptation to use this newly-found word. When writing the lyrics for the light opera *Mikado,* he used instead, in the interest of meter and rhyme, and we suppose, Victorian niceties, the word "maid."

The word *musume* has long since slipped into disuse among foreigners, its place being taken by other Japanese words easier to pronounce and spell, or now simply by *garu furendo* (girl friend).

The Bishop of Homoco, in his well known treatise on the Yokohama dialect,[3] used the spelling *moose me,* which people at that time thought to be as good as any, and beyond giving its meaning as "a woman," he seemed to studiously avoid the subject. At least we thought he was dodging it, because *moose me* at that time seemed to be one of the topics which all male visitors talked about, or boasted about, much as they boast to one another these days about their adventures in the Turkish baths of Japan. We concluded that there must have been something about a *moose me* which a man of the cloth, such as the Bishop of Homoco, should not discuss, and so we made a note on our cuff to do some research into the subject. Alas, we have never found the time to get around to it, an omission which we regret, because it has left us singularly unqualified to weight up a remarkable book which recently came under our notice, for it was then that the word *musume* again intruded upon our notice in a big way.

It was a very rare Japanese book printed a hundred years ago from carved woodblocks.[4] Apparently the worms found it to their liking, because it was riddled with holes. The title *Yokohama Kidan,* (Interesting Tales of Yokohama) was arresting enough, until upon opening the book we found that the English alphabet, and how to write Roman numerals, were among the interesting topics to which the reader was treated. Our excitement completely subsided when we came to the last sentence in the book—" . . . *any delicate matters have been omitted, which please note."*

We thereupon settled down to a study of that dull portion of the book, which was in fact a directory of the foreign residents of Yokohama of 1861-1862, in order of their places of residence within the Settlement, commencing with Lot No. 1 or *Ichiban.* It differed from all other directories which we have seen,

in that in addition to giving the name of the *danna-
san*, or master of the house, it also gave the names
of his principal employees, a departure no doubt designed to provide vital information for the Japanese
readers of the book. For example, the entry against
each house number was that of the foreigner living
there, not that of the firm which he represented. It
was therefore more of a personal directory, rather
than a business one. In those early days the foreigners usually lived in, or above, their offices, the same
building often serving the joint purposes of an office, a warehouse, and a place of residence. In this
directory, *danna-san's* name was followed in most
cases, but not all, by the name of a *musume*, a *kozukai* (servant), and a *betto* (groom). Upon making a
tedious count we discovered there were 79 *danna-
sans*, against which were listed by name 30 *musume*,
79 *kozukai*, and 52 *betto*.

We thus discovered that each of *danna-sans* employed a *kozukai*, from which it can be inferred
that servants were plentiful in those days; and that
the majority employed a *betto* also, from which it is
evident that most of them owned a pony or ponies.

We do not know that any other inferences can be
drawn.

Because the names of such Japanese supernumera-
ries for each household were given, the directory
must have proved of inestimable value to the Japanese tradesmen and shopkeepers of Yokohama. For
example, they had a ready reference of the name
of the *betto* to approach regarding supplies for the
stable, the name of the servant for supplies for the
house, and we suppose negotiations on general mat-

ters could have been carried to the heart of the *danna-san* by courtesy of the *musume*.

Without making a more exhaustive analysis of this remarkable book—which we do not now contemplate doing—we feel unable to offer any explanation of the duties or function of the thirty *musume*. We did however note that there were none in the residences of the Foreign Ministers (excepting the French Minister) nor in the homes of the missionaries, the clergyman, the Catholic priest or the doctor. The heads of some, or possibly most of the very important firms (but not all) and also the bank managers, so far as we could detect, did without *musume*, as also did those homes where a wife was in residence.

In those houses where there were two bachelors residing, we observed there were two *musume*. On the other hand, so far as we were able to discover, there were none in the homes of any of the senior consular officials, but there was one in the house of the Secretary of the British Legation, as also in those of some of his Continental counterparts.

We noted many other interesting things in this very old book, but found, as the author had warned, *"any delicate matters have been omitted, which please note."*

We then closed this rare and discreet old book. After having pored over it for many days, we had a feeling that each time we opened its covers, skeletons in the closets of a hundred years ago might come tumbling out. And so we carefully put it away, and will leave the bookworms undisturbed.

THE WHALERS
AND THE
BEACHCOMBERS

The dangerous practice of hunting whales commenced in Japan, as in most maritime countries, far back in time, too early for systematic record. At first, of course, only those whales which approached close to shore, or accidentally stranded, were attacked. Later men set out in ships, but, as the whales were killed off and became less numerous, the vessels had to venture further and further from land, and thus whaling became more and more dangerous.

In those early days the whales were taken more for the meat than the oil—whale meat was a common food in some parts of Japan from early times. The Dutch historian Hagenaar, who was in Hirado attached to the Dutch East India Company, has recorded that during the season of 1636 the Japanese whale fishers captured 274 whales,[1] which however the Dutch reported to be smaller and less fatty than the Greenland whales.[2]

In other countries also the hunt for whales had been going on for centuries. Most of the Norwegian whalers set out from Spitsbergen, the British from Hull. In fact all the North European nations were in the hunt; gradually they extended their activities into all the oceans. The first English whaler to visit Japanese waters was the "Emina" as early as 1788; she was followed by the "Syren" from London in 1819.[3]

When the Yankee whalers of New Bedford and Nantucket began to find their game scarce in the neighbouring waters of Massachussets and in the Atlantic, they moved south, rounded Cape Horn and began hunting in the Pacific. The first American whaler was on the Japanese whaling grounds about the same time as the "Syren." And of course the Russians were whaling off Japan also. They all hunted along the shores of Japan but were wary of approaching within gunshot range. When they came near to shore sometimes they could hear the temple bells being tolled in alarm, and at night they could see the beacon fires being lighted along the coast to warn the people that a landing might be attempted from a foreign ship.

Japanese records relate that in some places the shore-watchers counted over eighty foreign whalers passing by in a year.[4] "Black ships" was the name given to them by the Japanese, because, in addition to being painted black, they were smoky and sooty vessels—some too, thought them ships of ill omen.

The crews were tough sailors, they had to be to survive the long rough voyages. Some died by shipwreck, some died of thirst, and some of malnutrition or outright starvation. Little wonder that some in their extremity deserted their ships and came ashore

on Japan's inhospitable coast, risking the execution-
er's sword rather than remain on board those floating hells. Often whalers in distress would roam along
the Japanese coast in search of a secluded cove where
they could replenish their water casks, and perhaps
obtain supplies of fresh vegetables. Some made raids
on villages along the coast in the hope of obtaining
much needed supplies. Some of the raiders were captured and executed. Many vessels were driven off
with shot and shell and many were wrecked along
Japan's rocky coast. The survivors, if there were
any, were soon captured by the Japanese. Some died
during imprisonment, others were eventually deported on Dutch vessels through Nagasaki, often after
years of amazing experiences. Unfortunately being
men without education they could not record their
adventures, with the result that history is so much
poorer for the loss.

It is true that some of the seamen who landed
illegally in Japan committed outrages, but on the
other hand all the misdeeds that have been marked
up against them, may not have occurred.

It has been said that some of the whalers were
guilty of burning of villages and the slaughter and
plunder of cattle. The most cited case is that of
the outrages said to have been committed by the crew
of the whaler "Lady Rowena," as related by Richard
Hildreth in his book *Japan and the Japanese*, Boston,
1860. Hildreth states that in the *Sidney* (sic) *Gazette* of Feb., 1842, there appeared a paragraph
*"warning mariners to be cautious how they landed
on Japan, as a Japanese village on the east coast of
the islands, somewhere near 43 degrees north lati-*

*tude, had been recently destroyed by the crew of the
'Lady Rowena,' then in the harbor of Sidney (sic)
and whose captain openly boasted of the fact."*

The record of some of the whalers, and other trading vessels in the Pacific in the last century, is so
terrible that one hesitates to say much in their defence. On the other hand whilst the "Lady Rowena"
outrage, as reported by Hildreth, has been cited by
Japanese historians as an example of the lawlessness
which occurred along the Japan coast, there seems
to be no Japanese version or record of that case, and
every effort to discover corroboration has failed.

Recently when in Sydney, Australia, I visited the
Mitchell Library—a library which specialises in early
Australian records—and it was with feelings of suppressed excitement that I turned over the pages of
the *Sydney Gazette* of over one hundred and twenty
years ago and commenced reading from the first day
of February, 1842, in the hope that the news item
would yield a few more details than those quoted by
Hildreth. To my surprise there was no mention of
the "Lady Rowena." I thereupon searched through
ten years of that newspaper without finding any
mention of the vessel nor indeed even a single reference to the country of Japan. (That there should
have been no mention of Japan, even over a period
of ten years, is understandable, because that country
was then still secluded from the rest of the world;
her doors were still shut tight.)

I have since learned that I was not the first to un-
dertake that research. H. E. Wildes describes in his
book *Aliens in the East,* published in 1937, that he
was attracted by the same story and had looked for

corroboration but that a *"through search of the Sydney Gazette for the period failed to discover the notice, nor are there records in the customary maritime mediums of the time referring to the event."* In other words Wildes forestalled me by twenty-four years.

In addition to Sydney, Australia, I had a search made of the archives of Sydney, Nova Scotia, but again without being able to trace either the *Sidney Gazette* or the whaler "Lady Rowena."

Whence therefore the story of the *Sidney Gazette* and the "Lady Rowena" originated, and whether it has any basis in fact, remains a mystery.

Whalers working the northern Pacific had to establish their chief base for repairs in the Sandwich Islands (Hawaii) where they loaded most of their supplies. They were able to pick up some provisions, and some rum, in the Bonin Islands[5] (or the Ogasawara as the Japanese later re-named them) where at that time a small colony of English, Americans and Hawaiians had been established under the Union Jack, but more often than not the whalers were short of vegetables for long periods and had to subsist on a surfeit of salt junk. Occasionally they were lucky enough to get some turtle meat from turtles which then abounded along the shores of some Pacific islands.

The winds blow steadily and strongly around northern Japan in the seas where the whalers hunted. So strong are the winds that the Japanese coastal sailing vessels in the Tokugawa days did not attempt to beat against them. For example, the rice ships,[6] bound for Osaka, which sailed out of Niigata

on the west coast, would leave in the late spring and
head south to Shimonoseki and then up to Osaka.
The time taken for that 900 mile journey was three
to six months. They would then lay up in Osaka for
the winter and return in the early spring, a full year
being allowed for the entire trip. Such were the difficulties of navigation around the Japanese coast in
those days of sail.[7]

For the foreign whalers, the region was one of
tremendous hazards, because with the whole Japanese coast line closed to them, there were no ports of
refuge into which they could put for shelter.

After the Japanese had been forced to open a
number of ports to international trade—such ports
were known as treaty ports—much of the hardship
previously associated with whaling in these waters
was eliminated. The whalers were then assured of a
safe retreat against stress of weather. They could
enter those treaty ports for refitment or seek shelter
there from the treacherous typhoons—more treacherous then than now, because the only warning the
captain had was a falling barometer, the flight of
birds, and other signs which he could read in the
skies.

Once the treaty ports were opened, ample supplies
of fresh provisions could be obtained. At first the
cheapest meat obtainable was venison, wild boar and
bear's flesh[8]—most welcome luxuries to seamen after
the salt junk to which they had been accustomed.
Potatoes and green vegetables were likewise available in abundance. Water also was freely obtainable
although it was frequently contaminated because

Japan was then a cholera[9] and dysentery[10] ridden country.

In the off season the whaling ships were usually laid up in the treaty ports for several months—during which the crews were given plenty of shore leave, or took it. Some established agreeable domestic arrangements on shore, and, whilst their money lasted, lived the life of Riley in a new-found Garden of Eden, in their estimation second only to the Bonins or Tahiti.

Many seamen, after looking this new land over, decided to give up the hardships of the sea for the pleasure of a life ashore. They signed off and never went back to sea. Some started out on new careers in Kobe or Yokohama as shipwrights, tinsmiths, carpenters, butchers, coachmen, or tradesmen of various descriptions, making use of such qualifications as they possessed. Many, in all these categories, failed in their new enterprises, but some laid the foundations for what in course of time became thriving businesses.

There was the remarkable case of a Dutch sailor[11] who left his ship in Yokohama to become a godown keeper. Then when his employers closed their business and he was out of employment, he decided to seek work in Kobe. Travel between Yokohama and Kobe was then normally done by sea, but as the sailor was unable to pay for a passage by sea he determined to walk to Kobe—a distance of about 350 miles—despite the fact that in those days foreigners were restricted to travel within a twenty-five mile limit of the treaty ports, unless provided by the

Japanese authorities with a special passport. However when the Dutch sailor eventually arrived at Kobe he reported that he had met with the greatest kindness all the way. At the castles of two daimyo, where he applied for assistance, he was feasted—according to his account—sumptuously, before being put on his way. On approaching the forbidden city of Kyoto he was then taken in charge by Japanese officials who lodged him in a Japanese hotel before escorting him to Kobe, where he was handed over to the Dutch Consul—certainly a most extraordinary adventure at a time when Japan was an unknown country, even to most of the foreigners, who were then residing in the treaty ports.[12]

Other seamen, who were allergic to work of any kind, deserted their ships for the life of a beachcomber, until the harassed Japanese police herded them back into the Foreign Settlement where their consul could pick them up and ship them away.

To assist the consul in such constabulary duties, there was a constable on the staff of the British consulates, and a deputy marshal in the U.S. Consulates. That there was a real necessity for those guardians of the peace is evident from the frequent references which are made to those officials in the early Nagasaki British Consulate records, which I recently had the privilege of examining.

On the word of the British Consul, when writing to the Legation in Yedo under date of 11th October, 1859, we know that he was fortunate *"in engaging the services of a respectable constable—his name is Kettle . . . at the rate of 45 $ Mex. per month."* When the Legation questioned the necessity of paying a constable so much (or should we say so little), the Consul replied with some asperity: *"I have procured a man of intelligence and experience . . . I regret that the rate of wages should have appeared to you so high—for I confess that on reflection they had not so appeared to me."*

For living accommodation in the Consulate the constable had *"two little compartments nine feet square."*

It is of interest to read that Kettle threw in his job after six months, thereby seeming to demonstrate that the Legation had been wrong in believing that 45 $ Mex. was a munificent salary for a constable.

The Consul thereupon engaged *"as a substitute a man named Green, who was chief mate of a merchant ship . . . in all respects a suitable and competent person. He is a respectable elderly man . . . active and very useful, and in the capacity of outdoor assistance (so to term it) he certainly does not eat the bread of idleness."*

Whether the U.S. Consulates were equally fortunate with their deputy marshals is doubtful, because I found the following in an editorial in *The Japan Mail* of 12 March, 1872, protesting at the violence displayed by that official when making arrests:

Wm. M. Davis, the deputy marshal of the United States Consular Court, who, we believe, is a retired prize fighter, may be familiar to the public in connection with a charge of biting a man's nose off on the occasion of the last regatta.

In the early days of the Foreign Settlement, first in Yokohama, Nagasaki, and Hakodate, and later in Kobe, it was not unusual during the off-season to see anything up to thirty whalers and sealers anchored in the harbour for weeks or months at a time—and long thirsty months they were. The captains, officers, and crews, generally a tough living and hard drinking crowd, gathered on shore in the many saloons where they mingled with sea-faring men from the sailing ships and other vessels then coming to Japan in increasing numbers.

Love of liquor and a lack of sobriety was a characteristic failing of many of those sea-faring men, as may be discovered from a perusal of the early public telegraph code books, many of which provided ample facilities, whereby the ship's agents and others could apprise the owners at home of what was happening on their vessels. There were, for example, separate code words for:

> *The captain is drunk.*
> *The captain is very drunk.*
> *The captain is always drunk.*

And similar code provisions for the chief mate and other officers. Eventually the various mariners associations throughout the world made representations to the publishers of the telegraph code books that such code provisions were a reflection on the merchant marine, and so in course of time, as new editions of the codes were printed, those blunt but useful code provisions disappeared. Thereafter the ship's agents when sending a telegram to the owners could not comment upon the captain's lack of sobriety with the same facility and economy as formerly.

Besides the whaling vessels, many sealers were anchored in the treaty port harbours during the off-season, but their livelihood was not to last; the slaughter of seals proceeded at such a pace that the sealing grounds soon ceased to exist. Also offshore whaling gave way to modern whaling, involving long cruises. With those changes, the "black ships" disappeared from Japanese harbours, and with them disappeared many of the saloons in the Foreign Settlements, the brawls, knife fights, and other problems of the consuls, the foreign constables, and the Japanese police, which had grown out of the hard living of those sea-faring men.

The beachcombers rather than do hard work, begged or stole and were as great a nuisance to the Japanese as to the foreigners. They prowled about the Settlements, using the sale of mock coral trinkets, Hakodate salmon, or anything else as a pretext for entering a front garden and getting near a back door, whence by threats or stealth they hoped they might gain something.

They remained for some years, even after the days of extraterritoriality ended, but gradually, as the discomforts of Japanese jails became known among their fraternity, they also disappeared.

COBB & CO.,
OF YOKOHAMA

And out beyond the reach of rail,
As far as wheel-tracks go
The drovers round their camp-fire hail
The lights of Cobb & Co.
Will H. Ogilvie, 1895.

Most Australians, and New Zealanders also, know something of the stories of romance and adventure associated with the days of about a hundred years ago when the Royal Mail was carried by Cobb & Co., with six steaming matched horses—greys, roans, and bays all well bred, groomed and intelligent— kicking up the dust on the Otago roads of New Zealand or on the overland roads to the Australian gold-fields.

At night—what a sight—as the three big lamps of a coach, one on either side of the box seat and one towering in the middle, swept around a bend in the road and came nearer and nearer. The lamps—feeble things by to-day's standards—did not do much to illuminate the road ahead, but they were considered a wonderful sight a century ago, especially when the coach from the Ballarat goldfields came sweeping down Great Bourke Street[1] in Melbourne Town.

The first coaches had been imported from America. Suspended on stout leather straps, they represented the most up to date coaches for the rough roads of a new pioneer country. The old fashioned vehicles, rigid and unyielding with their iron-plates and bolts, had been breaking up on the rough roads of the Australian bush.

In 1853, four Americans, one of whom was Freeman Cobb, had started a line of coaches—Cobb & Co.—between Melbourne and the goldfields. Enormous profits were made and within a few years each of the partners had amassed a fortune. Freeman Cobb returned to California where he lost everything in wild cat schemes. Then he went to South Africa and started a coaching business to the Kimberley diamond mines. That business after changes in name was still in existence at the time of the South African War and did in fact transport some of the British troops, notably the Canadian Field Artillery Battery, to the front.

After Freeman Cobb left Australia, the company extended its operations throughout that continent, and by 1870 was harnessing six thousand horses a day and covering twenty-eight thousand miles of routes a week. Cobb & Co., carried the Royal Mail to the furthermost towns in Australia, miners to the gold rushes, and gold from the goldfields to the cities. Adventures and brushes with bushrangers—as bandits were known in Australia—were not infrequent, all of which is told in the song, stories, and drama of Australia.

The horse-coaching days of a century ago were commemorated in Australia in 1955 by the issue of a special postage stamp depicting one of Cobb & Co's coaches carrying the Royal Mail. Actually the company is still in existence in Queensland—in Toowoomba[2] and Brisbane—as a transport company.

Although the name of Cobb & Co., is a household

word in Australia, it is not generally known there, or in Japan, that there was a Cobb & Co., in Yokohama. There were in fact several coaching companies in the early days of Yokohama, and their coaches usually caried a flag with the distinguishing mark of the company, such for example as a black horse on a red ground.[3]

The flags of those early coaching companies were also displayed at the terminal points of the coach journey, and are reproduced in a number of famous Japanese woodblock prints of the early Settlement days. Such prints are now rare and are not usually seen outside of museums and specialist publications, but even in those places, if the flags are described at all, they are usually stated—quite incorrectly—to be daimyo banners erected outside an inn at which a daimyo was accommodated.

There is also a rare woodblock print[4] of the Bund of the Yokohama Settlement by Hiroshige II showing a number of foreign and Japanese merchants, European ladies in crinolines, Chinese compradores, and foreign seamen on the quay, bidding farewell to an American sailing vessel. A Japanese tea-house girl is also there, although whether to bid goodbye to an overnight customer departing on the vessel, or in an endeavour to collect an unpaid bill from a runaway patron, is a secret which Hiroshige did not reveal. The British Consulate, and prominent mercantile houses can be seen on the Bund, the French Consulate and Military Hospital on France Yama, and the British and French garrison barracks on the Bluff,[5] also one of Cobb & Co's coaches on the Bund.

The early foreigners, who at times had to make

use of *norimono* (Japanese palanquin) on official occasions and visits, considered them abominable contraptions, and a reproach to the ingenuity of the Japanese people. The Japanese, on the other hand, being accustomed to sitting cross-legged for long periods, thought them not uncomfortable, and some were rather amazed that the foreigners should have introduced stage coaches as a substitute method of conveyance.[6]

Despite an immense amount of research which has been done on the subject both in Japan and in Australia, the manner in which Cobb & Co., came to Yokohama is still in doubt. Some Australians[7] give credit to Cyrus Hewitt who it is stated took a team of coaches to Japan, but Japanese competition, it is said, soon ran him off the roads and he left Japan a ruined man. We know much about Cyrus Hewitt, and have even seen his name mentioned in a Japanese publication, but we do not believe he ever came to Japan.

A New Zealand historian[8] gives credit to the Hoyt brothers of New Zealand, proprietors of the Cobb & Co., Telegraph Line in Otago, who sold their business in March 1868 and sailed for Yokohama in ss "Albion"[9] and there started a line of coaches to Yedo (Tokyo). It is related that they sent for two Yankee drivers, Tom Sayers and Frank Rutherford. The former it is said found *"the unpleasant Japanese habit of executing criminals at the roadside got on his nerves and he retired."* Rutherford, it is said, died of smallpox in Japan in 1871.

When we traced Frank Rutherford's tombstone in the Yokohama Foreign General Cemetery, the Japanese custodian informed us that it is customary after fifty years have elapsed without any maintenance coming from friends or relatives to disinter the remains and bury them in a common grave, thus making the plot available for others. That information did not conform with our understanding that burials in that cemetery during the days of extraterritoriality were protected by special treaties, and, as this grave is probably the only link now remaining between Cobb & Co., of Yokohama and the famous Cobb & Co., of Australia and New Zealand, we contacted the Chairman of the Cemetery Committee and were glad to receive his written assurance that it is not intended to disinter the remains of Frank Rutherford.

We know the Hoyt brothers[10] did sail for Japan and did arrive in Yokohama in June, 1868, in ss *"Albion,"* in which they had acquired an interest, because one of them wrote a long letter which was published in the *Otago Witness* of 19 Sept., 1868, in which he described the voyage, the Yokohama Settlement, and the life of the foreigners there, the purpose of all of which was to warn any other of his countrymen against coming to Japan *"where nothing but disappointment awaits them."*

He related that *"there are immensely wealthy firms here, branches of business houses in China, long established, who do all that is to be done,"* and he reported that the merchandise brought by the "Albion," comprising *"goods of nearly every description and some stock"* remained unsold at the time of writing; even two pianos and one harmonium failed to find a ready buyer.

Knowing what we do about Yokohama of those days we can understand all that part of his letter, but knowing what we do about Yokohama of those days—a fact we now repeat—we are perplexed at his comment that *"The foreign population is but small; most of the gentlemen are bachelors,"* and wonder what interpretation he intended us to put upon it! We even wonder whether he intended to write: *"The foreign population is small; most of the bachelors are gentlemen!"*

Another New Zealand writer[11] states that the Hoyt brothers sailed for Japan, in partnership with the captain, as owners of the ss "Albion," but *"when she arrived in the East she belonged to only one of them. The ship returned to Sydney, the owner giving his unlucky friends a passage home; after he had done them at cards on board the ship."*

If this be true—which we doubt—it leaves us more puzzled than ever, as to when and by whom, was Cobb & Co., of Yokohama first established, although it would seem that the Hoyt brothers were interested in one or other of the early Yokohama coaching enterprises.[12]

Although Cobb & Co., in later years used to advertise that it had been established in Yokohama in 1867, we have not been able to trace the name in Japan earlier than 1st February, 1872, when an announcement appeared in the local papers that the coaching firm of Sutherland & Co., would thereafter be conducted under the name of Cobb & Co.

Sutherland & Co., had commenced regular coaching services to Odawara with stables at Fujisawa and Oiso to supply relays of horses. Also their

127

coaches had been running to Yedo, later to be known as Tokei, then Tokio, and finally Tokyo. That business, from 1st February, 1872, was conducted under the name of Cobb & Co., as already mentioned.

In the absence of a postal system and railways, all of which were to come later,[13] there was an urgent need for coaches for the conveyance of passengers,[14] mail, specie, and supplies, especially to the foreign legations in Tokyo; nevertheless, because of the fierce competition among the several coaching companies, profits were thin. There were other foreign coaching companies, and Japanese coaches were on the roads also, but the name of Cobb & Co., seemed to outlast most of them, and was still in existence at the beginning of this century.

Cobb's drivers were colourful characters, Americans, Australians, and New Zealanders, well paid and skilful, who had years of hard experience behind them before they came to Japan, and well they needed it—driving a coach and four along the narrow Tokaido of those days was no easy task. There was one named George, a negro, who was reputed to be exceptionally accomplished with the reins, another—we suspect an Australian—named Stephen Fitzgerald of whom J. W. Sutherland, director of the Yokohama company asserted in a consular court case, when giving evidence concerning one box of specie out of sixteen which went astray whilst Fitzgerald was driving in a drunken condition—not a particularly rare condition for Fitzgerald—"He is the best man we ever had!"

Business in the Foreign Settlements in Japan in those early days was in a state of flux. Many of the first arrivals, quite a few of whom came from the goldfields in Australia, were adventurous types who were jumping in and out of all manner of enterprises, starting new businesses, selling out in one and buying into another.

Despite much research, in several countries, little is known regarding Sutherland who appears to have come to Japan around 1867.[15] It would seem he was a well known figure in the community. At least we gained that impression after we had traced his name through the British Consular Court records and found he had figured in a number of cases—as a witness in 1872, a defendant in 1873, 1876, and 1877, a plaintiff in 1877, and also a juryman in 1877. He continued to live in Yokohama until the summer of 1889 when he left Japan with the intention of living in retirement in the south of France. However an obituary notice, which has been discovered in a London newspaper, shows he never reached France. He died in London on 11 Sept., 1889.

Our interest in J. W. Sutherland is that he originated a stamp for use on letters and packages carried by his company's coaches, although most probably he got the idea from the "Pony Express" stamps which had been issued by Wells Fargo & Co., some ten years or so earlier, when William F. Cody, otherwise known as "Buffalo Bill," was one of their riders carrying mail overland to Sacramento in California, or perhaps he had copied Burdell & Co., of Melbourne, Australia, who in 1854 had issued a stamp for use in the express service they operated for the carrying of letters and parcels to and from the goldfields in Bendigo and Ballarat.

Cobb & Co., Of Yokohama

Before the days of a postal system in Japan, the delivery of letters was mostly in the hands of letter carriers—professional runners—who were capable of covering considerable distances on foot at a fast trotting pace. Also it was customary for those operating coaching services and other transportation enterprises, to convey letters and packages from one town to another for a fee, but J. W. Sutherland appears to have been the only one who had special stamps printed. They were perforated and in two denominations, ¼ boo and 1 boo,[16] on pink and yellow papers and depicted a galloping horse with a rider blowing a horn. In addition there was the English lettering *"Sutherland & Co., Postage."*

Following the opening of the Japanese national postal services in 1871,[17] the Japanese Government prohibited the carriage of mail by the coaching companies, but in those days of extraterritoriality it was unable to stop the traffic on foreign-owned coaches. However, in course of time, when the senders of mail found the postal service more convenient and reliable, the letter delivery service of the coaching companies came to an end. For some years thereafter Cobb & Co., continued to carry currency and other items between Yokohama and the capital. Then gradually their business changed to livery stable keepers, and as such the name of Cobb & Co., carried on in Yokohama into this century.

Only nine specimens—all in a used condition—of the Sutherland stamps appear now to exist; they are owned by philatelists scattered around the world.[18] Although they are not recognised as true postage stamps, they are referred to in some philatelic publications and are looked upon as valuable rarities.

For years they puzzled collectors who believed they had been used in Hongkong. Later it was realised that the word *boo* was the manner in which the early foreigners in Japan spelled *bu,* a silver coin then equivalent to about a shilling. After that link with Japan was established, many years were still to elapse before the connection between the Sutherland & Co., stamps and the coaching service was discovered.

It seems unlikely that any further specimens of the Sutherland stamps will be found, but the nine genuine stamps which are known to exist will put the name of Sutherland & Co., and its famous successor, Cobb & Co., on the map in Japan for so long as there are stamp collectors.

SUTHERLAND & Co.

Postage 1 Boo.

THE ENERGETIC REV. M. BUCKWORTH BAILEY

> *I tooke a garden this day and planted it with pottatos brought from the Liqueu (Luchus) a thing not yet planted in Japan.*
>
> Richard Cock's diary, 19 June, 1615.

A hundred years ago the staff of a British Consulate in Japan at times included officials other than consuls and vice-consuls. There were often, for example, a constable, a goaler, turnkeys, and a chaplain.

Our interest in this article is in a consular chaplain, the Rev. M. Buckworth Bailey, pastor of Christ Church,[1] Yokohama, who was also the military chaplain to the garrison of British soldiers then stationed in Yokohama. The latter duty must have been an onerous one, considering the number of persons and influences in Yokohama conspiring to bring about the moral downfall of those soldiers, and the comparatively few persons interested in their welfare— for those were the days when soldiers in the ranks, in most armies, were generally left to look after and amuse themselves.

We do not, however, believe that the task of military chaplain would have been too heavy for the broad shoulders of the Rev. Buckworth Bailey, because he was an unusual man of many parts. He could use a hammer and a carpenter's saw, quite as effectively as he could deliver a sermon. Credit for the excellent taste displayed in the stalls and furniture of Christ Church, Yokohama, was given to his own manual skill and industry. He was also quite a cook, and he offered to teach Western cooking to the Japanese, and truck gardening also. In fact, he and another resident, "Public Spirited" Smith,[2] were given credit for providing the early foreign residents in Yokohama with most of their European vegetables.

But his name will live in Japan as being the founder, in 1867, of one of the earliest Japanese language newspapers—*the Ban Koku Shimbun Shi.* It was a neat production printed from wooden blocks on Japanese paper. Unfortunately it was not a financial success, and after only eighteen issues it went out of existence.

He had a good intellectual background, had graduated from Cambridge and was an author of sorts. The British Museum in London has two books by him—*A Guide to Church Hymnals,* and a book on cotton bag manufacture.

Considering that the nearest telegraph office[3] in those days was in Colombo, that there were no news services, no telephone communication, and of course no radio—in fact nothing faster than semaphore signalling and community gossip—it is surprising, that the foreign newspapers in the Settlements were able to find sufficient news items to fill their columns. The truth is they filched each other's news, which of course led to wars between them. On the other hand the Settlements were so small that a newspaper editor, who at times also had to act as type-setter, proof-reader and reporter, did not have to travel far to get his news. There were occasionally strange happenings within the Settlements, but not all the papers cared to risk offending their subscribers by printing the news.

The foreign newspaper editors attended all community meetings, whether related to municipal sanitation, church affairs, or club matters, and if the meeting was tame and unexciting it was possible, by some shrewdly phrased question, to create a diversion or stir up rancour in that feud-bound community—feuds seemed to carry on in the Foreign Settlements for as long as they did in the Kentucky mountains.

The annual meeting in 1871 of Christ Church on the Bluff in Yokohama, was serene enough until the reporter of *The Japan Herald* referred to the non-attendance of the parson at several funerals. Up jumped the Rev. Bailey in a furious rage—that is furious for a parson—and gave his impressions of *The Japan Herald*. The British Consul restored some degree of harmony by stating that the non-attendance of Mr. Bailey was caused by a disagreement between the Consular constable and the sexton, with which explanation the meeting had to be satisfied.

Perhaps it was because the Rev. Bailey had the energy and ability to do many things better than his fellow-men, that he was often in a storm centre. His

134

rows with the organist were as frequent as his rows with the church trustees.

Even such a worthy undertaking as the construction of a new aisle for Christ Church led to a storm in the community, which amused almost everybody but the church committee and the star actors in the drama.

The contract for the new aisle had been given to an American named Bridgens, who then sought to sublet it at a profit to others, but without any success because it was well known that the pastor, the Rev. Bailey, was skilled in many things besides ecclesiastical matters—one of which was building construction—and that he would almost certainly give the work a personal and more exacting supervision than even a professional architect, and so they refused to have anything to do with the construction of a building under the eye of the parson.

Bridgens, ired by his inability to farm out his contract at a profit, was careless enough to air among the community his personal opinion of Mr. Bailey, who thereupon went to the American Consul and asked for a summons against the contractor for defamation of character—under the laws of those extraterritoriality days Bridgens, being a U.S. citizen, could only be proceeded against in the U.S. Consular Court.

The U.S. Consul endeavoured to arrange an amicable settlement by persuading Bridgens to apologize to the parson, but, in doing so, Bridgens only made matters worse by tacking onto his apology the accusation that the Rev. Bailey swore in church and kicked coolies! No denial of these remarkable accusations was given, and so the matter had to rest there.

On another occasion there was a row in the community over the management of the hospital. The complaints which were voiced at the annual meeting caused tempers and temperature to rise. The heat was just about subsiding, when the Rev. Bailey rekindled the blaze with an allusion to a questionable alteration of a death certificate, and a rumoured dissection of a body.

A seaman had died in the hospital, but was not buried until several days later. The death certificate had first been dated the 8th day of the month, but then had been altered to the 9th. The hospital steward admitted to having altered the document, because he believed the doctor had made a clerical error, but Mr. Bailey was not willing to have the issue side-tracked in that fashion. He knew, or said he knew, the seaman had died on the 8th. Not unlikely he was right. He seemed to be right in most things—other than keeping accounts. But partisanship had been awakened. Some shouted "Eighth." Others yelled "Ninth."

The next day, J. R. Black of *The Japan Gazette* attempted to oil the troubled waters with a "let bygones be bygones" editorial, but Capt. F. Brinkley of *The Japan Mail* would not allow the matter to terminate in that fashion. He was one of the few doughty foreign residents who placed accuracy above the ruffled feelings of even those foreigners who believed themselves to be important persons in the community, and whose names appeared in the upper income brackets. And so Brinkley had the last word —or rather the last three words—by concluding his editorial comments with: *"But it was the Eighth! Eighth! Eighth!"*

The Rev. Buckworth Bailey's ecclesiastical accomplishments and qualifications were impressive—at least they impressed us when we read them. We even came to the conclusion that a man who was expert in so many things, must surely have been inexpert in at least one thing. And so, when we discovered that the Rev. Bailey was inexpert in bookkeeping, we were more understanding than many of his flock appear to have been.

The church trustees, for example, showed so little understanding that they resigned, and said point blank they would not serve while he remained as chaplain.

"Church affairs have reached a pretty bad state and something had to be done," said the chairman.

Then, as if that were not plain speaking, he proceeded to explain that he would be obliged to use plain language. He invited the padre to go home.

"It was a case of Mr. Bailey present and bad finances, or Mr. Bailey absent and good finances," said he.

In reading an account of the meeting, which proceeded to even plainer speaking, we found ourselves with the minority, and we even cheered when Mr. Bailey refused to go home "second class." Knowing some who always travelled "first," we would not have denied that pleasure to him.

Later on somebody, or everybody, discovered that

The Energetic Rev. M. Buckworth Bailey

"Mr. Bailey after ten years labour, was due to go home on sick leave."

In that fashion the Rev. M. Buckworth Bailey left Yokohama, but where he went the foreign press followed, knowing there would be a news story. And so we read in *The Hiogo News* of 1872, that on arrival in Kobe, from Yokohama, by the P & O "Aden" to connect with the ss "Nourmahal," it was found that the latter vessel would not be ready to leave for six weeks at least, and that the captain only agreed to receive him on board at a charge of ¥8 Mex (Yen) per day for board for himself and family—a substantial charge in those days, especially to one who had just been fired.

His enforced stay in Kobe did however give rise to an item of interest. It so happened that the first Union Church, then located on a site opposite the present day Daimaru Dept. Store, had just been completed and was ready for use, and so the Rev. Bailey officiated at a service. That was in 1872.

At the annual meeting of the subscribers of Christ Church, Yokohama, following Mr. Bailey's departure, one of the members while discussing the year's deficit, neatly rolled the year's happenings into two short sentences, spiced with vinegar;

"We have built a new aisle, bought an organ, and sent Mr. Bailey home. Future generations of residents should contribute their share of these expenses since they would enjoy the benefits!"

No matter what the Church Trustees may have thought of their first chaplain, the British Foreign Office bestowed upon him the maximum pension to

138

which he was entitled as a Consular Chaplain—little though it was—of £68 per annum.

Although it is ninety years since the Rev. Buckworth Bailey was given the ecclesiastical boot out of Yokohama, we are still cheering for him. Admittedly he did not have much idea of keeping accounts, but then he was not taught bookkeeping when at Cambridge.

Many parsons have come to Japan during the past century, but we shall continue to cheer for the Rev. M. Buckworth Bailey until there is another padre who is his alround equal as a newspaperman, teacher, cook, truck-gardener, carpenter, architect, builder, and an author on such diverse subjects as church hymnals and cotton bag manufacture.

HORSE RACING IN THE EARLY DAYS

The betting-ring, the crowd that
throngs the rails,
The usual dog, the chimney-pots
and veils,
The Stand with beauty crammed
and banners gay
Recall the glories of a Derby Day.
The Hiogo News, 14 Jan. 1869.

When the foreigners came to Japan over a hundred years ago, many brought with them their household furniture and their Chinese ponies. Some enthusiasts gave priority to the ponies, seemingly considering them more important than beds and dining-room tables. At least the ponies served as a means of getting about in those days, when no better mode of transportation existed. Then, in addition, horse-riding offered an agreeable form of physical exercise, and a more healthy one than that of the bowling alley[1] which also was popular then—the ponies carried them further away from the saloons whereas the bowling alleys were operated by the saloons.

Furthermore, in the eyes of the Japanese masses of those days, riding on horseback gave the foreigners prestige and privileges normally accorded only to the military and the ruling classes. The Japanese merchants, farmers, artisans, and lesser folk of those times had to walk.

It was therefore with some annoyance that the Japanese higher officials watched the foreign merchants, shopkeepers, and others riding—in fact galloping—about on horseback.

The samurai class demanded that merchants and farmers should bow down before them. It mattered nothing whether the farmer cultivated a hundred acres or tilled a single row of *daikon*, whether he was a merchant with a capital of 100,000 *rio* or just a pedlar with his whole stock-in-trade wrapped in a bundle slung across his shoulders. They were all required to humble themselves before the samurai. They were permitted to lead a horse, but not to sit on it.

It was not until 1871 that all classes of Japanese were permitted to ride on horseback, and to wear *hakama* (divided skirt) or *haori* (formal coat)—all previously the privileges of samurai.

During the first two years of the Yokohama Settlement, as related elsewhere, there were plenty of ponies being ridden madly by foreigners along the narrow roads, raising clouds of dust and occasionally knocking down a pedestrian, all of which angered the Consuls who were strenuously endeavouring to control any tendency to lawlessness on the part of their nationals, many of whom were out-and-out adventurers.

The desirability of a track on which the owners might test the speed of their ponies, without endangering the public, was apparent, but three years elapsed before a suitable area could be found on which to hold a race-meeting. In those early days much of the area which now comprises Yokohama was swamp and marsh land.

By the spring of 1862, a portion of the swamp in the rear of the Yokohama Settlement had been sufficiently filled in, to permit of a course, of about three-quarters of a mile round, being temporarily enclosed in preparation for two-days racing. During those two days all business activities in the Settlement closed down, so that everybody could attend.

On 1st and 2nd August of the same year, the second meeting took place. It was called the Autumn Race Meeting, although why that should have been so, when it was held in the hottest part of the summer, is not clear. It was then that Batavier,[2] one of the most remarkable little ponies ever to appear on a course in Japan, made his first appearance. He appeared to enjoy the thrill of racing, and had won every race he had entered. He won all his races at that meeting, and in the last event of the day was still so keen that he galloped two more laps before his exhausted rider could pull him up.[2]

Interspersed between the horse-races there were foot-races between servicemen of the various nationalities in Yokohama, all of which added to the excitement and rivalry of the times.

For several years after those initial meetings, horse-racing and sports in Yokohama largely lapsed because of the lack of a suitable ground. Whatever sports did take place were garrison meetings arranged by the English and French regiments. They were held on the garrison parade ground on the

Bluff or on the Rifle Range—both rather hazardous courses for horse riding. Steeplechases were arranged in the hills outside to the thrill of everyone except perhaps the farmers. In all of those military sports, "gentlemen in the community" were invited to participate.

Then in 1866 an excellent site for a racecourse was secured near Mississippi Bay and the Yokohama Race Club was formed. It all started in a small way—the first stand for example was a hideous contraption, but when heavily decorated with evergreens and bunting, it added colour and gaiety to the course.

At first there was great rivalry in racing among the *taipans* of the different hongs, but increasing weight eventually compelled most of them to abandon racing, although one did win a race even when he had reached the substantial weight of 182 lbs—such was the stamina of some of the horses. It became more and more necessary to use professional jockeys, who as a class soon learned all the tricks of the racecourse. Little wonder was it that there was a good opening for Australian jockeys who had been warned off race tracks in Australia for life. Some did well in Japanese racing, although loyalty among the racing fraternity was such that their past was not often talked about.

The foreigners in Nagasaki had been anxious to establish a racecourse, but had been unable to locate a suitable flat area of ground. In March, 1863, the Foreign Consuls addressed a request to the Governor *"at the instance of the whole community of Foreigners resident at Nagasaki, who through us re-*

quest your favorable consideration of an object which they have very much at heart," namely the renting of a suitable site for a racecourse. They then proceeded to explain that horse-riding was an exercise taken frequently by foreigners, and a favorite amusement is *"the race in which the speed of one horse is tried against that of another."*[3]

For several centuries the governors of Nagasaki had been faced with an endless series of problems arising out of the drunkedness of foreign sailors and others on shore. Perhaps it was the knowledge of that circumstance which prompted the Consuls to remind the Governor that *"the best way to keep off trouble and mischief is to provide men with healthy and harmless diversion."*

As the site requested was partly under cultivation by small farmers, it is good to know that nothing came of the request. It was not until ten years later in March, 1873, that a suitable area of flat land was secured near Isahaya, some fifteen miles outside of Nagasaki, and the first racemeeting was held by the Nagasaki foreigners. The *Nagasaki Express* of the time reported that the strange sight of the long procession of foreigners and their ponies on the outward and return journeys to and from the racecourse *"caused considerable commotion amongst the natives in the villages en route."*

When Kobe was opened to foreigners in 1868, nine years after Yokohama, horse-racing was already well established at the latter port.

In Kobe, where distances over which the foreigners required to travel were short, a pony was not really essential. The Foreign Concession was only

PLATE I

Charles Longfellow (on left) son of the American poet, Henry Wadsworth Longfellow, riding in a *kago* whilst touring Japan in the early 1870's. Note the *kago* bearers are clad only in loin cloths ; some have towels wound around their heads. See chapter, "Those Very Queer Japanese."

PLATE II

A street scene in a Japanese town in the 1870's. Children playing hop-scotch. See Note 1 re. "The Disappointed Rev. Wilton Hack."

PLATE III

View of Yokohama Foreign Settlement, looking along Water Street. Drawn by C. B. Bernard in 1882. The two-storied building on the right was the office of the Pacific Mail Steamship Co. at No. 4, followed by No. 3; then Walsh Hall & Co. at No. 2, later the site of the Hongkong & Shanghai Banking Corp. At the end, on the right, was Ichiban (No. 1) Jardine Matheson & Co. In the foreground on the left, chests of tea, destined for Chicago, are being loaded onto a hand cart. A *taipan* can be seen riding in a *jinrikisha*.

PLATE IV

Main Street (Honcho-dori) in the former Foreign Settlement of Yokohama, in the 1890's showing the Bluff in the background.

PLATE V

Grand Hotel, Yokohama, in the early 1890's. See chapter, "Those Very Queer Japanese."

PLATE VI

Nagasaki Harbour about 80 years ago. Inasa, or Russian Village, is across the harbour, left of center. See chapter, "The Wild Oats of the Grand Duke Alexander."

PLATE VII

One of the streets in the Yoshiwara licenced quarters in Tokyo, in the 1890's. This section of Tokyo at that time contained some of the most costly private dwellings in Japan, and was a small town in itself, occupied entirely by the demimonde. The quarters were completely destroyed in the earthquake of 1923. Licenced prostitution was abolished throughout Japan in 1957.

PLATE VIII

View of Ueno Park, Tokyo, during cherry blossom season, from drawing by C. B. Bernard in 1895.

about a half-mile square, and those who did not live within the Concession were close by on the fringe outside. Nevertheless it was a pleasure to have a pony, when the wages of a groom cost so little. It was pleasant to exercise it of a morning along the white sandy beach, right in front of where the Oriental Hotel is located to-day, or to trot along the path on the bank of the Ikuta river, which in those days ran down to the sea, along what is now the Kano-cho tramline. They could ride down to the mouth of the Ikuta river which was then about where the main Custom Gates are to-day, or they could ride up the river to the waterfalls at Nunobiki.

They could canter through the fields north of the Concession along a narrow winding path which years later came to be known as Kitanagasa-dori—meaning the north long and narrow passage—or they could gallop along Ikuta-baba, which was a soft leaf-covered path that led up to the temple.

All ages of transportation have had their reckless riders and drivers. Some foreigners used to gallop their ponies along Ikuta-baba to the danger of the wayfarers on foot to and from the temple. If detected they were liable to be punished severely by their consuls, who, in a sense, acted as "traffic cops" in those days, in addition to their other multifarious duties.

The need for a place on which to test the speed of ponies, without endangering the public, manifested itself in the creation of a crude track at the northeast corner of the Settlement, just west of the present Kobe City Hall, for that was the section of the Foreign Concession which was last to be built on.

The first games of cricket and baseball were played at that same place long before there was any Re-
creation Ground. Around the perimeter of the
ground the ponies soon wore a track and it was
there that Kobe's first race meeting was held on
Christmas Day, 1868, less than twelve months after
Kobe was opened. And what a day of excitement it
was—bright silks and riding colours, gaiety, spills
and thrills.

Or as the local poet expressed it:

"A noble race-course springs from out the sand.
The satin-coated steeds devour the ground;
Or fly the hurdles with elastic bound;
While each aspiring jockey tries his luck
And some show skill, and all show lots of pluck.
The betting-ring, the crowd that throngs the rails,
The usual dog, the chimney-pots and veils,
The Stand with beauty crammed and banners gay,
Recall the glories of a Derby Day.

Thousands of Japanese gathered to witness this
madness of the foreigners and so became infected
with their first passion for *keiba*—horse-racing. Order was maintained by a file of U.S. marines from
U.S.S. "Oneida"[4] *"in keeping the track clear and the
Japanese, of whom thousands were present, from
crowding the foreigners."*

All the races, with the exception of two, were for
foreign "gentlemen" riders—*"none but Subscribers
and Officers of the Navy may enter ponies or ride in
the races."* Among the important events were the
Celestial Plate for Chinese ponies, the Hiogo Hurdle
Race, and the Osaka Cup, but every event had its
thrills, of which the Kobe Plate, the opening event

for Japanese ponies, gave the spectators a hint of the excitement in store for them.

According to *The Hiogo News:*

"All got off well together, but the course near the Customs House was recognised by many of the ponies as leading towards their stables, and a general rush seemed to be made for them, much to the discomfort of some riders, for at this point, three of them parted company with their ponies."

The Japanese howled with excitement as they observed the gaily coloured jackets and the faces of the foreign riders take on a darker hue as they rose from the mud.

Included in the programme were several races for Japanese. There was the "Bettos Race" for Japanese ponies ridden by *betto*—Japanese grooms. Some of those men were cruel and mean to their animals, which maybe was why one pony administered a public castigation to its groom. First of all it threw him at the starting post, then butted him in the stomach with its head, after which it put on a ripsnortin' kind of can-can performance—first on its hind legs with its mane flung high in the air, then on its fore legs with its tail and hind legs high— to the immense applause of the Japanese spectators. It then wandered off the course back to its stable followed by the *betto* looking green and crestfallen.

The absence of a fence around the course caused further difficulties in the final race which was an extra for Japanese ponies ridden by *yakunin*—government officials. Six started but only four came in. The remaining two were last seen by the spectators bolting across country after having thrown their riders. Again the Japanese crowd yelled with delight.

And so came to an end the first race meeting held in Kobe. The foreigners went home surfeited with good food, champagne, and excitement, and the Japanese with expectations of better things to come.

Despite the waywardness of some of the ponies and the improvised course, the meeting had been such a great success that a group of the most influential foreign residents determined to stage something better. Within three months The Hiogo Race Club was founded, soon to be renamed The Hiogo and Osaka Race Club in order to placate the Osaka foreigners who had taken offence at the first name.

By arrangement with the Prefectural Office a piece of land about 6,000 tsubo in area—about five acres—was leased north of what is now the Hankyu Railway terminus and just east of Ikuta forest, where a course of about 1,200 yards was laid out.

That the Race Club's meetings were important events may be learned from an announcement in *The Hiogo News* that, in accordance with usual custom, it would suspend publication and "take a holiday during the Races," which was only fair considering that everybody else, barring the missionaries, laid off business during that period.

That the meetings were a social success can be gleaned from the fact that the consular corps donated a trophy, and also from the newspaper report on the Spring Meeting of 1871: *"Every fourth man was sporting a white chimney pot."* It is interesting to speculate on the fate of those fashionable headgear.

The foreigners were able to find a ready sale for their old bowler hats, but one never saw a Japanese wearing a white top hat!

That horse-racing achieved great things can be judged from the circumstance that it actually changed the face of Kobe, but whether for better or worse is a matter of opinion. That revolutionary happening came about in the following manner.

The construction of the railway line between Kobe and Osaka was commenced in 1870, but progress was slow owing to the number of rivers and watercourses which had to be bridged. Land speculators therefore had ample time to acquire land along the projected route through Kobe, which was to have been much higher up the Hill than at present; in that position it would have passed behind Ikuta temple, along what is now the hill tramline, thereby cutting off a portion of the racecourse.

The Race Club demanded a new and better course in exchange for that portion which would be lost to the railway, whereupon the Prefectural Office took advantage of the opportunity to demand from the Railway Department an extraordinarily large sum to cover the acquisition of land for a new racecourse. That demand, added to those which were being made for compensation by a number of foreigners, who at the suggestion of Japanese friends, skilled in municipal skullduggery, had leased land along the projected route of the railway in anticipation of being able to demand compensation for the loss of their rights, decided the Railway Department to change the plans. And so it was that in 1874 the railway was opened along the present route below Ikuta temple, much closer to the sea than had originally been contemplated.

The newspapers of the time contain lamentations and accounts of recriminations between the parties demanding compensation, each blaming the cupidity of the other for having made the "ante" so high, that the foreign advisers and engineers in the Railway Department altered the route of the railway rather than submit to the extortion.

With the opening of the railway and the appearance of an ever increasing number of *jinrikisha*, foreigners began to abandon the pleasure of owning their own horses, and so the Hiogo and Osaka Race Club went out of existence. Thereafter the gentlemen's silks were converted by their wives into bloomers, and the stewards' red coats were hung in wardrobes to be devoured eventually by the moths.

It yet remains to describe the most thrilling race meeting of all time in Japan—a thrill then no less great than to-day when in some motorcar races half a dozen roaring racing cars crash and pile over one another. Fortunately in those distant days, of nearly a hundred years ago, the thrills could be accompanied without loss of life and no greater mortality than that of dignity, top hats, crockery, and cream.

It all happened at the first race-meeting of The Hiogo Race Club on 17th April, 1869, on the racecourse already described, near where the Hankyu Railway terminus is located to-day.

The first misadventure occurred in the Hurdle Race. There were only three starters. All had gone once around the course when the stewards discovered that the leading pony was ridden by a gentleman who was not a "gentleman," or rather not a member of the Race Club. To the amazement of the Japanese spectators, who imagined they were witnessing something akin to a dramatic arrest, he was flagged by the stewards, disqualified, and compelled to withdraw. All this in the presence of thousands of spectators. Fortunately the miscreant was a foreigner and not a Japanese, and so he was able to face the humiliation with equanimity and did not feel impelled to commit *harakiri*[5] forthwith. What was his ultimate fate, or whether he subsequently decided to become a member of the Race Club, does not appear to be recorded in history.

The second mishap followed soon afterwards, in the race for the Challenge Cup.

The Governor and Vice-Governor of Hyogo Prefecture were present, also the foreign consuls and the flower of the foreign residents. The lesser adornments of the foreign community were there too, but not in the grandstand. The band of Her Britannic Majesty's ship "Rodney" added much to the gaiety of the occasion with lively airs. The ponies were gathering at the starting point. "They're off!" —a roar in ten or more different languages went up. The excitement was terrific, but when everybody stretched their necks and stood on tiptoes, the strain was too great. The improvised grandstand collapsed. Officials, crockery, champagne bottles, and sandwiches were all mixed up with ladies parasols, amateur bookmakers, and Japanese dignitaries. Flagpoles and bunting fell across the track. The ponies took fright and ran faster than ever before; indeed the two favourites—Tartar and Lightning—ran so fast that they raced four times around the course instead of only three. However by that time, the officials had disentangled themselves from the mess of bass drums, truffles and cream, and, although their vision was impaired, they were able to witness the finish. All in all, a day to remember.

THE
REMARKABLE
MR. SMITH

*The Foreign Affairs of Japan
have been under the malign influence of this crapulous dotard . . .
and the congenial crew with
whom he tippled.*
    The Japan Weekly Mail, 9 Dec.
    1876.

A hundred years ago—and for some time after that—the Mexican dollar was better known in Japan than any other foreign coin; it was also a coin known to millions more people outside of Mexico than in Mexico.[1] Compton Mackenzie[2] described it as *"the lineal descendant of the West Indian piece-of-eight, so familiar to pirates."*

Some Japanese newspapers, and also *The Japan Mail,* described it as *"an excrescence upon Japanese foreign trade."*

Some extremists—notably Mr. E. Peshine Smith—linked it with *"pirates,"* but not the same kind that Compton Mackenzie had in mind.

That the *The Japan Mail* did attempt to see the Japanese point of view,—and perhaps at times with overmuch effort—brought it in for much criticism, but it never allied itself with such beings as Mr. E. Peshine Smith, and in fact carried on a relentless war against him.

Both in what *The Japan Mail*[3] described as his

153

moments of *"fortuitous sobriety,"* or during his periods of inebriety, that *"crapulous dotard"* Mr. E. Peshine Smith, was prone to say many harsh things about the foreign community. *"Pirates"* happened to be just one of his mild expressions. *"Unprincipled rapacious thieves"* was a more favoured term. While it has to be admitted that there were such rascals —and many of them—among the early arrivals in the Foreign Settlements, it was unfair, but characteristic of Mr. Smith, to paint the whole foreign community with the same brush.

Peshine was just one of the many remarkable eccentrics who was able to latch himself onto Japan as an adviser during the early years of Meiji. It does so happen that he was an American, but not all were Americans. Perhaps the United States furnished Japan with more eccentrics than other countries just because Commodore Perry arrived here a year or more ahead of the others, and so, as it were, America had that much head-start on other countries.

At any rate, E. Peshine was more colourful than some of the stuffy English eccentrics who came to Japan. For one thing, after his abjuration of his own nationality, he habitually appeared in Japanese dress decorated with two swords—and that at a time when most Japanese samurai had discarded those dangerous appendages.

There were a few other foreigners also, who aped Japanese dress even on formal occasions.

There was for example the unusual Englishman, at a somewhat later date, who appeared at a British Embassy dinner dressed in formal Japanese attire, whereupon the Ambassador ordered that a *tatami* be brought in for his greater comfort.

The foreign directories of the eighteen-sixties and eighteen-seventies, or hong lists as they were generally called at that time, make interesting reading, and list many of the Europeans who then held positions in various Japanese Government Departments. Over five thousand[4] foreign experts in every field of human endeavour were employed over the years to teach the rudiments and point the path to the new mode of life and enterprise for which Japan had forsaken her feudalistic ways. Those foreigners were the guides, the helpers, and the servants. Their pupil proved to be quick at learning.

The Department of the Navy was largely staffed by Britishers, from directors down to several able seamen, the Yokosuka Arsenal with Frenchmen, the Imperial Academy of Medicine mainly with Germans. In the Railways there were European superintendents, engineers, draughtsmen, mechanics, engine drivers, clerks and yardsmen. There were foreign advisers and experts in every department, lighthousekeepers, miners, telegraphists, and foremen. In the Mitsubishi Mail Steamship Company, the forerunner of the Nippon Yusen Kaisha, there were ship captains, engineers, storekeepers and clerks.

Japan was fortunate in securing the services of many experts, but inevitably a few adventurers and fakes were able to insinuate themselves into some appointments.

Particularly was that so among the ranks of teachers and professors, who were hastily engaged locally when universities and senior schools began to spring up in Tokyo and other great cities. There was the notorious case of a butcher who secured an appointment as a professor at the Tokyo University, and who lectured with a pipe in his mouth and often in a top-heavy condition.

Whilst these strange intrusions into the realms of education and culture were taking place, it would seem there was a movement also in the reverse direction if we believe a queer entry in the *Japan Gazette Hong List and Directory of* 1876 stating that the proprietor of the Kobe Hair Dressing Saloon at No. 35, Kobe Foreign Settlement, was Prof. F. da Cunha!

But let us return to Peshine Smith.

Peshine was an American citizen with some legal qualifications but more political pull, and so it was that during the early eighteen-seventies he was recommended, at the request of the Japanese Minister at Washington, by the Secretary of State of the U.S. Government, for the post of International Adviser to the Japanese Foreign Office.

According to *The Japan Mail* of the time:

"Mr. Peshine Smith showed some traces of ability of a certain kind, during such lucid intervals as confirmed habits of inebriety permitted him to enjoy."

Over the five years or so during which he acted as adviser to the Japanese Foreign Office he caused much embarrassment to the U.S. Minister in Japan, who in turn openly expressed so much irritation and disappointment at the appointment, that Mr. Secretary of State Seward—or was it Mr. Fish—never claimed any credit for what was described as *"the worst appointment ever made by the Japanese Government."*

At one stage, during the course of his residence in Japan, Peshine refused to register at the U.S. Consulate as a U.S. citizen and was thereupon proceeded against for neglect by the U.S. authorities."[5] And then commenced one of the most amazing Consular Court trials of the Settlement days. There were many Consular Court cases which brought mirth to the foreign community—at least to those members not involved—but few raised as much derisive laughter as did Peshine Smith in court.

Mr. Smith conducted his own defence and kept the audience in roars of laughter much to the annoyance of the presiding Consul. In his opening address to the Court he boomed:

"I have been summoned here by the People of the United States, and . . . it says 'the people of the United States send greetings.' I take that as a great compliment, one of the greatest that a man could be paid . . . The summons announces that the people of the United States are my accusers—where is their counsel and upon what proof, what evidence does anyone assert that I am an American citizen? . . . I call upon them for a reply . . ."

Mr. Smith during interrogation pretended that he did not know when or where he was born, although he believed it was in New York, because his mother had told him so! However he argued that his beliefs were not evidence. He had to admit that he had voted in the United States; then, amid further laughter, he asserted that he may have done so illegally, and therefore the fact that he had voted was not evidence of nationality.

In reply to a question as to whether or not he knew that he should have registered at the U.S. Consulate, this exponent of international law replied:

"Had I been an American, I might have been expected to know something of the U.S. law, but being only a weak, ignorant, heathen Japanese, I could not be expected to know the law of a foreign nation."

He claimed that, as he was engaged by the Japanese Government, he could not serve two masters and therefore considered himself a Japanese. He then rambled into muddled rhetoric, but when he referred to the "Stars & Stripes," tears—some believed they were composed more of gin than salt—rolled down his cheeks in profusion.

The case was brought to an end by Mr. Smith being fined $10 Mex. and being ordered to register forthwith. Said *The Japan Mail* at the conclusion of the trial:

"The Japanese make no distinctions in regard to nationalities. In their eyes we are all foreigners, not merely Englishmen, American, Frenchmen or Germans. The honour of one is the honour of all, the shame of one, the shame of the others. We utterly object to being bracketed with Mr. Peshine Smith."

Not unnaturally *The Japan Mail* warned the Japanese Government:

"It is dangerous to act on momentous questions upon advice which has no better foundation than

*a fortuitous sobriety and the intrusion into its
archives of opinions which display delirium of
any kind."*

Hard words, certainly, but not as hard as those
which followed from time to time.

When E. Peshine retired from the Japanese Foreign Office and departed from Japan in 1876, *The
Japan Mail* had this to say:

*"The Foreign Affairs of Japan—have been under
the malign influence of the crapulous dotard who
left for Rochester in August and the congeniul
crew with whom he tippled . . . It takes time to
disinfect a public office from the noxious influence of men like Mr. Peshine Smith. No whole-
some doctrine can live, so long as the lingering
demon of this driveller remains unexorcised.
Nothing can be hoped for Japan so long as the
quirks and quibbles and florid ignorance of those
who thrive on Japanese credulity are permitted
to usurp the place of liberality, justice and good
sense . . .*

*If a loss may ever be said to be a gain, the
Japanese Government has received a solid addition
to its credit by the retirement from its service of
Mr. E. Peshine Smith . . ."*[6]

TRAVELS
TO OSAKA

We found Osaca to be a very great Towne, as great as London within the Wall.
Captain Saris' diary, 1613.

In these days of modern travel, when traffic can be seen converging from all directions at high speed on Tokyo, Osaka, and other great cities in Japan, it is difficult to imagine a time, just a hundred years ago, when Japan was about three centuries behind most of the civilised world in speed and all means of communication.

The fastest mode of travel was then on foot. Certainly horses were seen on the highroads but they were mostly packhorses. Only the samurai class were permitted to ride on horseback, and except in times of emergency galloping horses were rarely seen along the highways.

The Government couriers and the merchants' letter carriers[1] could cover on foot about thirty-five miles a day for several days on end, their dress in almost all weathers consisting of a loin cloth, a towel wound around the head, and nothing more. The rate of travel for the ordinary foot travellers generally averaged less than twenty miles a day. They made an early start and carried on at a leisurely pace until dusk, resting from time to time at the eating stalls, or the so-called tea-houses which were scattered along all the highways of feudal Japan.

160

Travelling after nightfall was avoided because of the dangers from robbers and outlaws.

Hours, indeed at times days, were wasted in fording or being carried across rivers, especially when they were swollen with rain. Then there were further delays at the barriers or check points.

During the two centuries the Tokugawa family had controlled Japan, they had developed a highly effective spy and security system, of which the barriers were just one of their measures of control. Travel was slow because the Tokugawas did not encourage road or bridge building. The more difficult the lines of communication, the greater were the obstacles which beset any insurgents rash enough to rise against them.

The difficulties of communication were such that even the delays in transporting rice often exposed one part of the country to distress and famine whilst another district may have been wanting an outlet for its surplus.[2]

Yedo and Osaka although connected by the best road in the country, were a fortnight or more apart for the ordinary foot travellers, and even a trip from Kobe to Osaka was quite an adventurous undertaking. When Sir Rutherford Alcock, the first British Consul-General to Japan, visited the Kansai in 1861 to inspect several possible sites for the future Foreign Settlement, he and his party did the trip from Kobe to Osaka on horseback in eight hours, which was considered fast travelling.

"We had to cross a succession of rivers, some over plank bridges, almost too fragile for horses . . . Others had to be crossed in boats and several

*were forded . . . Much of the corn had been cut
and some was still on the ground . . . The cotton
planted on each side of the rows of corn as an
alternative crop was just appearing.*"[3]

Cotton was grown in Japan from ancient times
to supplement the needs of the farmers, and the results were seen in the home spun fabrics worn by
so many of the people. In most districts the cotton
was planted along the edges of the fields, between
the rows of corn, or on embankments as marginal
crops.

When Japan began to emerge from seclusion and
develop into an industrial nation, the population
which had previously fluctuated around 30 million
soon began to increase, until to-day it is more than
three times that figure. And so it was that the cotton plants have long since disappeared from the
countryside between Kobe and Osaka and elsewhere
in Japan. The cottonfields of Japan had to give way
to ricefields to feed the increasing population, and
the ricefields in turn are now making way for tall
re-inforced concrete apartment blocks to house the
growing population.

Following the opening of Kobe and Osaka in January, 1868, Wm Rangan & Co., of Yokohama, whose
coaches carried a flag depicting a black horse on a
red ground,[4] established a coaching service in Kobe.
It was, however, soon found that the roads out of
Kobe were so few and narrow that there was not
as much scope for coaching services as in Yokohama, where coaches ran daily to Tokyo and also to
Odawara, carrying mail, parcels, bullion, legation
despatches, and passengers.[5]

Rangan's therefore had to abandon the idea of operating a coaching service between Kobe and Osaka, but in November, 1868, eleven months after Kobe had been opened, they established a Pony Express[6] between the two ports. That surely is a claim to fame. The courier departed from Kobe daily at 7 am, and set out on the return journey from Osaka about 2 pm the same day.

Gradually the road to Osaka was sufficiently improved to encourage one of the foreign residents of Kobe to attempt the journey by pony and trap. He achieved some local notoriety by getting through. However two months later communications between the two places were temporarily suspended when a rider—the local newspaper said a "gentleman"—on horseback upset one of the bridges, so frail were the structures then.[7]

In March, 1871, the first *jinrikisha*[8] journey from Kobe to Osaka was successfully made, whereupon the Osaka authorities issued a notification to the effect that the new fangled conveyances, known as *"jinrikisha"* must henceforth be licensed. The fare for the trip to Kobe was set at 6 bu, the equivalent of which came to be about 1½ yen, or 1½ U.S. dollars in those times.[9]

Before long, *jinrikisha* journeys to and from Osaka became commonplace. Thereafter travels between the two towns, whether by land or sea, did not receive much publicity in the local newspapers unless something unusual occurred, such as a ferryboat stranding on the Osaka Bar or the boilers blowing up en route. The latter misadventure was not as rare as may be supposed.

By the end of 1871 there were a dozen or more ferryboats plying between the Kobe and Osaka Foreign Settlements. The fare was around $1 Mex. although Capt. Gibson of the "Race Horse," who threw in sandwiches and beer free, charged $2 Mex. Freight was $1 Mex. per ton, and treasure 1/10%. (The Mexican Dollar was then equal to about one Yen or one US$.) Some of these ferryboats also conducted a mail service whereby for a small fee the subscriber could send as many letters a month as he pleased —a concession on the part of the promoters which did not require much courage, because in those days before the age of typewriters and stenographers, when everything had to be written in longhand, the number of letters was kept to a minimum. Letters carried by the ferryboats had to be picked up on arrival by the addressees—a list of all mail remaining uncollected was circulated in the Settlement—a system which despite its defects seemed to work well enough in those small communities.

Delays and mishaps on the voyage to Osaka were not unusual. Most of the ferryboats had already seen the best years of their life on river service in China; some even had their boiler tubes repaired with wooden plugs.

The first ferryboats, the "Flying Cloud," "Staunch," "Race Horse," "Rising Sun," and "Ohen Maru"—all famous names on the Kobe and Osaka waterfronts of those days—were owned and operated by foreign firms, who, in most cases, soon sold out to Japanese and apparently were glad to pass on their vessels, complete with hazardous boilers, before they blew up for the last time.

The best known was perhaps the "Ohen Maru" or OLD HEN MARY, as known to some foreigners, or HOWLING MARY to others. The excitement arising out of her frequent strandings, including eight days on the Osaka sandbanks, and many boiler mishaps, became a feature of life in the Kobe and Osaka Foreign Settlements until she ended her days in a typhoon in July, 1871, which storm also wrecked the Kobe waterfront.

A trip on a Kobe-Osaka ferryboat was at times something worth writing to the Editor about, and this a Kobe foreign resident did in *The Hiogo News* of 3 Dec., 1868:

"I have been to Osaka and I am happy to say I have got back. Osaka isn't much of a place, nothing to speak of in fact. We started at 1 o'clock on the superior steamer the "Old Hen Mary" and her gallant captain boldly breasted the surging flood, and turned her bow down stream which didn't seem to please Mary, for she showed a disposition to go down the river sideways. When the captain, after vainly trying to get her to go ahead, gave in, she sulked again and made up her mind only to go backwards. The Captain put out ropes to all the junks and the Japanese let them go; the mate swore, and the crew pushed with long poles. After awhile she started down the river.

Everything went merry as a marriage bell until we reached the bar, and then it seemed as though one letter of the bell was changed. The water was breaking and foaming, and the boat was puffing and blowing and . . . she commenced to roll much to the disgust of the mate who put

*his glass to his eye . . . and said it was "Bad, Sir,
very bad," and looked so hard at the breakers
that he nearly made a hole in his glasses.*

*After awhile the steamer concluded to go back
to Osaka and went sideways . . . and drifted slowly up the river. We then took a native junk to
Kobe, fully convinced that a trip to Osaka fur-
nishes many incidents for the notebook of a traveller."*

The Kobe and Osaka railway, which was opened
in 1874, was a success right from the opening day.
The promoters announced with pride that the gross
receipts on the first day amounted to $442 (i.e. Yen)
and to $525 on the second day![10] Certainly most of
those passengers bought tickets for the thrill of travelling at the high speed of something more than
twenty miles per hour, but even when the novelty
had worn off, the popularity of the railway as a
means of travel to Osaka was firmly established,
as may be judged from the fact that during the last
week of September of the same year, 16,775 passengers[11] travelled from Kobe to Osaka!

In February, 1873, the *Hiogo News,* with a hint
of better things to come, had announced with pro-
phetic pride, " . . . *the small beginning of that which
some day must become an important enterprise. At
1 o'clock the first passenger horse coach left Kioto
for Osaka. According to the illustrated placards
which are to be seen in various parts of this city,
these coaches are to run each way twice a day."*
Those uncomfortable coaches, little better than
boxes on wheels, were considered fast means of travel, but not as fast as the railway which three years

later linked Osaka to Kyoto, to the great dismay of many, such as the porters, ferrymen, and jinriki-sha-men, who thereby lost their livelihood. The river boatmen also took fright and began planning to carry passengers from Osaka up to Kyoto for 6 sen (sixteen trips for a yen!) and down stream from Kyoto to Osaka for 3 sen (thirty-three trips for a yen!) [12]

In the years that followed, travelling to Osaka by land or sea ceased to be an adventure worth talking about, until of recent years, with the immense increase in motor traffic, the dangers to life and limb, encountered by all who travel on the road to Osaka, have become far greater than they ever were in the less enlightened past. [13]

THE
DAUNTLESS
MR. McLEOD

> *Mr. N. McLeod, whose researches
> in Japan have satisfied him that
> the people of this country are of
> Jewish family, has just given an-
> other work to the world. We have
> not had the advantage of inspect-
> ing a copy.*
>
> *Japan Weekly Mail* 23 Oct.
> 1875.

Mr. McLeod was a stout-hearted, frugal, and religious man who started his career in Scotland in the
herring fisheries, and ended up in Japan as an in-
dependent missionary.

When he decided to forsake Scottish herrings for
bigger fish, he shipped before the mast to Japan.
He arrived here just over ninety years ago. At first
he secured employment in the countinghouse of a
foreign hong. History does not record whether or
not he was a good bookkeeper, but the hong soon
went bankrupt.

Personally we think that was just a co-incidence,
and that no more significance should be attached to
it than to the fact that the famous Scottish hong of
Findlay Richardson & Co., Ltd., went into voluntary
liquidation precisely six years after we became associated with it!

After the failure of the hong, McLeod started a
business of his own in Kobe and Osaka, where, ac-

cording to his own words, *"he made money when it was practicable in the two penny half penny line he was then engaged in,"* but he frankly stated that *"kissing the golden calf pleased him not."* He lived in the Osaka Foreign Concession for some years, but much of his time and all his available means were spent on what he termed *"travel and researches."* He seems only to have embarked on trade in order to gain the wherewithal to pursue his pet religious notion, namely that he had discovered a part of the Ten Lost Tribes of Israel in the Koreans and the Japanese—*"at intervals resuming business to provide the needful for this purpose."*

Whatever the Israelites or the Non-Israelites, the Japanese or the Koreans, might feel about that discovery, it should be conceded by all that few men can have thrown themselves body and soul more enthusiastically into proving a theory than did Mr. McLeod. According to his own words he continued his labours through sickness and other untold difficulties, and often without a single dollar in his pocket.

He became a preacher and pamphleteer, sparing neither his body, his pocket, nor his mind, in the presentation of "proof" that the Koreans were descended from Japhet and the Japanese from the last king of Israel.

To that end he spent his entire savings in the publication of several books, one of which will most probably go down in history as among the most remarkable books on Japan. The latter publication was a combination of two of his major works, namely KOREA[1] AND THE TEN LOST TRIBES

OF ISRAEL and AN ALBUM AND GUIDE BOOK OF JAPAN.

It was privately printed in Yokohama in 1879, and now ranks as a very rare volume among unusual literary curiosities.[2]

The dedication of this oddity—runs to over 90 words and embraces more than half the world, to wit:

> *Dedicated to Great Britain, America, Germany, France and the other Teutonic nations of Europe, the supposed representatives of the Royal House of Judah, and the seed only of the Royal House of Ephraim, and the children of Israel, their companions and to the Jews or Judah who are with them, also to China, Japan and Korea, the Shin dai or Celestial race of which are supposed to represent Royal House of Israel or Ephraim and the Ten Lost Tribes; or all the House of Israel called Jacob, his companions and fellows.*

We should like to reproduce the preface of this quaint book, but refrain from doing so because of its length and the thought that few people would have the patience to read it through. Certainly they would not have the breath to read it aloud, because it consists of a single sentence of 606 words. The spelling is unorthodox and the punctuation queer, but just what percentage of those oddities may be the fault of the printers, and how much Mr. McLeod's notions of English, is not clear.

The whole preface does however represent a recital of woe and hardship. It is an autobiographical account of the trials and tribulations which beset him in the pursuit of a literary career, and at the same time a declaration of faith in his own belief of the Israelish origin of the Koreans and Japanese. It is a confession that he could not have persevered in his work had he not *"been convinced of the identity of part of lost Israel in Japan,"* and it is an admission that nothing but the discovery that the Japanese *"answer in nearly every particular the various prophets' descriptions of lost Israel"* sustained him in the face of fire, shipwreck, and disaster. It describes the losses which he suffered at the hands of embezzlers, frauds, insolvents, and conspirators, most of whom according to his experience were booksellers and publishers. It is a paean of thanks to his financial backers—those foreigners who were friends during all his extremities, even when he had become *"bimbo,"* as he expressed it. Finally it is a voice of hope that *"this present edition which is only a small one, may meet with as good and ready a sale as its predecessors."*[3]

There is hardly a dull page in the book. The lost tribes of Israel keep turning up in the most unexpected places.

Unlike the Osaka apprentice boys of Tokugawa Japan, who were taught by their masters to look on the ground so that they might never miss the opportunity of picking up a lost coin, Mr. McLeod was ever looking forward and upward. In doing so, he discovered signs of the lost tribes even among the birds of the sky, and the temples on the mountain tops.

On one page we read that Queen Victoria was descended from King Zedekiah's daughter, and on others that some of the purest Israelish blood flows in the veins of the Imperial princes of Japan, or rather we should say it did once flow because the knowledgeable Mr. McLeod was writing eighty years ago. Doubtless some of the Kyoto geisha of Ponto-cho,[4] who might viciously speculate on the origins of their rivals in Gion across the river, should know that according to Mr. McLeod the Gion festival occurs on the same day as the feast of the tabernacles and is *partly the remains of that feast.*

When not harping on the lost tribes, our author throws in advice calculated to assist foreigners in Japan in their everyday problems. Much of it no doubt was valuable advice, although some is quite out-of-date in these changed times of motor transportation.

For example, in those days any foreigner of importance kept one or more horses,[5] and maybe a buggy, a brougham, a phaeton, or a landau. Some of the lesser foreign folk had wagons, drays, or carts, instead of carriages, but they of course were the tradesmen, and as such suffered certain disabilities, but on the other hand were spared the irksome social duty of having periodically to distribute a handful of visiting cards among their equals or betters. Anyhow, as foreigners, they all could afford to employ Japanese grooms, or *betto* as they were called.

The experienced Mr. McLeod warned his readers that, unless supervised, the *betto* would deliberately feed the horses stale and musty corn and beans so that they would not eat so much, and he then proceeded to explain another of the tricks of the betto's trade:

The Dauntless Mr. McLeod

*The proverb saith bring a horse to the water, but
you can't make him drink; you have only to corn
him well and give him plenty of beans and he
will drink like a fish, but if the betto himself has a
likeness for corn he greases the horse's mouth so
that he won't look at the oats.*

There are also a few tips on housekeeping, but
none to equal the advice which was given, by a foreign lady of much experience, to my wife when she
first came to Japan twenty-five years ago.

*"You must of course, my Dear, keep a housekeep-
ing account. And if you are ever short, just put
it down to fish, put it down to fish, my Dear."*

The book is illustrated with many pages of excellent fine-line Japanese engravings—the work of
a master craftsman—but it is not easy in all instances to follow the reason for the inclusion of
the illustrations. There is for example a drawing
of the *"Supposed Chains of the Kings of Israel
brought to Japan with Jinmu Tenno,"* followed by
a picture of a very stout Japanese wrestler, but
how the latter fits into Israel is not explained.

Then there is a set of 48 illustrations of Japanese life, such as *"Wine Bibber," "Poor Girl Sold
to Beelzebub," "Husband absent, wife bakes cake
for herself,"* etc. The picture which intrigued us
most had been censored by Mr. McLeod who had
added the explanation *"Heathen picture left out."*
Being as we are, we could not help trying to imagine just how naughty it could have been.

Such rare books as this are not easy to come by.
Actually our attention was first drawn to it by a

friend—at least he called himself a friend—who
suggested we might find therein much in common
with Mr. McLeod!

Actually we found the substance of the book to
be a hotchpotch of facts, theories, parables, and
wild imaginings thrown together in a manner which
made us rather giddy. Much of the information contained in the guide section is now out-of-date, as
will be gathered from the following words of advice to a tourist whose rickshaw may become bog-
ged on a country road:

> *Should the tourist on an ancient mountain road
> ever stick in the mud, there are always plenty of
> pack horses returning, and for a consideration he
> can trace one ahead of his jinrikisha coolie, and
> thus get up steam, no fear of coming to grief as
> the steed is homeward bound, and fed on Japa-
> nese bran and stubble ends, tandem Japonicum
> is a shade better than one horse power.*

That sentence is a fair example of Mr. McLeod's
involved literary style, but the grammar and the
punctuation are rather above his average.

There were many facts in this guide which stirred
and fascinated us, particularly a comparison of the
widths of the nostrils of the three largest Daibutsu
in Japan[6]. We were amused at such oddities that
plums in plum pudding spoil the digestion, but we
were deeply interested in the transportation and
hotel charges of those days.[7] For example, the normal
tariff for *jinrikisha* was seven sen (seven hundredths
of one yen) for two and a half miles, or half a yen
for a whole day. After much concentration and cal-
culation we discovered that we could have travelled

two thousand five hundred miles by *jinrikisha* in those days for the same cost as a ¥70 taxi ride to-day. Had we chosen to hire the *rikisha* by the day, we could have retained it for 140 days for the same ¥70.

Foreigners were expected to pay one quarter of a yen per night for lodging at the best hotels and inns, provided they supplied their own food. After re-whittling our pencil for further calculations, we discovered we could have stayed in one of those hotels for 16 years 5 months and 10 days for the same cost as one night in a tourist hotel to-day. Such in fact has been the decline in the purchasing power of Japanese currency over the past century.

A few years before Mr. McLeod's sojourn in Japan, the purchasing power of Japanese currency may have been even greater, judging from the following item-ised expense account, reproduced from another source, of two Japanese samurai who whiled away the 18th and 19th March, 1860, in one of the licenced houses in the Yoshiwara, whilst waiting to partici-pate in an assassination plot:

For Tamayoshi (one of the girls)	2 bu
” Chitose (the other girl)	2 ”
” a singing girl	1 ”
” drinks	1 ”
” fish	2 ”
” rice	10 tempo
Tips for servants	½ bu

The total cost of those two days frolic in the licen-ced quarters was equivalent to 5s 3d per head, all in, at that time about U.S.$1.[8]

But let us return to the writings of the good Mr. McLeod.

The Dauntless Mr. McLeod

We gather that most foreigners in those days when staying at a Japanese hotel preferred to provide their own food rather than risk the table d'hôte, because in Mr. McLeod's words *"unripe food, some badly cured fish and dykon are only waiting their doom for the Imperial sentence to condemn them to banishment for taking the lives of his loyal subjects."*

Ever before Mr. McLeod, during the writing of this book, was the ambition to out-do Kaempfer[9] by producing a standard 12 volume work on Japan. He planned to have *"Illustrations similar to Kaempfers, but it will contain a more accurate and detailed account of the origin of the Japanese with a description of their Jewish belongings."* Unfortunately his ambition was never achieved. It seems that the reading public of the time did not have the same regard for the worth of his writings as did Mr. McLeod himself.[10] When he died he was still a good nine volumes at least behind Kaempfer.

When Mr. McLeod gets off the subject of the lost tribes he covers a wide field. Among many other things he commiserates with the Scotch, berates the Fenians, slugs the Devil, and offers Japan an interesting piece of advice, namely that she should amend her naturalization laws and so make it easy for a few Rothschilds to become naturalized Japanese, and thereby *"soon turn the tables of political economy in favour of Japan."*

And so the good Mr. McLeod rattles on page after page. In the absence of many full stops it makes exciting but exhausting reading. Finally we arrived breathless and panting at the end of this amazing book. We had finished the last sentence—a mere 219 words in length—at a gallop, and then found ourselves clutching wildly at the full stop which fortunately was there at the end!

Japan has changed so much since Mr. McLeod wrote his *magnum opus*, that his *"Album and Guide Book of Japan"* was a loss so far as guiding us around Japan is concerned, but the book altogether was a rare find in that we learned something we could never have imagined, namely that Queen Victoria was related to the Emperor of Japan via one of the lost tribes of Israel.

THE
DISAPPOINTED
REV.
WILTON HACK

*All emigration of Japanese out of
the Empire will be resisted.*
Japanese Minister for Foreign
Affairs, 1877.

When the Rev. Wilton Hack was a missionary in
Nagasaki around ninety years ago, the country had
just emerged from the feudal stage and had a population of about thirty-three million, or close to a
third of what it is to-day.

Before the foreigners came to Japan and began to
purchase silk for export abroad, there had been some
sericulture but not much more than was necessary to
clothe the ruling and privileged classes, and to provide luxurious clothing for the better-class courte-
sans (both male and female), the geisha, the actors,
and a few others who were accustomed to live in the
lap of luxury. Then, of course, there were the wealthy
merchants, but they had to be careful not to flaunt
their silks overmuch, in case they became entrapped
by the sumptuary laws, which prohibited the wearing of silk fabrics by the common people.

Then also, an ostentatious display of wealth and
finery might even encourage some ambitious person,
who stood in favour with the local authorities, to
endeavour to evoke a new edict of benevolence or
tokusei, whereby in certain cases the differences be-

178

tween rich and poor, between those in debt and those living on usury, or between the fortunate and the unfortunate, could be equalized. *Tokusei*, or the old law of benevolence was in the law books, but not easily evoked. At times, however, when the burden of the people became over desperate, they took the law into their own hands, and mobbed and plundered an over avaricious pawnbroker or a merchant who flaunted illgotten wealth. The authorities might then even shut their eyes to the crimes of the mob, looking upon it as a justifiable expression of *tokusei* or the old law of benevolence.

When the Rev. Wilton Hack first came to Japan there was more homespun cotton clothes to be seen than silks, because the poor could not afford anything else, and the mass of the people were poor. There were plenty of mulberry fields then, but not as many as later, when, for some decades, the prosperity of Japan rode on the back of the fragile silkworm.

Cotton fields were common, and cotton plants were to be seen growing along the edges of the fields, but as soon as Japan began to enter the industrial age, the space previously devoted to cotton was given over to producing more silk for export, and more rice to feed the rapidly increasing population.

Wilton Hack was here before Japan was an industrial country. He saw the farmers working from dawn to dusk, generally with no greater reward in those days than to keep starvation from their doors. Most of the products of their labour went to the landowners and their overlords, in order to pay the crushing burden of land rents. The farmers produced silk and grew rice, but many neither dressed in the former, nor ate the latter. Mostly they dressed in coarse homespun cottons and ate barley and millet, except on holidays and in case of sickness. Some farmers were always so poor that rarely, even on festival days, could their families taste rice. For some people rice was such a remote dish that they had little expectation of eating it except on their death bed. The enquiry "Has he tasted rice?" indicated that a person's end was so close it was presumed he was being treated to rice.

Famine and epidemics were the two factors responsible for the population of Japan remaining more or less stationary at about 30 million during the early nineteenth century.[1]

About the time Hack came to Japan, which was long before the days of Federation in Australia, and when that continent was divided into States each with its own government, the State of South Australia was endeavouring, although without much success, to open up and develop the vast Northern Territory of Australia.

Hack had been most favourably impressed with the courage, the energy, and skill displayed by the Japanese farmers, even when working under conditions which yielded them little of the fruits of their labour and little hope for the future. He became convinced that they would make good colonists in the Northern Territory of Australia, where the climatic conditions, although severe, were not much more trying than those to which they were accustomed.

He visualised that if three to four hundred Japanese farmers, and also skilled workers accustomed to mining and pioneering operations, could be induced to emigrate to the Northern Territory, bringing with them *"a years provisions, tools and everything necessary to guard against privation,"*[2] the experiment would go a long way to developing those areas, and it would yield important benefits to those Japanese who were willing to emigrate.

In July, 1876, when on a visit to Australia from his mission work in Japan, he wrote to the South Australian Commissioner of Crown Lands suggesting that the Japanese would make good colonists, and offering "to lay the matter before the Japanese Government" when he returned there. His suggestion was studied by the South Australian Government, but the Cabinet did no more than approve of his visiting the Northern Territory and *"obtaining what information he can with a view to his disseminating the same in Japan."*[3] When Hack, who was a missionary without personal wealth, asked for financial assistance towards his travel expenses back to Japan, he was informed, after much official deliberation, that £50 would be made available to him. With that modest sum, and a letter of introduction to the Japanese Minister for Foreign Affairs, Hack set out for Japan on a mission which might perhaps have changed world history, had it met with any success.[4] He was ahead of the times in Japan.[5] He soon exhausted his funds and his private resources hanging about Government offices, endeavouring to secure interviews and interest the Japanese authorities in his proposals.

Those were times when there were clan rebellions in Japan and when echoes of the once popular cry of expel the barbarians could still be heard against foreigners. Finally, in reply to his enquiries as to *"whether your Government is willing to allow Japanese subjects to emigrate to the Colony of South Australia,"*[6] the Japanese Minister for Foreign Affairs replied with determination that *"all emigration of Japanese out of the (Japanese) Empire will be resisted by the (Japanese) Government."*[7]

Traditionally the Japanese authorities distrusted the foreigners. Furthermore a few of the clans distrusted some of their own countrymen perhaps even more. Parts of the country were still in a state of insurrection, and the authorities were determined to keep all malcontents at home under their watchful eye, and in any case were too intent then upon conserving their manpower to give much encouragement to the emigration of skilled workmen, or at least not to a country so far away as Australia.

Hack was of the opinion that *"had his object been merely to obtain coolie labour no difficulties would have been placed in his way, but the ground of objection was evidently that he wished to obtain the more respectable classes, such as artisans, farmers etc."*[8]

Poor Hack's vision of a great scheme, and an early development of the Northern Territory of Australia, came to nothing. He had exhausted his own funds and borrowed money from his friends. He had nothing to show for his efforts or his perseverance. When he and his family arrived in Nagasaki in April, 1877, seeking a passage back to Australia, they were penniless. The British Consul in Nagasaki thereupon opened a subscription list among British nationals in the port to enable Hack and his family to return to Australia, and thereby raised the modest sum of Mex $251 (about £60 sterling). Hack gratefully accepted this sum, which he said *"made the future less gloomy in appearance."*[9]

The facts regarding this strange episode in Japanese history have sometimes been distorted and often related otherwise than we have told them. In popular newspaper articles it has often been said that Hack was a paid publicity agent of the South Australian Government; that he was sent to Japan as an emissary to open negotiations for the entry of 100,000 coolie indentured labour, and that his mission was to open up Northern Australia to the Japanese, all of which imaginings are far from the simple facts.

Nevertheless, many may be inclined to join us in marvelling that Wilton Hack's idea, which not unlikely would have greatly benefited the Northern Territory of Australia and also Japan, and perhaps have changed history, was considered by the South Australian Government to be worthy of no more than fifty pieces of gold as travel expenses, and by the Japanese Government as an idea to be *resisted*.

THOSE
VERY
QUEER
JAPANESE

Oh, Japanese
You're welcome to this shore!
We greet you as we greet the
        Orient breeze
Whose rustling robes have swept
        the perfumed seas;
You come as welcome as the ear-
        liest peas—
Can soul of man say more.
        The New York Illustrated News,
        26 May, 1860, on the occasion
        of the visit of the first Japanese
        Embassy to the U.S.A.

In the early days Japan was an unusual place inhabited by strange people. Most of the foreigners thought the Japanese to be very queer, but they did not realise that the Japanese considered them to be equally queer. The fact is, by to-day's standards, both were queer.

For one thing most of the foreigners were overdressed, and most of the Japanese were underdressed. Most of the foreign gentlemen—an expression freely used in those days, because the rest of the males didn't count—wore coats on all occasions even when having a friendly drink in the club, and if you know anything of the drinking habits of those days you will know what a formidable performance the wearing of coats in the bar in summer time must have been. Little wonder many of them died of so-called heat stroke. However, they mistook the symptoms and made a wrong diagnosis, and instead of cutting down on their drinks they added another article of clothing—namely an inch thick pith helmet to protect them from the sun. The ladies also, by to-day's standards, were overdressed in that they wore as many petticoats as the Japanese court ladies wore underkimono, and that is a great number, as anyone who has been present in a court lady's boudoir during dressing or undressing time, will know.[1]

A large proportion of the Japanese wore very little at all in summer and not a great deal more in winter. For example, the letter carriers[2] and couriers of those early days, the rickshawmen[3] and the coolies—a permissible expression for labourers in those days—in summer time wore only a loin cloth and a towel wound around the head, but even if we exclude the towel there was still about ten times as much yardage in their costume as in that of some of our favourite cabaret entertainers of to-day, so surely some of the criticism which our forefathers levied against the nudity of the Japanese people was a little unfair.

Apart from the temples, it would seem that the nudity of the Japanese people was the feature which most impressed the early tourists, judging from the travel books written by visitors to Japan, of wh'ch books there was an annual crop. They were almost uniform in their contents. Generally an opening chapter describing their arrival in Yokohama and visit to the great "Dieboots"[4] at Kamakura, followed by a chapter about the nudity of the Japanese people, one about the temples of Nikko, another about the nudity of the Japanese people, with a final chapter about curios. The latter chapter generally took one of two forms. Either it was a glowing account of the wonderful curios to be bought in Main Street, Yokohama—and they were wonderful compared to the contents of a souvenir shop these days—or alternatively a lamentation that Japan had been stripped of her curios[5] and that nothing old or genuine remained. That was around eighty or ninety years ago!

The Japanese officials of those days should have our sympathy, because certainly many tried hard enough to understand the ways of the West in the matter of dress, and they must have been bewildered to note the horror in which the naked human frame was beholden by even some of the learned *gaijin*. Maybe they had heard of that remarkable meeting of the Asiatic Society of Japan in 1880 to hear a paper by Professor Conder on "Japanese Dress." Prior to the reading of the paper, it had been arranged for Dr. Faulds, another learned member, to introduce a certain Japanese male, by way of illustrating the heights to which tattooing had been carried. But the exhibition of a semi-naked person—and a Japanese "coolie" at that, as some of the members chose to regard him—was too much for some of the savants. One member thereupon moved that *"the specimen should be relegated to the exterior of the premises, where if anyone who desired might examine him critically."*

That was not the end of the matter. As with all

wrangles in the community, it was continued in the correspondence columns of the Yokohama English-language newspapers where Dr. Faulds expressed regret that *"the apparition should have so alarmed any of our weak-nerved savants."*

With the opening up of Japan to an increasing tourist traffic, the authorities became so concerned at the bad publicity the country was receiving over the lack of dress of the lower classes, that anti-scanty clothing regulations were framed. Those regulations added to the duties of the police, and were particularly difficult to enforce during the summer months, especially when many people kept just within the law by wearing jackets made of mosquito netting.

Very few of those travel authors mentioned the foreign residents, from which we must suppose that they did not consider them of much importance. To one who has lived over forty years in Japan, this came as a sobering discovery.

We have remarked that both the foreigners and the Japanese of that period were rather queer. There is plenty of evidence forthcoming from both sides. The fact is the customs and habits of both were a source of never-ending amazement and amusement to the other. The foreigners laughed loud and long at the Japanese, but as few of them moved in Japanese circles they could not hear the Japanese laughing at them. And that is still true to-day.

For example, the management of the Grand Hotel of Yokohama, in their advertisements made a feature of the front verandah from which visitors could view the quaint customs of the natives on the Bund[6] below. That was just a veiled invitation to come to

Japan and see the queer Japanese. The tourists came by the thousands and enjoyed every bit of it.

They travelled everywhere and did everything. "Pushing into the interior" was the way some described their adventures.[7]

They insisted upon a geisha party.[8] They ate Japanese food. In short they were determined to try everything. Some even insisted on sleeping in a Japanese bed, and all that. And you know how thorough some people can be.

Of course they stayed at the Grand Hotel on the Bund at Yokohama as did all tourists in those days. After "Number Nine"[9]—a hostelry of another kind—the old Grand Hotel lingered in the memory of more visitors to Yokohama, than any other place.

Some of the menfolk spent most of their time in the bar just drinking, while others with great patience and finesse attempted to tap the barboy for information about "getting around" Yokohama, tactics which always achieved their aim, because the barboy was an old-hand who knew exactly what they were angling for. He was able to put them under the care of a rickshawman as a guide. Thereafter they had no trouble, or rather perhaps we should say their troubles only began!

The others sat on the verandah drinking stone ginger beer or sarsaparilla or some other favourite soft drink of those days, whilst they gazed and laughed at the Japanese on the Bund below them, quite oblivious, however, that among the throngs there were often organized tour parties from the country, who had been brought along by their guides especially to see the queer *gaijin*—the curious be-

whiskered men from the West with their wives who
wore hats almost as large as umbrellas—indulging
in their strange custom of drinking whisky on the
hotel verandah.

We have laughed a lot at the queer Japanese over
the years, but they were having their laughs on us
too.

Actually, conducted tours are nothing new in
Japan. The Japanese got the idea quite as early as
did Thos. Cook, and when the Yokohama Foreign
Settlement was opened it became an even more popular tour place for the farmers and country bump-
kins from the interior than a trip through the
Yoshiwara. At least they knew what they would see
in the Yoshiwara, whereas on entering the Foreign
Settlement they would be in a new world, the wonders of which would be explained to them by knowledgeable guides.[10]

Those were the days before overseas steamers
called at Shimizu, and Nagoya. Green tea was therefore delivered to foreign merchants in Kobe and
Yokohama, where it was roasted in tea-firing godowns[11] preparatory to being shipped abroad. The
work was done by females to the accompaniment of
songs generally of an erotic nature. The smoke from
the fires seeped out of the ventilators in the roof of
the godowns, and the air was heavy with the aroma
of burnt tea.

All the Settlement property holders who were not
engaged in the tea business, considered the tea-firing
godowns to be an eyesore, and they thought they
should be moved outside the Settlement into the native quarters; some even suggested they should be

moved to the garbage disposal area. On the other hand those foreign merchants, who were making their money out of tea, never could see anything unsightly about a tea-firing godown.

When the Japanese moved away from the front of the Grand Hotel, the foreigners on the verandah laughed at their strange shuffling walk, they laughed at the clip-clop of their tall *geta,* and wondered why they did not topple off those clumsy footwear, but they never realised that the throng was gathering outside the tea-firing godown in the rear of the hotel, where the guide was describing to those country visitors that the building was a foreign bath house.

He explained the clatter and the singing as that of the Japanese servants bathing their foreign masters, who on such occasions, he stated, drank vast quantities of tea. Then pointing to the smoke coming through the roof he explained it as indicating the lavish manner in which foreigners waste fuel.

Having thus convincingly explained away the salacious songs, the smoke, and aroma of tea, he apologised that he could not take them inside because, he said, foreigners are strangely sensitive about being seen taking a bath!

And so the country folk returned to their hamlets in the mountains with wondrous tales of the queer foreigners, and their families rocked with laughter at the telling.

That Japan and the Japanese—and the foreigners too—of a hundred years ago were more than queer was pungently reported by one writer in the following words:

"The first overlapping of the selvedges of the two

civilizations was not a winsome spectacle. The licentiousness of the first visitors from the ships and terrific greed and covetness of the traders outraged the native sense of propriety. On the other hand, the horrible obscene orgies in the religious festivals or matsuri, and the display of pornographic pictures and phallic emblems in the temple processions surprised even those familiar with India and the Pacific islanders."[12]

Even so, at least one foreign storekeeper in Osaka seemed to think that the market was not satiated with pornography, because he added his mite. *The Hiogo News* of 26 July, 1871, protested that he was doing quite a business in a peep-show machine with stereoscopic art pictures from Paris.

Considering the number of nude forms to be seen in Japan in those days, we would have thought that when it came to paying for a peep-show that no nudes would have been considered good nudes—maybe, however, the novelty of a foreign nude could be an attraction.

We have no idea how naughty those pictures were, and doubt that they were very nude. We rather venture a guess that few people would pay a copper coin these days to see them. More than likely they were pictures of chorus girls dressed in long lace-up black leather boots, bloomers, corsets, and long-sleeved underwear. But we doubt whether even those sights could have been nearly so thrilling for a Japanese of the old-school as the back neck line of a geisha.[13]

Around a hundred and fifty years or so ago when the Japanese proletariat used to purchase woodcut

prints for a copper coin a sheet, to use as pin-ups in
their rooms—prints which to-day fetch great prices
—the pictures which were intended to create pas-
sionate reactions showed the hair-line at the back
of a woman's neck, or the glimpse of a small portion
of a red undergarment against the flesh of her ankle
or wrist. Such simple sights were believed to stir
the passions of even the most stolid men. They were
born of established conventions in *kabuki* plays that
a geisha could encourage a man, for whom she had
a passion, by giving her neck a twist, or by allow-
ing a small portion of her red underkimono to show
against her bare arm or ankle. Needless to say the
kabuki theatre in those days was considered by the
upper circles to be distinctly low brow. Even so, that
vulgar entertainment—so high brow now—attracted
all classes. However the wives of samurai, when
visiting a *kabuki* theatre would often take the precaution of wearing cheap clothes and having their
hair done up in the fashion of the common people,
to avoid recognition.

The old fashioned conventional Japanese idea that
red cloth can inflame a man as well as a bull, seemingly prompted the official Japanese broadcasting
station in 1945 to warn all women, prior to the landing of the Occupation Army, to avoid wearing red
under kimono and to convert their kimono into wartime working garments, with the sleeves closely tied
at the wrists and with the trousers drawn in at the
ankles with tapes. The women of Japan hastily obey-
ed only to discover later that they had thereby destroyed the souvenirs which the first Occupation
troops coveted most and for which they were will-

ing to pay the highest prices—namely a kimono. In the resulting scarcity of kimono, it naturally happened some of the G.I.'s had secondhand Japanese bath robes and bedgowns palmed off on them as genuine Japanese kimono!

After recently reading a *Japan Mail* editorial of 1887 reporting that some European prudes had been shocked at the gleam of flesh among the Japanese female clam gatherers, near Yokohama, who of necessity rolled their sleeves high and tucked up their kimono, thereby exposing a little more than the ankle whilst squelching about in the mud flats of Mississippi Bay, we are no longer disposed to laugh at any old-fashioned Japanese gentleman even if he is thrilled with the back view of a geisha's neck, strange though it may seem.

It had never been necessary for a geisha to disrobe to reveal that she paints and powders her face, neck, and shoulders until she is whiter than a plaster-of-Paris bust of a Roman emperor. However, the number of holes that once were made in the paper *shoji* at Japanese inns, through which everyone from the manager to the kitchen boy might apply an eye, was abundant evidence that foreign female nudes were novelties, but the peeping was done in a spirit of genuine investigation—at least we were told so—to determine whether foreign women are white from the neck down, or whether they bear a colour line around the upper portion of their torso, as do the geisha.

The times have changed, the customs, and the people also.[14] Much of the quaintness—and the queerness too—of earlier days has passed away, and with them

some agreeable pleasures of simpler times. Gone, for
example, are the days when many Japanese bathed
in a tub outside in the street in view of all passers
by, and a lather of soap was considered to be an
ample cover of one's nakedness.[15]

We live now in times when even the elements, no
less than people, behave differently to a century ago,
as anybody can verify by examining paintings and
sketches of those times. In those days even the wind
was less uncouth than now, it invariably blew umbrellas and gentlemen's coat-tails upwards but ladies
skirts downwards—a genteel happening depicted by
many artists of our very proper Victorian era.

However, we have noted the same phenomena in
Japanese woodblock prints of the same period. And
so, despite the nudity of the Japanese people of those
times, it would seem we foreigners did not have a
monopoly on modesty.

THE WILD OATS
OF THE
GRAND DUKE
ALEXANDER

> *Troops, guns, priests, ikons, wom-*
> *en—all became involved in one*
> *disorderly rout.*
> *"The War in the Far East"* by
> The Military correspondent of
> *The Times*, 1905.

Nagasaki in its heyday was the busiest port in
Japan. It was a great coaling station and therefore
a port which, in those coal-burning days, few ships
to Japan could pass by. Most vessels called there;
consequently the majority of tourists and visitors to
Japan in those times had the opportunity of a trip
through the Inland Sea—a place which comparatively few visitors now see.

A tourist to Japan in the eighteen-eighties, watched the coaling at Nagasaki from the promenade deck
of a passenger ship and described it:

"The coal junks cluster around the vessel . . .
Queer undersized mannikins briskly fill rows of
baskets, each about as big as a small flower-basket
and holding a small shovelful. These are snatched
up by old hags and passed along a double row of
bright young girls, who hand them rapidly up the
gangway ladder and empty their ridiculously tiny
contents into the ship's bunkers. Lilliputian ur-
chins collect the empty baskets and redistribute

them throughout the junks . . . The entire opera-
tion is accompanied with never ceasing merriment
and cracking of childish jokes . . . As for their
clothing—what can be said about that which
amounts to next to nothing . . . They substitute
their clean chemises for their coal-labour slips
under our very eyes with as much indifference as
an English young lady would change her gloves."[1]

That description was true enough, except that the
merriment and the jokes were more salacious than
childish, and represented a running commentary on
the tourists, who were gazing at them from the
decks above, quite oblivious of the fact that they
were the target of much ribald humour.

Nagasaki was then the gateway to Japan. Chinese
exchange shops, dealing in currencies of most countries of the world, were located at strategic points.
They were familiar with coins which few people
these days have ever seen, such as "pieces of-eight,"
Carolus dollars, and special U.S. "trade dollars."

There were souvenir shops in great numbers. All
sold the famed Nagasaki tortoiseshell ware, also
Satsuma and egg-shell porcelain, elaborately decorated with samurai and ladies of the Yoshiwara,
prettily decked out with the badges of their profession—the large-sized bamboo hairpins which stuck
out from their heads like the rays of light from the
halo of a saint. Some of the souvenir shops specialis-
ed in other *objets d'art*, transactions which were
conducted in whispered conversations at the rear
counter.

Prior to the Russian occupation of Port Arthur in
1898, Nagasaki was the winter rendezvous for the

The Wild Oats Of The Grand Duke Alexander

Far Eastern Squadron of the Russian Fleet. The vessels coaled[2] and picked up food supplies, whilst the crews picked up girls in that cheap market. Usually the fleet lay off Inasa, also known as Russian Village because so many of the Japanese there spoke some words of Russian. Madame Chrysanthemums[3] and Madame Butterflies were ensconced all over the town. The Russians found pleasure and the Japanese found profit during the winter months when the fleet was in port.

The Russian convict ships on their way around the world, from European Russia to Vladivostok, sometimes touched at Nagasaki when in urgent need of water or supplies, but only a few ship-chandlers and others were allowed on board those gloomy hulks. They slipped out of port as quietly as they came in.

In the Inasa Foreign Cemetery nearby, which contains some of the oldest foreign graves in Nagasaki, and many of great historical interest, there was a Russian naval section. The graves are still there, although mostly covered with rubbish and deep grass. Unhappily much of the cemetery was stripped of its metal, presumably during the war and is now in a shocking state of neglect. Much money has been spent on the so-called House of Madame Butterfly, which returns handsome dividends to the City, but seemingly none remains to preserve the history of early Nagasaki which is written on the tombstones in the old Inasa Cemetery.

But let us return to Nagasaki in the days of its glory.

The Wild Oats Of The Grand Duke Alexander

Signboards in Russian abounded in Nagasaki in those days. In addition some Japanese shops also hung out signs in English and French. Rickshaw stands were located almost everywhere within hailing distance. There were bars and saloons at every thirsty point. There were dubious places of entertainment in the back alleyways for the seamen, but the more respectable houses of iniquity to which tourists were welcomed, and which had been soliciting foreign patronage for well over three hundred years, were located higher up town around the old quarter of Maruyama.[4] They did not find it necessary to hang out signs in any foreign language.

We are indebted to Grand Duke Alexander of Russia[5] for a helpful description of how more discreet companionship—but I have no doubt equally professional—could be secured in Nagasaki. His information is a bit out of date now, because he was writing of 1886 when he was a junior officer on a Russian warship[6] which conveniently wintered in Nagasaki—that was before Monsieur Pierre Loti or Signor Puccini had found a glorious source of royalties in the heart-breaking stories of Madame Chrysanthemum and Madame Butterfly.

In his memoirs the Grand Duke tells us how O-Machi San arranged everything. She was a Japanese widow who ran a first class restaurant, the fame of which had spread throughout the Russian Far Eastern Fleet. *"She was considered a godmother to the Russian Navy . . . She employed Russian cooks, spoke Russian fluently, played Russian melodies on the piano, and on the guitar, served hardboiled eggs and spring onions with fresh caviar, and created in general the atmosphere of a typical Russian inn on the outskirts of Moscow."*

I believe the oldtimers will bear me out that we had nothing to equal that in our young days in Kobe. But what seems to have been more important than her culinary and musical activities, was her extra-curricular service in providing comforts for the Russian officers. If we are to believe the Grand Duke—and why not?—*"She exacted no fee for this additional service, doing it from sheer goodness of her heart. She thought she should help us to take back to Russia a pleasant memory of Japanese friendliness."*

The specific part which O-Machi San played in that *entente cordiale* business was to arrange the introduction of a number of "débutantes," and then, when the officer had made his choice, draw up a marital contract for a period of from one to three years depending upon the length of stay of the cruising man-of-war in Eastern waters. At the end of that period "the wife" might transfer her affections to another officer, but generally the first had been sufficiently generous for her *"to have saved enough money to obtain a place in the community."*

Evidently those Russian naval officers moved in higher circles than some of the French naval officers. Lieutenant Viaud, alias Pierre Loti, used the local laundryman as his interpreter and matrimonial agent. Furthermore the laundryman was not actuated by the noble altruism of O-Machi San, but was quite frank in stating that in return for his services he expected to get Loti's washing.

However to return to the Grand Duke, although

then only twenty-two years old, he must have been hard to please, because, according to his story, O-Machi San had to parade no less than sixty of Nagasaki's best daintiness before he made his choice. He almost had us believing that his decision was influenced solely by *"a sapphire blue kimono embroidered with large white flowers"* which she wore, because that was all he mentioned about her.

Wedding dinners used to follow each marital contract which O-Machi San pulled off—and what affairs some of them were. Among other things the table was loaded down with *"bottles of vodka sealed with the Imperial double eagle, the unavoidable piroski, the borsch, the blue boxes of caviar placed on a huge block of ice and the mammoth sturgeon occupying the center of the table."*

The "wives drank next to nothing," which is something that could not be said for their "husbands." The Grand Duke tells us that the "toy-women" were treated well and with due respect. To flirt with the "wife" of another officer, or for any of the "wives" to ogle another "husband," would have been considered a grave breach of etiquette. Whether such breaches did in fact occur is not mentioned.

From 6 o'clock every evening the Grand Duke was free to leave his ship and go ashore, where he devoted much time to the study of the Japanese language, but perhaps not from the standard grammar books, because his Japanese conversation seems to have had a local flavour.

It was about that time that the Grand Duke, up to then serving incognito, was ordered by his cousin, the Czar of Russia, to represent him on a state visit to the Emperor of Japan in Tokyo.[7]

At the banquet the Grand Duke was seated on the right of the Empress and took the opportunity of engaging her in conversation. The Empress was almost convulsed with suppressed laughter, but the Japanese prince nearby dropped his head in shame, in an effort to suppress his tears, upon hearing the Empress being addressed in Nagasaki tea-house slang. Fortunately a gale of laughter spread down the table and the peace of the world was thereby saved. The Grand Duke believed it must have been *"the gayest banquet in the history of the Empire."*

The Japanese Prime Minister seems to have been impressed, because when escorting the Grand Duke to his carriage after the banquet he enquired how many language lessons the Grand Duke had taken, and they slyly added, "I wish I knew her name."

From Tokyo state banquets, the Grand Duke returned to an incognito existence and the grind of life in Nagasaki. As mentioned, he was then only twenty-two years old. Eighteen years later during the Russo-Japanese war he appears to have been treading the soft carpets of St. Petersburg,[8] but in World War I he became Commander-in-Chief of the Russian Air Force.

Anyhow after reading the Grand Duke's memoirs we began to understand more about Japanese naval strategy in the Russo-Japanese War, but we do not recall ever having heard that O-Machi San was honoured for her contribution towards winning it.

DEMON
TILES*

*Fiogo (Hyogo) is the last good
harbor we come to in our voyage
from Shimonoseki to Osacca, and
is much frequented, that upon our
arrival there we found no less
than three hundred barges lying
at anchor. The city of Fiogo . . .
is built round the semi-circular
shores of its harbour . . . behind
appears the top of a barren mountain, which they say hath very
rich mines, yielding a good quan-
tity of gold.*

Dr. Engelbert Kaempfer, 1694

Of recent years great banks, hongs, and steamship lines have been celebrating their centenaries or
publishing details of their progress over the past
century. In marvelling at the immense achievements
which have been accomplished by some of the famous
names in the Far East, it should be remembered
that for each who succeeded there were a score, nay
a hundred or more, who failed or closed down, un-
successful and disheartened.

Among the startling failures were such princely
hongs as Dent & Co.; among the spectacular ones,
the Oriental Bank Corporation.

*This article first appeared in *The Mainichi Daily News* of
25 June, 1960.

Demon Tiles

Then there was the ambitious American firm of Walsh & Co., later Walsh Hall & Co., which was doing a fabulous business and had purchased in Yokohama and in Kobe, the best business sites available, curiously enough No. 2 Bund in each port. At Kobe they had built magnificent premises, far grander than any others in the Settlement—an immense two-storied wooden-frame building, cement faced, with extensive offices on the ground floor and palatial residential quarters above for the manager, with drawing and dining-rooms grand enough for a mayoral reception.

In line with Japanese tradition the *oni-gawara*—the demon-tiles or master tiles placed at the ends of the ridges of a tiled roof—were especially moulded. Originally, demon-tiles were intended as charms to ward off fire and ill-luck; later they were generally regarded as ornamental pieces, and as such were often decorated with the trademark of the firm or with the family crest—a proud announcement, set high on the building, of the social eminence of those living beneath the roof, and a warning also to the birds of the air to take care!

The Chinese character for "water" moulded on an *oni-gawara* was known to be particularly effective in preventing conflagrations from spreading to a building so protected. Other designs depicting the mask of a demon were known to be able to block the entry of evil spirits or ill fortune. Japan has progressed a long way during the past hundred years. Nowadays there are scientific fire-extinguishers, foam, and other complicated means of preventing fires from speading—but unfortunately nothing so simple as a Chinese character stamped on a tile!

With the tendency to modern forms of architecture, the tile makers found themselves with stocks of *oni-gawara* for which there was no ready sale. However during the Occupation period when there was a craving among Occupationaires to acquire Japanese antiques, some of the curio dealers discovered that by treating those tiles, and by giving them a dash of gilt, they could produce plausible curios, seemingly of great age. The addition of a wooden stand or case, and the inclusion of a certificate soon transformed that particular *oni-gawara* into a genuine relic of Hideyoshi's castle or some other historical building.

Of more recent times *oni-gawara* have even been introduced into Japanese flower arrangements. While rather bizarre in such settings, they do however show off to greater advantage than some scraps from the junk heap which now often find a place in modern Japanese floral arrangements.

When Walsh Hall & Co., built their grandiose office and residential quarters at No. 2 on the Bund in Kobe, they, or their contractor, ordered special demon tiles, presumably in the hope of protecting the firm against the hazards which were ahead. However, instead of a trademark or any mystical design the Japanese ideographs for "American No. 2" were moulded on the face of the demon-tiles— "American" being the nationality of the firm and "No. 2" the address. Walsh Hall & Co., was doing an enormous business; the partners were looked upon as merchant princes, and everyone recognised it as ranking among the No. 1 American firms. Then suddenly, following upon heavy overtrading, speculations, and trade reverses, they were obliged to curtail their operations, whereupon the Hongkong & Shanghai Banking Corporation[1] took over their premises in both Kobe and Yokohama. Thus it was, in that same palatial establishment in Kobe, the great British banking institution consolidated itself in Japan's foreign trade, but I have often wondered whether anyone was aware of the coy joke perched on the roof high in the sky.

Quite obviously those demon-tiles on the roof of the Kobe premises proved to be "good joss"[2] for the Hongkong & Shanghai Bank, but nevertheless the legend thereon set on the topmost peak of the building of that great British bank slyly said "American No. 2"!

The bank's customers when entering the building often watched the seagulls gathered in a neat row on the topmost ridge of the building, with their leader perched on the demon-tile itself; perhaps they wondered what the gulls were talking about!

The shades of the past that gathered about that building disappeared well over half a century ago, when in 1900 it was replaced by a larger red brick edifice—the same building which was gutted, but not flattened, in the bombing of 1945. The looters— Japanese contractors who made fabulous fortunes during the Occupation days—soon however flattened it, and other foreign buildings in the Settlement, in order to secure building material at no cost with which to construct high priced buildings and other facilities for the Occupation Forces.

Anyhow the records of the gutted and looted red

brick building, and of the earlier wooden frame building with the demon-tiles, still remain in photographs.

Should anyone wish to-day to verify my story of the demon-tiles, let him think up some excuse for calling upon the manager of the Kobe Branch of the Hongkong & Shanghai Bank, and then, when in his office, devise some means of being left unattended for just half a minute. Thirty seconds will be ample time within which to make use of a magnifying glass which should be secreted in a pocket. A glass of about the same magnification as that which Sherlock Holmes used, will be ample to examine the photograph on the wall and to read the legend on the demon-tile.

That photograph was in fact presented by us to the Bank some years ago, but until now we have kept as a closely guarded secret the coy joke hidden high on the roof. Perhaps it is that pride in the growing strength of sterling has now encouraged us to share with you this jest, once enjoyed only by the birds of the air and the ghosts of the former occupants of the building!

CHASING THE HOPE DIAMOND

> *A diamond is valuable tho' it lie on a dunghill.*
>
> Thomas Fuller—*Gnomologia*, 1655.

The Yokohama Foreign Settlement was one of the strangest places in the world. Not everybody knew that. Most of the foreigners who resided there were quite unaware of the intrigue and dramas that were taking place in the back alleyways. Their knowledge of happenings in the port was generally limited to the confines of their circle of friends and the particular club to which they belonged. There were a few, however, who knew something of the happenings in the byways and backways of that unusual place, and who used to say that the world's queerest people always turned up sometime or another in Yokohama, and generally left again with their secrets undisclosed.

Nowadays most people have heard about the Hope Diamond—the most fabulous diamond of all times, which, according to legend, had been plucked from the head of an Indian idol, and was believed thereafter to bring disaster to its possessor. For long periods it disappeared or its existence was forgotten. Then suddenly it would come again into the news with reports of trouble or tragedy to its owners.

Chasing The Hope Diamond

That amazing sparklet—to use the terminoloegy of the criminal world—was owned by Mr. Harry Winston, the internationally known jeweller of New York. It was securely locked away in a vault known only to Mr. Winston and a few others. It seems reasonable to suppose that Mr. Winston often dreamt that gangs of crooks were planning to rob him of his precious diamond.

As the owner of such a fabulous jewel, it was inevitable that he would receive many letters from queer people the world over. Indeed, I understand that most of the crackpots in the United States had written to him at one time or another. Certainly he must have viewed with suspicion some of the letters he received.

In 1958, Mr. Winston gave the diamond to the Smithsonian Institution in Washington. There were some people who said that by this munificent gift he sought to escape the curse which the diamond carried to its owners.[1] However Mr. Winston insisted that it had never brought him any bad luck, and that business had never been better.

Few people know that there is a connection between the fabulous Hope diamond and the Yokohama Foreign Settlement of more than half a century ago. There is a story—a strange one—of intrigue, love, hate, vanity, and greed, hidden among the shades of the old Settlement. For more than a decade I have pursued it, and in the process have amassed a file inches thick. Gradually the jig-saw puzzle began to fit together, but there were still some gaps. It was with the idea of learning something of those missing links that I wrote to Mr. Harry Winston. Perhaps he turn-

ed my letter over to his lawyers. Maybe he relegated
me to the ranks of the crackpots. At any rate he did
not reply.

Also I sought information from a friend of long
standing then resident in England, David H. James,[2]
for who else could have known as much of the early
Settlement days or the Far East of those times as he
who had been closely associated with Japan since
1884, when he first arrived in this country.

I knew that he had had experiences on the Yokohama waterfront as had fallen to the lot of few other
foreigners, and that he had then left Japan to join
the U.S. Army and fight in the Spanish-American
war. I knew that he had fought in more wars since
then than many people have read of; in the Klondike
Gold Rush he had searched for gold in Yukon; served
as a war correspondent in the Russo-Japanese War;
knew something of diamonds as far back as the
Transvaal days of 1905, when he went to South Africa at the request of Dr. Morrison, the famous Pekin
correspondent of the London *Times*, to report on
conditions of Chinese labourers in the mines; that he
had then joined the Imperial Light Horse to fight
against the Zulu Rebellion where he was seriously
wounded; and I knew he had been one of the foreign
experts in the China Customs.

Then World War I came, where he was seriously
wounded and gained the coveted Military Cross. Med-
ically unfit he then organized Chinese labour battal-
ions in France, and then again he was in war in the
ill-fated Siberian campaign.

Always closely associated with the Far East, he
saw most of the important happenings in Japan, and

then, when well over sixty years of age, he was captured as an officer in the British Army in Singapore, and thereafter spent three and a half years as a prisoner of war in Japanese hands in Changi and the notorious Omori Camp in Tokyo, a place now euphemistically re-christened Heiwa-jima or Isle of Peace.

In response to my enquiries he was able to provide me with some leads, and seemingly he became so infected with my enthusiasm for discovering more details of the link between the Hope diamond and the old Yokohama Foreign Settlement, that he also wrote to Mr. Harry Winston without knowing that I had already done the same. And so it came about that that gentleman in New York received two letters, almost simultaneously, from opposite sides of the earth. There is some reason to believe that Mr. Winston thereupon imagined that a squeeze (again to use the terminology of the underworld) was being made upon his diamond by a gang of international crooks. There are also some grounds for imagining that the two letters ended up in the files of the F.B.I., as did many other letters addressed to him whilst he owned the diamond.

Now let us digress for awhile and trace out the life history of an unusual woman.

She, that is to say the lady who figures in this story, was born in Bethlehem, Pennsylvania, in 1869, the daughter of an ironworker of German parentage. At the age of ten she made her first stage appearance, which was so successful that friends, with faith

in her talents, sent her to Paris to study. She returned to the United States while still in her teens and
became a chorus girl in a burlesque show—and what
a show it was.

She then made her debut in opera as "the girl with
the foghorn voice."

In 1887, she was at the top of the bill-boards of the
Chicago Opera House. Then one night, as the curtain
was rising, the stage manager was dumbfounded to
learn that she had departed for New York with a
wealthy married man. Later on, in response to many
frantic and imploring telegrams, she returned to the
show. The experience may have given her a taste for
married life, because when she did decide to marry
she had three husbands—not of course all at the same
time, but almost one after the other.

Her string of hits continued in many cities in the
United States, and then in Australia, where her name
was linked to several prominent men—and wealthy
of course. One of them had opals the size of pigeon
eggs, and a few diamonds too.

In London she was a great hit. Even the Prince of
Wales, later Edward VII, found her so. She called
him "Eddie," and he called her "Maysie."

She met Lord Francis Hope, heir to the Duke of
Newcastle and possessor of the celebrated Hope diamond, and hit him so hard that they were married,
despite the bitter and united opposition of the entire
family of the noble lord. The Duke was reported to
have offered Lord Francis a million dollars in a vain
attempt to avert the marriage. If this report is anywhere near true it just shows what snobs the English

are—unless of course it throws some light on the reputation of our heroine! At any rate she thus became Lady Hope.

Maysie used to say—although I personally do not believe her—that throughout her life she only wore the diamond twice. Some people, however, believe that disputes about that fabulous sparklet were the reason for her running away from England and from her noble lord, and returning to the stage in New York. Others hinted that something, other than disputes, accounted for her turning her back on English dukes and baronets, for the favours of beer barons of New York. At any rate Lord Francis chased after her and for awhile they lived together in a flat on Thirty-Fourth Street. At that point Captain Putnam Bradlee Strong, son of a one-time mayor of New York appeared on the scene as a frequent visitor to the flat.

Then the Duke of Newcastle arrived and carted his heir off to a hotel. It seems, or at least it seems to me, all that was just too much for Maysie, because soon afterwards she gave up coronets for Tammany Hall, and eloped with Captain Strong, the reckless playboy of New York. And what an elopement it was. At least Maysie said so, when she boasted that the gallant captain was at that time absent without leave from a military assignment on which President McKinley had sent him to Paris.

It was about the happenings which took place around that time that some of the gaps appear in the jig-saw puzzle of which I was speaking earlier in this article. Therefore I shall skip that period and leave those of my readers who care to do so to refer to the front pages of the Chicago and New York newspapers of those days, wherein will be found frequent mention of our heroine, of the disappearance of jewels, of quarrels and reconciliations, and vague talk of diamonds and paste.

At any rate Maysie and the captain came to Japan and set up housekeeping in Yokohama where they decided to transform their state of elopement into one of marriage—a tardy but honorable step on the part of the gallant captain. And what a sensation that caused. Not everybody in Yokohama by a long chalk was invited to the wedding, but everybody talked about it.

The men looked forward to partaking liberally of highballs, mint juleps, and other expressions of Tammany hospitality, whilst their wives hoped to see the Hope diamond. Certainly a few of the favoured ones were given a quick peep into Maysie's jewel box. Their eyes opened wide at the glittering sight. It was only a brief glance, but it might have been sufficient for a New York fence to mutter: *"Them's not genuwine rocks."*

Maysie and the captain staged dinners on a grander scale than even the diplomats. On some occasions the guests were required to dress in Japanese costumes. Her Roman dinners served after the vogue of Nero became the Mecca of diplomatic officials. That was the way in which Maysie described them, but she had a greater flair for drama than truth.

If we are to believe Maysie, those were hectic days with a newly acquired but wayward husband. Her own antics in Yokohama society, even if somewhat less sensational than those of her husband, were something to talk about. One night, on the occasion of the Benten *matsuri* or festival, she paraded down Benten-dori, all decked out in her diamonds, pearls, and rubies, in an illuminated rickshaw. She stole the show. At least that was her story later in life, when she was seeking to cash in on her past. Never had tongues wagged so much in the tea-party circles on the Bluff since the time, some years before, when Mrs. Carew poisoned her husband, the secretary of the Yokohama United Club, with arsenic. There was even more gossip and imaginings than when young Mr. Dickinson of the Hongkong and Shanghai Banking Corporation was required by the judge of Her Majesty's Consular Court in Yokohama to give evidence regarding certain tender love letters which he had written to Mrs. Carew.[3] Unfortunately the writing was so illegible that the judge could not read them, and thereupon called upon the embarrassed young man to stand up and read them aloud to the Court. I am sure all romantic minded people will agree with me when I say that no English judge has ever made a more monstrous demand than that!

But let us return to the side of the lady of our story. Maysie divorced Captain Strong in 1910, by which time the world at large had ceased to talk much about her or the Hope diamond. Also she was growing older. However, she had other adventures. For example she formed a friendship with the Sultan of Johore—and he had diamonds too—and she spent a year or so on a rubber plantation. Then later, as she slid downhill, she lived in a world far removed from diamonds whilst working as a janitress in a

214

Seattle shipping office. Then she operated a chicken farm, and later a tea-room.

Her third husband was Captain Smuts, formerly an officer in the British Army and a distant cousin of the Boer general—the one who became the famous and honoured prime minister of South Africa. Thereafter diamonds did not figure in her life. Although she insisted that her married life with her third husband, spent in a cheap Boston lodging-house, was a great success, her husband came close to dying there when a bullet lodged in his chest. Certainly he told the police that the bullet was accidentally discharged whilst he was cleaning his own revolver.

Maysie died at the age of 69 years, worth then about $16.50, that being the wages due to her at the time of her death.

And so it was that the gay May Yohe died—for that was her name—the one-time Madcap May as some of her friends called her, the engaging American actress and sparkler, the one-time toast of the Prince of Wales, the favourite of theatre-goers in several continents.

She was the lady who wore the Hope Diamond. She was the one who could have told us when and where she saw it last, and something of the details of how, for awhile, the most famous diamond of all time went into another period of hibernation. She could have told us of diamonds and sparklets, genuine and paste, and the part the Yokohama Foreign Settlement, or some of those in it, played in all those happenings.

Chasing The Hope Diamond

There have been people in Yokohama of those times who have been prone to explain their lack of success in life to the ill luck which, it is said, pursues all those who have come directly under the influence of the Hope Diamond, but beyond that they do not chose to be more precise.

There are some people, still living, who know some of the details of those curious happenings in the Yokohama Foreign Settlement of more than half a century ago, but, until they chose to come forward with the piece that will complete the jig-saw puzzle and add proof to the story I have to tell, that story must remain untold, at least until all connected with it are dead.

MUSINGS
ON A
CENTENARY*

> *All argument is against it, but all
> belief is for it.*
>
> Dr. Samuel Johnson, 1778.

In September, 1958, the Orient Line's luxur
cruise ship "Orsova"—soon to become a part of the
Orient and Pacific Line's fleet—arrived in Japan
from Australia with some 1400 round trip tourists
aboard,[1] all looking forward to going ashore, hoping
to get even a distant glimpse of Fuji,[2] to discover
somebody in a kimono[3] whom they might be able to
photograph, to purchase a transistor radio for themselves and some souvenirs for friends back home, and
maybe to eat one Japanese meal and see a geisha. In
short to "do" Japan in about three days, weather
permitting.

The arrival of 1400 tourists from Australia, with
money to spend, was an item of sufficient importance
to be covered at great length by the newspapers of
Japan. The Kanagawa Prefectural Police Band was
at the pier to welcome them with the Australian soldiers' most popular wartime tune—"Waltzing Matilda."[4] A bevy of attractive young Japanese ladies
dressed in gay kimono was also there to ensure that

---

* This article in an abbreviated form first appeared in *The
Mainichi,* on 7th November, 1958. All calculations of time
are therefore from that date.

the tourists would have at least one opportunity of seeing Japan's national costume, now fast disappearing.[5] There were real chrysanthemums and artificial cherry blossoms.

Flash bulbs flashed and much space in the newspapers was devoted to photographs of the great occasion. It was a great occasion, in that apart from all other considerations those Australians—the largest tourist party to come to Japan from Australia up to that time—brought goodwill, forgot the war, and purchased over thirty-five million yen at the legal rate.

Interviews were sought by newspaper reporters with the ship's agents, officers, and passengers, all of whom enthusiastically commented upon some phase of the great event.

It was, however, a surprise to me that nobody, not even the P. & O. Co's officials, as agents for the ship, seemed to be aware that the arrival of the "Orsova" was in the nature of a centenary, and a tourist centenary at that, and so indeed an event of greater importance than we read about in the press, or perhaps than most people imagined.

Furthermore it was a centenary, reckoning centenaries with the elasticity which Japanese sometimes calculate such events; or, if we are to be more exact than the Japanese usually are in such matters, it was really the ninety-eighth and a half anniversary of an event in which the P. & O. figured prominently and which put them on a pedestal for all time in the tourist trade of Japan.

In short, I believe, as I shall now set about to show, the P. & O. can fairly claim to have brought the first tourist party to Japan about ninety-eight and a half years ago, and thus to have inaugurated that which developed into the luxury cruise ships of to-day, of which the arrival of the "Orsova" was such a striking anniversary event. That surely is a big claim to distinction, and one that should be rememberd, considering the importance of the tourist trade and the fact that the economy of Japan might long since have foundered had it not been for the endless stream of foreign currency which that trade brings into the country.

However, so far as I am aware, neither the P. & O. nor the Orient Line have ever laid claim to the centenary event which the arrival of the "Orsova" marked. Or perhaps it was that the directors of those great companies, unacquainted with Japanese customs, did not reckon that ninety-eight and a half is sometimes near enough to a hundred.

I shall now quote from the diary of H.B.M. Consul,[6] Nagasaki, by way of proving my contention that it was the P. & O. Company which inaugurated Japan's tourist trade. Under date of 21st May, 1860, Queen Victoria's Consul made the following entry in his diary:

Wrote a note to the Custom House that:

"The steamer 'Aden' which arrived here this morning brought a large number of passengers on a pleasure trip to Nagasaki. Her Majesty's Consul requests that the Superintendent of Customs will be so good as to exchange for the passengers $200 a day 4 days in advance."

The "Aden" was a P. & O. vessel on the Shanghai/Nagasaki run, but she was not the first P. & O. vessel to arrive in Japan. The "Azof" was the first, arriving in Nagasaki on 3rd September, 1859, but there were many foreign vessels earlier than that. However, the "Aden" was probably the first to bring a party of tourists on a pleasure trip.

Mention in the Consul's diary of $200 refers to Mexican dollars,[7] truly an insignificant amount compared to the thirty-five million yen which the "Orsova's" passengers spent.

But the times have changed. Whilst the Finance Ministry officials must have chuckled with glee at the news that the Australian tourists had purchased thirty-five million yen to spend ashore, the Finance Authorities of ninety-eight years ago would not have allowed the tourists on the "Aden" a single copper cash of Japanese currency to spend, if they had had their way. It was only that they did not feel strong enough to withstand a blistering protest from the Consul that they allowed his very moderate demand of 200 Mexican Dollars worth of Japanese currency for the tourists of the "Aden" to spend.

The early treaties had specified that the Japanese should exchange foreign currency for Japanese currency on the basis of weight for weight, but they made no mention of the amount. In those days the price of gold in Japan in terms of silver was much lower than in the world outside. Consequently anyone who exchanged foreign currency, such as Mexican dollars, for Japanese currency, could then purchase Japanese gold and some other commodities at a comparatively small outlay. The Japanese authorities fearful of the consequences of opening the country to foreign trade and alarmed at the prospect of their country being drained of its gold reserves, sought to restrict the exchange of foreign currency into Japanese currency.

And thus it was that the first tourist party landed in Japan from the "Aden" about ninety-eight and a half years before the "Orsova" tourists arrived, but without any band of welcome and with little money to spend ashore.

In Japan, ninety-eight and a half years can be near enough to a centenary, or many seem to think it can, and apparently the Governor of Kanagawa Prefecture and the Mayor of Yokohama did likewise. Indeed I might say that most of the important foreign firms in Yokohama and Tokyo appeared to share that view, as I shall shortly demonstrate.

Yokohama was opened on 1st July, 1859, and yet the City of Yokohama celebrated its centenary in May, 1958, more than a year too soon, despite the fact that the 50th anniversary had been correctly celebrated in 1909.

And so it was that in May, 1958, on the occasion of Yokohama's felicitous celebrations of its so-called centenary, the important foreign shipping firms and some other institutions in Yokohama and Tokyo published congratulatory messages in the newspapers on the occasion of what they also erroneously described as "the 100th anniversary of the opening of the port"—all in fact except the U.S. Consulate-General in Yokohama. The latter offered congratulations but avoided all reference to a centenary, apparently because it perversely believed that ninety-eight and a bit is not a hundred! The P. & O. Branch in Yokohama, on the other hand, performed the difficult feat of walking an arithmetical tight rope by cunningly calculating the same period in two different ways in order to arrive at two different results— one that would be pleasing to the organisers of Yokohama's so-called centenary, and one that would demonstrate that the company really can calculate. Their congratulatory message read: *"The Peninsular and Oriental Steam Navigation Company, themselves the oldest Line regularly calling at Yokohama, take this opportunity to express Congratulations and Sincere Thanks to Yokohama Port on its Centenary. P. & O. ninety-nine years in Japan."*

At first I found myself sharing the belief of the U.S. Consulate-General, and thereupon sought an explanation from a friend in the Yokohama Municipal Council as to how a centenary could be celebrated before even the ninety-ninth anniversary.

I was at first supplied with an involved explanation that under the Japanese system of reckoning ages a person is one when born, and two on the first birthday. Therefore applying the same principle to centenary celebrations, he argued that the first "anniversary" of Yokohama's opening was in fact on its opening day, and therefore the centenary or hundredth anniversary would be celebrated ninety-nine years after the event and not a hundred![8]

In reply I pointed out to my city-councillor friend that this explanation, although exciting but mentally exhausting, could hardly account for celebrating Yokohama's centenary a year too soon, because, a few years before, the same dignitaries in Kanagawa and Yokohama—the same governor and the same mayor—had celebrated the centenary of Commodore

Perry's landing at Yokohama exactly one hundred years after the landing, not ninety-nine. In fact during the post-war period there had been quite a rash of centenary celebrations—much like an outbreak of measles—but each was a hundred years after the event, not ninety-nine.

To all that my friendly city-councillor replied that ninety-nine, or even ninety-eight and a half is really very close to a hundred, and that while from a point of view of history it might not be accurate, yet it is near enough, with which view it was hoped, in the circumstances, I would be satisfied. When I obtusely sought more information as to what the circumstances were, it was subsequently explained that the official celebration of Yokohama's centenary a year too soon was for political reasons, or as it was more gracefully expressed as a pleasing gesture to the popular mayor of Yokohama before his term of office expired, with which it was hoped I would agree. And I do indeed—acquainted as I am with the customs of the country. All of which explains how it is that, while I am familiar with Dr. Johnson's and Daniel Webster's conception of a centenary, I do now assert that the arrival of the "Orsova" marked the centenary of the arrival in Japan of the first tourist cruise ship, namely the "Aden" of the P. & O. ninety-eight and a half years before.

Of course my American friends might seek to detract from the halo which I have placed upon the P. & O. by contending that Silas E. Burrows of Boston, New York, and San Francisco, brought the first tourist party to Japan in his clipper ship "Lady Pierce" in July, 1854, just fifteen days after Com-

223

modore Perry had departed from Japan. But I will
have none of that.

Undoubtedly Silas E. Burrows was a great man.
The Japanese Government's spokesman of the time
even went so far as to insist that he was a greater
man than Commodore Perry, which was certainly
saying a lot, and furthermore they thought that
Silas' clipper ship was a better vessel than the "Sus-
quehanna" and all the other famous U.S. warships
of the time. The spokesman did not mince words and
called a ship a ship. He thought that Perry's ships
had too many guns and too many fighting men on
board, whereas Silas E. Burrows' clipper, the "Lady
Pierce," was a "beautiful ship."

There is no record that the U.S. Secretary of State
of the time took up the cudgels on behalf of his country and set the Japanese right in their beliefs about
the U.S. Navy. The fact is Silas E. Burrows' clipper
really was a beautiful ship—he had spent enough
money to make her so.

So beautiful, indeed, did they consider the "Lady
Pierce" that, with Burrows' approval, they had artists draw her from all angles, draughtsmen take
dimensions, and shipbuilders study and record her
tackle and fittings. In fact they told Mr. Burrows that
the Emperor was intending to honour him by having
two vessels built exactly the same. But that was perhaps fair exchange for the exceptional treatment
which they had accorded him. After all the authorities in the capital had issued instructions that he
should receive similar hospitality to that which had
been displayed towards the United States envoy,
Commodore Perry. Whilst the Commodore may not

have been pleased when he heard of that, Mr. Burrows was most gratified.

From a long article[9] which appeared in the London *Times* of 18 October, 1854, and in the New York *Times* of 31 October, 1854 (it is interesting to note that London scooped New York by a fortnight) it is evident that Burrows had determined to be the first tourist to visit Japan and had spared no expense to fit out his own vessel in the most elegant manner to impress the Japanese. And how he impressed them. They told him frankly *"your ship, the 'Lady Pierce', is the first foreign vessel that has been received by us with pleasure."*[10] That was intended as a slap at Perry. Then they elaborated:

"We understand what ships of war are; also what whaling ships and merchant ships are; but we never heard before, till you came here, of such a ship as yours,—a private gentleman's pleasure ship,—coming so far as you have, without any money making business of trade, and only to see Japan . . ."[11]

Burrows arrived in Tokyo Bay, or the Bay of Yedo as it was then known, intent upon visiting the city, much as the tourists of the "Aden" were intent on going ashore at Nagasaki to see the sights, or the tourists of the "Orsova" of "doing" Tokyo. Actually, however, Mr. Burrows never got nearer than ten miles to Tokyo. After dropping anchor in the bay he listened to a speech of welcome, and learnt that a pilot and an escort would conduct him immediately to Shimoda, an unimportant port that was maintained as a kind of back office in which to receive visiting foreigners, both V.I.P.'s and lesser folk.

To quote a young Dutchman, named Heusken,[12]

who sadly enough was assassinated a few years later
by a two-sworded samurai, Shimoda had little to recommend it other than its oysters and its lasses. I
believe he mentioned its attractions in the reverse
order. The samurai did not kill him because of his
fondness for lasses and oysters, but just because he
happened to be a *gaijin*.

But let us return to the "Lady Pierce." Burrows
had brought back to Japan a shipwrecked Japanese
named Deyenosuke (or Dee-yee-no-skee as he appears
in the ship's log) who was the sole survivor of a
crew of fifteen men belonging to a Japanese junk,
which had been blown out to sea and had drifted
helpless for about seven months, before being picked
up near the Sandwich Islands, or Hawaii as they are
known to-day.

Burrows had also brought with him a large number of presents, but these were refused. The Japanese authorities said:-

*"You offer us, as presents, all the rare and beauti-
ful articles you have in your ship; but we have received orders from the Emperor[13] that we must not
tax your kind feelings by taking anything from
you, as you have already been sufficiently taxed returning Deyenosuke.*

*The Emperor also directs that all the gold pieces
you have presented to the Japanese must be collect-
ed and returned to you, and to say that he alone
can make presents in Yedo Bay. He has directed
that presents be made to you in Shimoda—."*

At Shimoda, Burrows was given a royal welcome
and presented with gifts of silks, porcelains, and

lacquerware, but he did not think much of Shimoda or of the future prospects of trade in that unimportant corner of the country. When he came to buy coal, and was offered at $28 a ton, grade far inferior to that which could be bought outside of Japan at $8 a ton, he came to the conclusion that the Japanese were deliberately pricing themselves out of the market, so as to kill the trade that they had been forced by Perry to enter upon.[14]

Whilst anchored in Japan waters, Burrows had thrown open his ship to visitors. Several thousands came on board and were provided with refreshments including champagne. Everything was open to inspection, even the ship's silver, but not even a single article was stolen. Prominence was given to this circumstance in the London and also New York *Times*[15] as being a remarkable event—and indeed it was. It is most improbable that Burrows would have had that experience in other countries of the world at that time.[16]

The Japanese spokesman concluded a speech of farewell with the statement:-

Your visit to Japan in the 'Lady Pierce has been attended with great interest to us, and you will not be forgotten by the Japanese. We hope we may meet you again, and we hope you will come back to Japan.[10]

And so Silas E. Burrows took his departure from Japan. Certainly he was the first bona-fide tourist— even if he was not permitted to do any touring. He came under his own steam, or rather sail, but he was not in the tourist business, and the "Lady Pierce" did not bring the first party of tourists to Japan. That distinction, I contend, belongs to the P. & O. and the old "Aden."

From those curious beginnings, the tourist traffic to Japan has grown until it now represents one of Japan's most important sources of foreign exchange. But no longer can those tourists—those strange *gaijin* who used to come with immense wardrobe trunks and sometimes with their own bedding—afford the time or the money to travel leisurely through the country for weeks on end. Touring is now planned to fit into a brief period between arrival and departure times of overseas vessels or aircraft, and a budget not usually designed to meet the high prices now prevailing in Japan. Many stay on board ship, much as Silas E. Burrows had to do, and leave again after a brief trip ashore to see what they can of the country once known as *Mikadoland*.

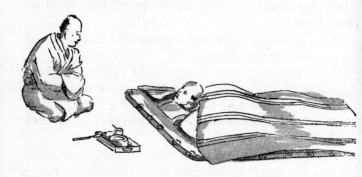

MISS
BUTTERFLY
AND
MISS
CHRYSANTHEMUM

> *On one side of the road a large
> wooden house almost devoid of
> apertures, and of evil aspect.
> What, that sinister-looking house
> the 'Garden of Flowers'? The jin-
> rikisha-man assured me it was,
> and seemed very sure of the fact
> . . . I wish in the first place to
> speak to one M. Kangourou, who is
> interpreter, washerman, and mat-
> rimonial agent.*
>
> Pierre Loti—*Madame Chrysan-
> thème* (1887).

We have just returned from Nagasaki a little off
colour. These days we often go to that delightful
place, but always return in the same condition.

The fact is that while we have a strong digestion
which, on our travels, delights in such indigestible
delicacies as octopus, squid, and abalone, we just
cannot stomach some of the literature and so-called
history which is now being fed to tourists arriving
in Nagasaki.

Having once done a bus tour of that city and listened to the conductress recite the romantic but ca-
lamitous situations in which Mesdames Butterfly and

Chrysanthemum became involved, and then having watched the tourists, Japanese and foreigners, stream into the former Glover mansion, the so-called "Madame Butterfly House," hoping perhaps to see her bedroom or at least her bed, we felt we could not take any more of that ballyhoo. However, it was amusing to note that some appeared to be slightly resentful at finding the bedroom door was locked.

On every visit—and they are frequent—it is becoming increasingly difficult to avoid the extravagant nonsense about Madame Butterfly's house; it is advertised on notice boards, in the guide books, and in many forms of tourist literature. Mesdames Butterfly and Chrysanthemum, appear to be as well known in Nagasaki these days as *Mikki Mausu*, Rikidozan, the "grunt and groan" wrestler, and other celebrities of modern times.

At first when the Nagasaki City authorities decided to whip up the tourist trade by putting on the "Madame Butterfly House" hoax, they described it rather obliquely, or shall we say with calculated ambiguity.

But now the gloves are off. The Butterfly romance, we are now being told, really happened in the Glover mansion, and both the lady and the house are now been given a prominent place in the tourist attractions along with the memorial to the twenty-six Christian martyrs, and the other truly historic monuments of Nagasaki's past. We say this in sorrow more than in anger, because we always receive the most kindly treatment from all the officials there whose assistance we seek in our researches.

It is sad to know that most of the tourists, both

Miss Butterfly and Miss Chrysanthemum

Japanese and foreigners, who visit the delightful villa overlooking the harbour, leave believing they have seen the actual house wherein the Madame Butterfly romance and tragedy occurred, and they will remember it as such, rather than as the home built in the early days by the highly respected British merchant, Thomas B. Glover, who lived there with his wife and children.

On our last trip to Nagasaki we visited the International Cultural Hall which among other things serves as a museum and houses the relics of the atomic bomb explosion. It is located at the opposite end of the city to the "Madame Butterfly House," but even so we could not escape her or Madame Chrysanthemum.

It so happened that our visit co-incided with the busy marriage *shiizun* (season) in autumn, a time when hired bridal wigs and kimono are worn by many different brides on the same day, and the same morning coats and striped trousers are donned by many different bridgerooms, one after another, as quick as the changes can be effected; also a time when trains and hotels are booked out with honeymooners. Two floors of the Cultural Hall had to be given over to relieving the pressure on the demands for space for wedding receptions and banquets.

The international tourists who happened to be viewing the museum at that *shiizun* thus had the thrill of seeing some fast moving wedding receptions. Indeed the crush of spectators was such that a person had to be on the alert to avoid being propelled into a wedding to which he did not belong.

In this atomsphere of bustle—we shall not say

231

gaiety, because the Japanese never appear to look
happy at wedding ceremonies—it came as not too
great a surprise to find that Madame Butterfly and
Madame Chrysanthemum had both been given a place
in the Cultural Hall, along with the hired wigs, the
rented trousers, and the wedding banquets. In this
centre of culture, on the floor devoted to the early
history of Nagasaki, there is displayed on a large
notice-board, in Japanese and in English, the "History of Nagasaki in brief," which tells of the arrival
of the Portuguese, the introduction of Christianity,
the entry of the European merchants, the martyrdom
of the twenty-six Japanese and foreign Christians,
the suppression of Christianity, and the events which
led up to the re-opening of the country from the self-
imposed seclusion. Then, tacked on to that history
which will live as long as Japan lives, is the remarkable statement:

> With the above historical background, Nagasaki
> has seen many sad incidents on one hand, but some
> interesting romances of world-wide fame on the
> other. Of the international romances happened in
> Nagasaki after the restoration of Meiji (1868),
> those of "Madame Butterfly" and "Madame Chry-
> santhemum" stand foremost in scope and color . . .

Neither of these ladies, nor their love affairs, were
mentioned in any guide books in pre-war days. It
was only in the post-war period, when it became
evident that Japan's economy might have to rest
more upon the shoulders of the tourists that upon
the frail back of the silkworm, has so much prominence been given to these "romances."

"Madame Butterfly" is a fictional character and as

232

such has no place in Japanese or in American history. Madame Chrysanthemum was real, and although we do not doubt Pierre Loti's word that she was "pretty and fascinating enough," the fact remains she was just one of many many "semi-professionals" in Nagasaki.

Her claim to fame rests solely upon the fortuitous circumstance (as described in an earlier chapter) of how the local laundryman, combining pimping with the washing of linen, secured a position for her with a French naval officer, who later under the pen-name of Pierre Loti, had the urge to boast to the world of his bitter and sweet experiences and of his fond recollections while *"beneath me Nagasaki lay asleep wrapt is a soft light slumber, hushed by the murmuring sound of a thousand insects in the moonlight, and fairy like in its roseate hues."*

Instead of homing with Loti for a couple of months, her fate, during that summer of 1885, might have been an episode in a back room of some shanty down Creekside as the partner of a sailor, or of a "marriage" with one of the other officers of the French war-vessel "Triomphante," that is to say with men without the gift of expressing their thoughts in words such as flowed from Loti's pen. Actually there were at least four others from the quarter-deck of the same vessel, including the doctor and a midshipman, who were keeping girls on shore under similar arrangements to the Loti menage—ill-matched couples, partners for a month or so. It is evident therefore that the arrival of the "Triomphante" meant good business for the laundryman.

Had Kiku-San, or Madame Chrysanthème as Loti

dubbed her, been snapped up by one of the other men, then her name would not to-day be written into the scrolls of Nagasaki's history alongside that of the twenty-six martyrs.

When speaking of those two ladies, we prefer to refer to the one as "Miss Butterfly" and to the other as "Miss Chrysanthemum." Why must we pretend that it was otherwise? Nevertheless we sympathise with each, for certainly both must have hoped that their alliances would assume a more permanent and less clandestine form. Why cannot we face up to the fact that in the one instance the fictional U.S. naval officer, and in the other the real French naval officer, both deserted their girls, who incidentally, according to their codes of behaviour, were faultless once they had linked up with those gallant officers? I have no doubt that the fictional Miss Butterfly and the real Miss Chrysanthemum both hoped that their temporary spouses would be stout enough to marry them.

If therefore the Nagasaki authorities are determined to include these two girls (or were they not women?) among the glorious company of those who really made history in Nagasaki, can they not be referred to, correctly and sympathetically, as "Miss Butterfly" and "Miss Chrysanthemum"?

It is customary to refer to them as "girls," but were they not women? For one thing, Miss Chrysanthemum was an inveterate smoker. She would even get up three times during the night to smoke, which seems more like the act of an experienced woman than a girl. The noise she made in doing so, used to wake Loti and annoy him immensely.

Prices were cheap in Nagasaki in those days. Nevertheless twenty yen a month for the services rendered seems pitifully little to us, even after making allowances for depreciation in the yen. No wonder Loti, after deserting his girl, described Nagasaki as "an unlooked for Eden." Nevertheless it did not remind him of apple blossoms. On the contrary he thought *"the atmosphere to be laden with a curiously complicated odour, something besides the perfume of the plants and soil, arising no doubt from the human dwelling-places, a mingled smell, I fancied, of dried fish and incense."*

We can only hope that the laundryman passed on to poor Kiku-San a sufficient percentage of the "take" for her to look back upon the period as being a reasonably profitable one, even if it was not for her exactly a Garden of Eden experience. But we have our doubts, because Loti realised the pimp was *"a cunning fellow"*—*"of the lowest type, a rascal of the meanest kind."* Loti being an artist of words, referred to him as a "matrimonial agent," rather than a pimp. Incidentally, although it may sound ridiculous, that pimp, in line with the fashion of the times, wore a bowler hat and white gloves.

We have no doubt that Loti's opinion of the man was correct, because at the first meeting as soon as his requirements were made known, the laundryman had no great difficulty in recalling a girl whom Loti said was *"absolutely what I want"*—and a virgin at that, according to the laundryman.

However that might be, the gallant lieutenant was prudent enough to have the menage recorded at the local police-box, much as an ordinary business transaction, and he was careful to pocket a certified copy of the record for his own protection.

And so even at that early stage of the game, the affair did not appear to display any of the qualities of a "great international romance" worthy of being perpetuated in an International Cultural Hall.

He confessed in his book that he had chosen her to amuse himself, but soon he tired: *"After all, I do not positively detest this little Chrysanthème,"* but *"habit turns it into a makeshift attachment."*

There was however a good streak in Loti; he did hope she had no thoughts whatever of what was happening. And yet sometimes under the green gauze mosquito-net he used to wonder *"what thoughts can be running through that little brain."* It would have been obvious to most men. She knew he was an officer. Perhaps she was wondering whether he would prove to be her hero. She had the answer a few months later when he sailed away.

Perhaps it was to salve his own conscience, that he decided *"it is a hundred to one that she has no thoughts whatever. And even if she had, what do I care? I have chosen her to amuse me."*

In the meantime complications were beginning to develop in the several little houses on the hill.

Frequently the officers were detained on board on duty for several days on end. At such times the sailors from the lower deck roamed the town and made social calls upon the girls on the hill. In the absence of evidence to the contrary we assume that nothing more than innocent indiscretions were involved, but the officers were not so sure. They seemed to think that like Caesar's wife their girls should be above suspicion. The lack of harmony which resulted was so disturbing to the neighbours that the police prevailed upon the landlord to evict some of the couples.

That was not so in Loti's house.

At no time did he have any complaints about Kiku-San's behaviour, but even in his house events seemed to be moving towards the climax of a Greek tragedy, from which it was only saved because Loti had already tired of his girl.

His best friend had fallen in love with his Kiku-San, and she seemed to be in love with him in a lady-like way; the landlady's daughter had fallen in love with Loti, and Loti pretended to be in love with no one. Nevertheless Kiku-San's behaviour continued to be exemplary, but Loti was never sure—"*I should hate her, my 'mousme,' if she were to entice him into committing a fault.*"

Once when three of the group had to share the same mosquito net to escape the mosquitoes, it was she who maintained the proprieties by insisting that Loti should sleep between her and his best friend.

But Loti was chafing at the restraints upon his freedom.

"*I should have been charmed. In reality, however, I am not charmed. It is only Chrysanthème, always Chrysanthème, nothing but Chrysanthème.*"

A picture so different to the great love theme that the Nagasaki city authorities, and the bus girls and guides of the tourist parties, would have us believe.

"*When night closes in . . . we sleep on the floor . . . under a gauze mosquito net . . . dark as the shades of night . . . it envelops . . . us like a tent . . . I feel as if I were acting for my own benefit*

*some wretchedly trivial and third-rate comedy . . .
I find her as exasperating as the cicadas on my
roof . . . what a pity little Chrysanthème cannot
always be asleep . . . In this manner at least she
does not bore me."*

Such were the sentiments of the male partner to a
so-called foremost "international romance," and such
was its "scope and colour."

Loti described his last visit to the house on the hill:
*"She recognises me from afar, and laughing as
usual, runs to meet me. I announce our departure,
and a tearful pout suddenly contracts her childish
face . . . it turns to a fit of laughter, a little nervous
perhaps, but unexpected and disconcerting . . ."*

And so Loti took his departure and deserted his
girl, telling the world that she dissolved their "marriage" with a laugh. Could it be that Loti was striving to protect himself from his own conscience, by
pretending not to know that the Japanese often
seek to hide their emotions with a nervous laugh?

*"She prostrates herself on the threshold of the
door, her forehead against the ground and remains
in this attitude as long as I am in sight, while I
go down the pathway by which I am to disappear
for ever.*

*As the distance between us increases, I turn
once or twice to look at her again; but it is mere
civility . . ."*

While the "Triomphante" was sailing home
through the Yellow Sea, Pierre Loti, the great lover,
threw out of the port-hole his last remaining souvenirs of the summer spent with Miss Chrysanthemum.

In that fashion Loti walked out of the story—and out of our esteem.

Such are the facts of Pierre Loti's great love for "Madame Chrysanthème" as he chose to call her, and as told by himself in his world-famous book of the same name. (The italicized portions of this article which are shown in quotation marks are all from the authorized English edition of that book).

Among the tourist sights of Nagasaki—and one well worthy of a visit—is the Suwa Shrine, but the bus girls and the tour guides now focus the attention of their charges upon its romantic attraction rather than upon its religious aspects. They tell, with due emphasis, of how Pierre Loti used to frequent the Suwa Park with his "beloved Madame Chrysanthemum," and they point out the bronze profile of Loti resting upon a pedestal, which according to the inscription in French is a *souvenir de ses ami de Nagasaki*. As there is no indication as to who his friends were, we hope we shall be pardoned for wondering whether it was Kiku-San, the laundryman, and the landlady's daughter who donated that memorial to Nagasaki City, because we do not know that Loti had many, if any, other Japanese friends.

Close to the Loti pedestal there is a notice board, erected by the City Authorities, which gives him credit for having introduced Nagasaki to the world. We would have thought the Portuguese, Dutch, and English merchants, and the Christian missionaries and martyrs had done that a good 250 years before Loti came ashore to quench his ardour.

The official "Guide to Nagasaki" states that the profile was the gift of the French Government, a circumstance which does not appear to be mentioned elsewhere. Anyhow after reading all the tourist literature on the subject we are left with the feeling that somebody is trying to fool someone.

Loti had no great regard for Japanese temples and shrines, nor for most things Japanese, other than the green of the countryside, the roseate tints beneath the moon, the chirping of the grasshoppers, and Kiku-San when asleep. He had many hard things to say about the people, their houses, their way of life, their food and their temples:-

". . . let the sanctuary be ever so immense and imposing in its sombre gloom, the idols ever so superb, all seems in Japan but a mere semblance of grandeur. A hopeless pettiness, an irresistible feeling of the ludicrous, lies at the bottom of all things."

Loti did in fact visit Suwa Shrine with Miss Chrysanthemum, much in the same way as they visited curio shops, or as when they called on some of her less fortunate friends in some of the less fortunate tea-houses, where the going was harder than in their house on the hill.

After such outings they had to climb the hill to their home:

"To what purpose, good heavens, do I clamber up every evening to that suburb, when it offers me no attractions, whatever? . . ."

"All this which I should find amusing in anyone else—anyone I loved—provokes me in her."

These do not sound much like outings with one's beloved.

Even when attracted by other *"mousme,"* he held

back from any switch-over, telling himself *"it would only be another take-in."*

In pre-war Japan, when the Japanese were less conscious of the art of advertising and ballyhoo than at present, the name of Pierre Loti was seldom mentioned in Japan, and then more by the foreign community than by the Japanese. That was understandable for there was little for the Japanese to admire in Loti or in his book.

Half a century or so ago, foreigners in Japan although well aware of his literary genius which had earned for him a place in the *Academie Française*, had little regard for his writings concerning Japan. The dreadful inaccuracies, his treatment of his affair in Nagasaki, and the manner in which he dealt with the life and culture of the Japanese all went a bit against the grain.

The *Japan Mail* in 1888 referred to him as a naval officer interested more in Venus than in Mars.

Nowadays his name and that of the woman with whom he experimented in living are being emblazoned about Nagasaki, but the true details are either not known or are being submerged in the mist of the legend of a beloved romance.

Perhaps we treat Loti too harshly; some folk may say we are looking at him through the wrong end of the telescope, because after all both the fictitious Miss Butterfly and the real Miss Chrysanthemum were both "semi-professionals" operating through panders.

Nevertheless considering that Loti, after living with Kiku-San for several months (during which time he certainly was unfaithful to her in word if not in deed) sailed away and deserted her, we fail completely to understand how he has qualified for honourable mention in Nagasaki, and how he has earned a place of distinction in one of Nagasaki's most famous Shrines.

There is no reason to believe that Pierre Loti left Nagasaki without paying to Miss Chrysanthemum what was due under the arrangement with the laundryman, and this we feel is about all that can be said in his favour—surely not enough to earn for him a place of honour in Suwa Shrine. If Loti is worthy of a place there, why not the laundryman also? It was his salesmanship—and Loti's ardour—that brought about the circumstances that led to Loti being put on the pedestal.

If it is desired that one of the trio be honoured in Suwa Shrine, or that a monument be raised to the Loti-Chrysanthemum menage, why not have the brave but pitiful little Kiku-San on the pedestal rather than Loti—the artist, the officer, but certainly not the hero of a great romance?

On Loti's own admission she was actuated primarily by the economic necessity of contributing to the upkeep of her mother and seven brothers and sisters, none of whom, including herself, appears to have had a father!

Whether or not she profited at all from the laundryman's deal is not recorded. If she did, then we shall feel happier every time we visit Nagasaki. And we do visit that delightful city frequently to see again more worthy sites, such as those made famous by twenty-six men and boys—the Japanese and foreign Christian martyrs—who really gained a place, and a glorious place it is, in Nagasaki's history.

Those sites will live in men's memory, long after the pedestal in Suwa Shrine and the Cultural Hall itself have crumbled away. They will be remembered as long as religions survive upon this earth.

". . . not to have written a book about Japan is fast becoming a title to distinction."
Basil Hall Chamberlain—*Things Japanese* (1890).

A somewhat disjointed series of
staccato notes, which leaves one
with the misleading impression that
Mr. Pound's shirt cuffs have been
sent to the printer instead of to the
laundress.

Philip Guedalla—*Some Critics*.

AN EARLY ENVOY FROM RUSSIA

Pages 24 - 31:

1. This and other excerpts are from *A Narrative of My Captivity in Japan*, by Captain Golownin, 1818.

2. Smallpox was a dreadful scourge in Japan until compulsory vaccination was introduced in 1874. In those days babies suffering from smallpox wore little red caps.

   Richard Cocks, chief of the English East India Company's house in Hirado, wrote in 1613 that "above 2600 persons are dead in Langasaque (Nagasaki) this year of the small pox."

3. Japanese hand-made paper, is strong because it is made from long fibres. Since olden times it has been used for scores of purposes for which the West had not normally used it, such as for fans, lanterns, umbrellas, raincoats, clothes, and in lieu of pocket handkerchiefs, glass win-

dows, walls and string, and for hundreds of other purposes.

The Japanese had mastered the art of paper-making at a very early date, and, it is said, were turning out a wide variety of fine paper as early as the eighth century. Certainly when the Portuguese came to Japan in the sixteenth century they were astonished at the fine paper that was available. Jesuit missionaries thereupon set up a printing press, where many books were printed on Japanese paper for use in their colleges at Nagasaki and elsewhere.

THE FIRST AMERICAN TEACHER

Pages 32 - 39:

1. According to James Murdoch's *"A History of Japan,"* Vol 3, the Dutch East India Company, during the 198 years of its existence, paid dividends to a total which represented an annual average of 18%. Considering the risk, that was a poor return. During the latter years of its existence there were substantial losses.

2. On the occasion of the centennial celebrations of the ratification of the Japan-U.S. Treaty of Amity & Commerce, the *Asahi Evening News* of 12 Nov. 1960, published the names of 298 U.S. citizens in the religious, educational, economic, industrial, political, diplomatic, social and cultural fields, who had been named for commendation for the significant contributions they had made to the development of Japan during the past hundred years or so. Ranald MacDonald's name was included in that list.

3. E. W. Clement's *"A Handbook of Modern Japan,"* Chicago (1913).

Notes

THE TOWNSEND HARRIS CALUMNY

Pages 40 - 56:

Bibliography:

W. E. Griffis, *Townsend Harris, First American Envoy in Japan*, New York, 1895.

J. H. Longford, *The Story of Old Japan*, New York, 1910.

Carl Crow, *Harris of Japan*, London 1939.

M. E. Cosenza, *The Complete Journal of Townsend Harris*, Tokyo, 1959.

Japanese pamphlets, newspapers, and magazine articles.

1. W. E. Griffis, author of *Townsend Harris—First American Envoy in Japan*, (1895), *The Mikado's Empire*, (1876), and other excellent books on Japan.

2. Harris acted as Consul General from August, 1856, until Jan. 1859, when he became Minister Resident of the United States in Japan. He left Japan in 1861.

3. Harris, while en route to Japan, stopped for about six weeks in Siam in order to negotiate a commercial treaty with that country, although his salary did not commence until he arrived in Japan.

4. See chapter "Queen Victoria's Present" in *"Shades of the Past."*

5. Townsend Harris' treaty was signed on 29 July, 1858. It was followed by a treaty between Great Britain and Japan on 26 Aug. 1858. Later in token of appreciation of the valuable aid and co-operation which he afforded Lord Elgin in negotiating that treaty with Japan, Harris was presented with a magnificent gold box by Queen Victoria.

6. See chapter "Queen Victoria's Present" in *"Shades of the Past."*

7. Carl Crow, "Harris of Japan," p. 11.

8. *The Barbarian and the Geisha* by Robert Payne, New York, 1958.

9. "The Barbarian and the Geisha," 20th Century-Fox

production, 1958, filmed in Japan with John Wayne as Townsend Harris.

10. A popular form of ballad, which is a mixture of story-telling and chanting, to the accompaniment of *samisen* (*shamisen*).

11. The term *"ketojin"* (hairy barbarian) was used more frequently in earlier days than now, when referring to foreigners, because in those times many foreign men had moustaches and beards. It is doubtful, however, that the Japanese were fair in applying it to foreign women. Those foreigners, who will confess to having surveyed a naked but unshaven Japanese woman, will know that some grow patches of hair in the strangest places, such as the side of the leg near the knee-cap, the upper thigh near the hip bone, and even in the centre of the back.

12. Harris on arrival at Shimoda was accompanied by his secretary, Henry C. J. Heusken, who acted as Dutch interpreter, because at that time Dutch was used more than English in Japan. Heusken was assassinated in Yedo in 1861.

13. Perhaps, if the American film producers had been aware of the fact, they could have argued that the idea of a geisha accompanying a diplomat on such a mission is not farcical, by pointing to the precedent set by one of Japan's delegates to the World War I Peace Conference in Versailles in 1919. Prince Saionji, head of the delegation, took along his favorite geisha, and brushed off all criticism by saying that if he had to travel around the world as seventy years of age in the interests of his country, he would at least select his own personal attendants.

14. The purpose of Harris' visit to Yedo was to hand over a letter from the President of the United States to the Emperor of Japan, who at that time was incorrectly believed to be the Shogun (i.e. Tycoon). In delivering the letter to the Shogun, Harris therefore delivered it to the wrong person. (see "The President's Letter" in *Shades of the Past.*)

Notes

Sir Harry Parkes, who succeeded Alcock, and arrived in Japan in 1865, was accredited (according to his credentials) to the Court of the Tycoon. They were addressed to "His Majesty," and Japan was referred to as "His dominions." By that time, it had come to be realised by the foreign diplomats in Japan that the Tycoon was not the Emperor. Sir Harry Parkes therefore did not present his original credentials, but awaited the arrival of a new letter accrediting him to the Court of the Mikado. (F. O. Adams *History of Japan*, Vol 2, 1875).

15. See *Asahi Evening News*, 22 June 1961.

16. See *Asahi Evening News*, 25 July, 1961.

THE FIRST BRITISH MINISTER TO JAPAN

Pages 57 - 78:

1. Lord Elgin—8th Earl of Elgin and Kincardine—had visited Japan in July, 1858, for the purpose of arranging a treaty of amity and commerce, following which Alcock was then sent to Japan to head the British diplomatic mission to be established there, as provided for in Elgin's treaty.

2. Nowadays usually spelled "Edo." The spelling of "Yeddo" gave way to "Yedo," which was generally used by foreigners in the Settlement days. An alternative spelling of "Jeddo" was a legacy from the Dutch in Nagasaki and was used by some early writers. Alcock related that during his stay in Japan, letters intended for the British Consulate at Jeddah on the Red Sea were occasionally delivered to him, and *The Japan Mail*, 8 May, 1872, also reported that mail intended for Jeddah found its way to Japan.

On 29 Oct., 1868, the Emperor left Kyoto to take up residence in Yedo, which thereafter became known as "Tokio," meaning eastern capital, now usually spelled Tokyo.

249

Notes

3. He arrived at Nagasaki on 4 June, 1859, and then proceeded in H.M.S. "Sampson" to Yedo.

4. See *Shades of the Past*, pp. 51-61.

5. *The Capital of the Tycoon: A Narrative of a Three Years' Residence in Japan.* London, 1863.
   Alcock stated he had two objects in writing that book: "*To give the results of a careful study of the singular people among whom my lot had been cast, and to throw some light . . . on . . . Western diplomacy in its struggle with Eastern character and Eastern policy.*"

6. Alcock became consul at Fuchow in China in 1844, and continued in the diplomatic service in China and Japan until 1871. In 1820, Harris, at the age of sixteen, started business in New York as a dealer in chinaware. He continued in business until the early 1850's. In 1854 he was appointed a U.S. Consul. After seven years in the diplomatic service he resigned on the grounds of ill health.

7. See photograph, plate II, in *Shades of the Past*.
   In the absence of a suitable alternative it was customary in those days to assign a Buddhist temple, monastery, or retreat, for the accommodation of diplomatic representatives. Cho-o-ji and Sai-kai-ji had been assigned to the Dutch and French Ministers respectively, and Zempuku-ji in Azabu to Townsend Harris the U.S. representative.

8. See *Shades of the Past*, pp. 26, 65, 179.

9. In a good Japanese residence fine timbers free from knots and imperfections are used in an unpainted condition, even in the bath room.

10. Tozen temple would be a more accurate rendering, inasmuch as the "ji" indicates temple. However Tozenji Temple (and other such cases) is in accordance with common usage, just as Shimbashi Bridge and Kyobashi Bridge are used by Japanese and foreigners alike in English writings and conversation, rather than the more correct renderings of Shim Bridge and Kyo Bridge. On the other hand Japan's famed mountain used to be commonly referred to as Mount Fujiyama in English writings, a redundancy which has since been corrected to

Mount Fuji or Fuji-san. When Japanese refer to the
famous mountain they call it merely "Fuji," or more
formally "Fuji-san."

11. This and other quotations, for which no source is
cited, have been taken from *The Capital of the Tycoon.*
Tocado was one of the many spellings adopted by the
foreigners of those days for the Tokaido highway.

12. See *Shades of the Past,* p. 178.

13. In those days more Japanese, especially officials,
understood Dutch than English, because of contacts with
the Dutch trading establishment at Deshima in Nagasaki over a period of more than two hundred years.
Alcock in *The Capital of the Tycoon,* published in 1863,
describing his arrival in Yedo in 1859, when he found
few Japanese capable of acting as interpreters of English, wrote:-
> *"At Yeddo I offered to have a class of youths taught
> English, if the Government would select educated boys
> and send them to us. They appeared to receive the
> proposition with great pleasure and promised . . . to
> make a selection, but it was yet to be done when I
> left at the end of three years."*

See also *Shades of the Past,* pp. 37-50.

14. The Tokugawa clan, which had been governing Japan
for over 250 years through the Shogun, was striving to
keep the Emperor out of politics, secluded and powerless
in his palace in Kyoto. Townsend Harris relates in his
Journal under date of 28 Jan. 1858, that the Tokugawa
officials with whom he was negotiating *"spoke almost
contemptuously of the Mikado, and roared with laughter
when I quoted some remarks concerning the veneration
in which he is held by the Japanese. They say he has
neither money, political power, nor anything else that is
valued in Japan. He is a mere cypher."*

15. See *Shades of the Past,* pp. 80-88.

16. On several occasions diplomats visiting the old Japanese styled palace crashed their heads against the low
traverse beams, and at least one was laid out cold for
several minutes. On the other hand the low traverse beams

saved Laurence Oliphant's life when assassins attacked
the British Legation—the blows of the two-handed
swords were turned aside in the semi-darkness by the
low beams. (For attack on the Legation see *Shades of
the Past*, p. 65).

The difficulty about shoes and the hazardous cross beams
were two factors which decided the Japanese at an early
date to construct a foreign styled palace for the Emperor.

17. See *Shades of the Past*, p. 309.

One of the early references to taking off one's shoes appears in a book written by an Englishman, Peter Heylin,
and printed at Oxford in 1625:

> *"The soyle and the people participate much of the
> nature of China, but that the Japonites are more
> superstitious: as washing their children as soone as
> borne, in rivers, putting off their shoes before they
> enter into the dressing chamber."*

18. Fashions in Japan changed slowly in the days when
she had isolated herself from the world abroad, and for
that reason the Japanese were suspicious of any changes
in the dress of the Dutch on Deshima. The dress and
behaviour of the Dutch in the early part of the seven-
teenth century became precedents for the next two centuries, and any departures therefrom had to be explained. The Dutch tried as far as possible to humour the
Japanese, and so for a long time they continued to dress
like Van Dyke pictures, even although those fashions had
long since changed in Europe.

See also note 10 re "Yokohama the Wild West of the
Far East," for further information re *Illustrated London
News*.

19. See also: *Journey from Jeddo into the Interior of the
Island of Nippon, with Ascent of the Volcano of Fusi-
yama* by Rutherford Alcock, Esq., H. M. Minister in
Japan. Communicated through Sir R. I. Murchison
(Proc. Roy. Georg. Soc., V, 1861. pp. 132-135).

20. In late June, 1957, 4,000 officers and men of the U.S.
Marines, 9th Regt. climbed Fuji with packs and bivou-
acked on top. They encountered unseasonal snow with
freezing temperatures.

Notes

21. Townsend Harris wrote feelingly about palanquins (*norimono*): "... *The Japanese norrimon (sic) will compare with the celebrated iron cage of Cardinal Balne of France, in which the poor inmate could neither lie down nor stand up. In the norrimon the Japanese ... place their feet close together and then sit on their heels ... a position that they assume and keep without annoyance, from long practice, and from the great flexibility of their joint, but which is almost unattainable by a white man and is absolutely unendurable.*

    I had a norrimon made for me seven feet long, and in it I put a mattress and pillows, which made it as comfortable as the Indian palanquin; but, of all modes of travelling, the camel, the elephant, and the palanquin are the most fatiguing."
    Quoted by Hildreth in *Japan and the Japanese*, Boston, 1860. p. 545.

22. Alcock did not mention Miyanoshita by name, and in fact the first mention of that place in any foreign book appears to be by Le Comte de Beauvoir in *Pekin, Jeddo and San Francisco. The Conclusion of a Voyage Round the World*. John Murray, London, 1872, where he describes a visit to the hot springs of "Mionosha."

23. See also *Shades of the Past*, pp. 312-322 for a description of Fuji at close hand.

24. To-day, a hundred years later, the same custom persists, except, alas, the priests have long since lost their monopoly to the hawkers and others who now sell the staffs at all the starting-off places around the base of Fuji.

25. Edward Barrington de Fonblanque, who was one of the party, related that upon arrival at the top—"*having sufficiently recovered breath, we proceeded to climb to the highest point of the crater, where Mr. Alcock's standard bearer unfurled the British flag, while we fired a royal salute from our revolvers in its honour and concluded the ceremony by drinking the health of Her Gracious Majesty in champagne iced in the snows of Fusijama.*"—*Niphon and Pe-che-li; or, two years in Japan and Northern China*, London, 1862.

Notes

26. The first occasion on which Fuji was successfully climbed in midwinter is said to have been on 11, 12 and 13 Feb., 1922, when Lt-Comdr. T. Orde Lees and H Crisp. members of the British Air Mission attached to the naval training school at Kasumigaura completed the climb. Both were experienced mountaineers. Orde Lees was a member of Sir Ernest Shackleton's Antarctic expedition of 1914-16. Much preparation, organization, and a preliminary reconnaissance were features of the climb. They started from Gotemba without guides, porters or horses and arrived back forty-eight hours later. They were assisted by two colleagues who helped them haul their gear, packed on a small sledge, as far as the hut at the 4,700 feet level.

    (Condensed from report in *The Japan Chronicle*, 19 Feb., 1922, and *The Japan Advertiser*, 25, Feb., 1922.)

27. Alcock's successor, Sir Harry Parkes, accompanied by his wife and a large party of friends, made the ascent in Oct., 1867. Lady Parkes thus was the first foreign woman to climb Fuji.

28. *Handbook for Central & Northern Japan*, by E. M. Satow and Lt. A. G. S. Hawes (1881) p. 111.

29. ". . . those who do not mind the odour of oil paper (abura-kami) will find sheets of it stretched over the quilts by far the best protection against fleas." *Murray's Handbook Japan*, London, 1913.

30. The *Mainichi Daily News* reported that during one day and night in August, 1962, "more than 15,000 climbers swarmed over Mt. Fuji. They formed unbroken lines to the summit from the five starting points at the foot."

31. See *Shades of the Past*, pp. 214 and 250, re "scum of the earth" episode.

32. See "*Private Journal John T. Comerford--an English Surgeon in Japan in 1864-1865*." An extract from the journal is reproduced in *Miscellanea Japonica I* by Frank Hawley, published privately, Kyoto, 1954.

33. Probably the tea was made by Japanese servants in the traditional manner of preparing Japanese green tea,

Notes

by throwing the tea leaves into a tea pot containing hot water which had not been brought to boiling point, a method many, if not most, Japanese servants still follow.

34.   Edward H. House, an American journalist, once associated with the *New York Times*, came to Japan and established his short-lived journal *Tokio Times* (1877 1879) wherein for a consideration he championed Japan's cause, and waged unremitting war on some of the foreign legations, on all the Foreign Settlements, and most of the foreign newspapers in Japan. Sir Harry Parkes, who succeeded Alcock, was even less to House's liking, and the latter once boasted that the purpose of the *Tokio Times* was *"to write Sir Harry Parkes out of Japan"*— a task however in which it failed.

35.   See Appendix

36.   Quoted by Alcock in *The Capital of the Tycoon.*

37.   According to ancient records silk had its origin in China before 2000 B.C. The secret of its production was probably introduced into Japan early in the Christian era. It was the favoured material for both clothing and bedding of the upper classes, but the vast majority of the population could not afford it, and at times under the sumptuary laws were forbidden to use it. After Japan was opened to foreign trade in 1859, sericulture was developed, the market for silk goods was widened, and to some degree it came within the reach of a greater portion of the people.

38.   Visitors to Japan in those days were amazed that the Japanese coolies—an expression rarely used these days— went about almost naked, even when the ordinary person considered the weather to be cold. Some visitors even likened the Japanese to the Indians of Tierra del Fuego, near the Antartic tip of South America, who were able to survive near freezing temperatures without clothing.

39.   See *Tales of the Foreign Settlements in Japan* p. 64

40.   *The Capital of the Tycoon*, Vol. 2, p. 378

41.   Japanese are considered to be notoriously unpunctual for business engagements. On the other hand when Japanese receive a dinner or other social invitation from a

foreigner, they assume the host means they should come at the hour stated, and so they can be depended on coming right on time. The punctuality too of Japanese trains is something which visitors to Japan marvel at.

42. One of the members of the Mission maintained in great detail a journal of the trip under the title (translated) —"*A Confused Account of a Trip to Europe as by a Fly on a Horse's Tail.*" In addition to many quaint passages and commentaries on the foreign countries which were visited, it also contained an immense amount of details and measurements of things seen, dimensions of rooms, widths of hotel passageways, description of furniture, and in particular details of guns and fortifications.

43. These were not by any means the first Japanese to visit Europe.

According to Murdoch and Yamagata—*A History of Japan.* 1903, p. 68, the first Japanese who ever set foot in Europe was:

"*When Xavier left Japan on November 20, 1551 . . . he was accompanied by his two body-servants, Matthew and Bernard the Satsuma man. The former died at Goa, but the latter reached Lisbon safely, whence he was sent on to Rome. He shortly returned to Portugal, when he entered the 'Society of Jesus' and ended his days at the College of Coimbra.*"

The first Japanese seamen to visit England probably were the fifteen seamen who sailed as crew members on the "Clove" when she returned to England from Japan in 1613. When they arrived back in Japan in 1617 a labour dispute arose between them and the English East India Company, in which the Japanese authorities supported the English. See M. Paske-Smith, *Western Barbarians in Japan and Formosa*, p. 22.

44. Alcock was recalled to London in 1864 and then appointed Minister at Pekin.

Notes

"INSTANT" PROFESSORS

Pages 79 - 84:

1. Following the introduction of Instant Coffee into Japan
(now one of the great coffee drinking countries of the
world) the Japanese seized upon the word "instant" and
introduced it into their own language to describe anything that comes about quickly and with ease. On the
occasion of a woman stealing a newborn baby from a
maternity hospital, and later pleading that she did so
because she wanted a baby of her own, the infant was
described in the Japanese press as the "instant baby."

Thousands of foreign words are now to be found in
Japanese dictionaries, including many such as *insutanto*
(instant) which have been given a new twist. For example, *abekku* (from French *avec*—meaning *with*) has
the dictionary meaning of *lovers*, but is also used to
denote any of the activities of an unmarried couple. It is
interesting to note that ninety years ago there were
Japanese who viewed the changing times with so much
alarm that they even visioned the dangers of "avec"
arising out of an innocent jinrikisha ride, for we find
in 1873 the Japanese newspaper *Nagasaki Shimbun* de-
ploring the new custom of a man and a woman riding
together in one *jinrikisha*. From "avec," other expressions have evolved. Nowadays scattered around the country there are thousands of hotels popularly known as
"avec hotels." The *Mainichi Daily News* of 17 Dec. 1962.
when reporting a fire at one such hotel stated: *"A total
of 44 persons who put up at the 22 rooms of the hotel
dashed out of the rooms in gowns and pajamas."*

Another example *arubaito* (from German *arbeit*—
meaning *work*) has the dictionary meaning of work done
by students to earn their keep, and pay their way through
college or university. The word is now even used to
designate anyone who does part-time work.

Many far stranger distortions of English words are
now in current use in Japan, and are to be found in
modern Japanese dictionaries, e.g. *rimokon* meaning *remote control*, *masukomi* a contraction of *mass communication*, and *zenesuto* which is derived from *general
strike*.

257

Notes

Another overworked new word is *romansu* (romance), which is even considered appropriate by a firm of manufacturers to use as a brand name for their rolled toilet paper.

Among new words now in the course of being introduced into the language is *darin* (darling), but the current indications are that it may develop a somewhat comic twist and be strictly of the masculine gender, unless, of course, Japanese males succeed in reversing that tendency.

In the years immediately preceding the Pacific war, the use of foreign words was discouraged; notices in English were removed from railway stations, and even the signboards giving the names of stations in Roman letters were taken down—all in accordance with the ultra-nationalistic policy of the times. The present development of the Japanese language is a complete reversal of that policy.

2. The word *typhoon* is thought to be derived from the Chinese *tai fung* (in Japanese *tai-fu*) meaning *big wind*. These "big winds" known to Americans as hurricanes, or cyclones to Australians, are most apt to strike Japan during August and September, when the rice crop is ripening for harvest. Generally they are accompanied by heavy rainfall, causing mountain slides and overflowing rivers, which often lay waste great areas of land.

3. In 1875, C. W. Brooks, Japanese Consul at San Francisco, delivered an address to the local Academy of Sciences on the subject of *Japanese wrecks picked up adrift in the North Pacific Ocean and stranded upon the various outlying islands and shores of the N. W. Coast of America and the chain of islands extending from Hawaii to Japan*, in which he listed such wrecks. The substance of his lecture was reproduced in *The Japan Weekly Mail*, 3 April, 1875.

4. James Murdoch "*A History of Japan*" (1926).

5. R. Hildreth "*Japan and the Japanese*," Boston, 1860.

6. In 1868, when the Emperor took up residence in Yedo, the name was changed to Tokyo, meaning *eastern capital*. The *Edokko* (Yedokko), or natives of Edo (Yedo), were

258

proud of the old name and were unwilling to adopt the new one, and so in a rebellious spirit insisted upon using the ancient, and therefore more elegant, pronunciation of *Tokei*. Eventually however they fell into line, and all called it Tokyo.

In the British Legation's translations of Japanese documents around 1869, the rendering *Tokei* was used.

YOKOHAMA: THE WILD WEST OF THE FAR EAST

Pages 85 - 105:

1. So described in the documents relating to the charter of incorporation of the English East India Company granted by Queen Elizabeth I of England to "The Governor and Company of Merchants of London trading into the East Indies."

2. Miss Grace E. Fox dealt with this subject at length in a learned paper entitled *"British Policies and Prospects at the Opening of the Japanese Ports"* which she read at a meeting of the Asiatic Society of Japan on 26 May, 1958.

3. The name "Yokohama" signifies "opposite shore" in relation to Kanagawa.

4. George Smith, Bishop of Hongkong, *Ten Weeks in Japan*, 1861.

5. Sir Ernest Satow, *A Diplomat in Japan*, p. 29, 1921.

6. *"The Customs House contains also the local Treasury and the subordinate branches of other departments of the State. Here accordingly a number of two-sworded officials are squatted on their mats, busy reading, writing, cyphering and going through their various forms of business . . . They are very painstaking and methodical and upon the whole correct clerks."*

   Niphon & Pecheli by E. B. de Fonblanque, London, 1862.

Notes

7. George Smith, Bishop of Hongkong, *Ten Weeks in Japan*, 1861.

8. E. B. de Fonblanque, *Niphon & Pecheli*, London, 1862.

9. See Note 9, concerning "Those Very Queer Japanese."

10. See index for references to *Illustrated London News*. According to James Murdoch's *History of Japan*, Vol. III. p. 568, as early as 1842 the Dutch in Nagasaki were ordered *"to supply . . . illustrated books and journals . . . and ere long, such publications as the Illustrated London News began to find their way to the Council room in Yedo Castle."*

 In 1956, I saw in the lower basement storerooms of the Ueno Public Library, Tokyo, piles of unbound copies of early issues of the *Illustrated London News* which possibly had been moved there from the Imperial Palace, and may have represented those numbers which had been received against the subscriptions placed by the Tokugawa Shogunate.

11. In 1859, three crew members from a Russian war vessel were slashed to death whilst on the way back to their ship at night. In the following year the Chinese servant of the French Vice-Consul was cut down in the middle of the day, and later two Dutch sea-captains were horribly assassinated in Main Street one evening. In Yedo and elsewhere there were other murders.

12. *A Lady's Visit to Manila & Japan*, 1863, by Anna d'A. (Mrs. Anna d'Aguilar).

13. See Appendix.

14. According to the *Hongkong Daily Press Chronicle and Directory for China, Japan and the Philippines* for 1865, the following fifteen insurance companies were represented in Yokohama at that time: Universal Marine Insur. Co., Commercial Union Insur. Co., Queen Insurance Co.. London & Oriental Steam Transit Insur. Co., London & Lancashire Insur. Co., Phoenix Fire Insur. Co., Union Insur. Co., North China Insur. Co., Imperial Insur. Co., China Fire Insur. Co., Northern Insur. Co., The Royal Insur. Co., Batavia Sea & Fire Insur. Co., Yangtsze Insur. Assoc. of Shanghai, Sun Fire Office.

By 1877 the list had increased to twenty-eight companies.

15. See *Tales of the Foreign Settlements in Japan*, p. 209.

16. Sir Ernest Satow, *A Diplomat in Japan*, London, 1921.

17. We are reminded of the great Hiroshige's entry in his journal where he recorded: "*On the way back from the theatre got into bad trouble by falling into a stream. That was an evening of great drinking.*"

18. See later chapter entitled "Cobb & Co., of Yokohama."

19. Lotteries became a great craze in the Settlements, especially in the Kobe Settlement during the year 1869. According to The Hiogo News, the prizes offered comprised lots of land, cash sums, a velocipede, a music-box, and other items. Some of the land lots then raffled would have a value to-day of more than 50 million yen, but at that time some owners were already regretting their purchases made a year earlier, and were seeking to dispose of them by lotteries.

20. "*One of the biggest items of leisure spending in 1961, according to a white paper issued by Government Economic Planning Agency, was gambling..at horse and bicycle racing and in other forms,*" *Asahi Evening News* 12 Dec. 1962.

YOKOHAMA MUSUME

Pages 106 - 110:

1. *Ten Weeks in Japan,* by George Smith, D.D., Bishop of Hongkong, London, 1861.

2. See *Madame Chrysanthème,* Chapter III.

3. *Exercises in the Yokohama Dialect,* by the Bishop of Homoco, *Japan Gazette* Office, Yokohama, 1879.

4. *Minato-no-hana. Yokohama kidan,* Chinji Gokakoku Yokohama Banashi (1862).

Notes

THE WHALERS AND THE BEACHCOMBERS

Pages 111 - 121:

1. See *Voyages des Indes* by Hendrick Hagenaar.

2. See *Japan & the Japanese* by R. Hildreth, 1860.

3. See *Whalers & Whaling* by E. Keble Chatterton.

4. W. E. Griffis in *The Mikado's Empire*, 1876, states: "*The 'black ships' of the barbarians passing Matsumae (Fukuyama, near Hakodate) in one year numbered eighty-six.*" Hildreth in *Japan & the Japanese*, 1860, reversed the number and gave it as sixty-eight, although he may not have been referring to the same year. He wrote: "*Siebold states that sixty-eight square-rigged vessels mostly no doubt American whalers had been counted by the Japanese as passing Matsumae and Hakodate in one year.*"

5. A Japanese named Ogasawara discovered the islands in 1593, but owing to the laws which forbade Japanese people or ships from going overseas, the islands remained uninhabited. The name Bonin is a corruption of the Japanese *munin* meaning uninhabited.

   The islands were visited by American and English whalers and in 1827 Capt. Beechy of H.M.S. "Blossom" landed and nailed on a tree a copper plaque with the inscription that he "took possession of these islands in the name of His Majesty King George."

   In 1830, the English consul in the Sandwich Islands (Hawaii) arranged for a small party of colonists to settle there. Later they were joined by shipwrecked sailors from British and American whalers, beachcombers, and sea-waifs, who remained there because of the delightful climate and the alcoholic idyllic pastoral life, which seems to have been marred only by a continual plague of myriads of cockroaches. Some of the men derived a living from supplying rum, vegetables, and other supplies to the whalers. Others scratched a living catching albatrosses and turtles, and a few who wanted to work joined the sealing ships.

   In 1877, Japan annexed the islands, but the Europeans and half-caste settlers remained. Although they intermarried with the Japanese they continued to speak English as much as possible. Their women folk mostly wore Japanese *geta* (clogs), wide brimmed straw sun hats of many strange forms, and European dress, usually of the Mother Hubbard style (see note 1 re "Those Very Queer Japanese.") After Japan opened regular shipping services to the Bonins, or Ogasawara as they called them, the Japanese population increased.

The carefree life of the islanders began to change. In the early part of this century many young Bonin Islander girls came to Yokohama. Some became well known in the saloons and other houses where they were popular because of their good looks and ability to speak English. Some made good.

6. See H. Wigmore's "Introduction to Prof. Koda's *Edo and Osaka*," quoted by Skene Smith in *Tokugawa Japan*, 1937.

7. "*Japan had of course no foreign trade, but along the coasts of the three islands there was a ceaseless movement of produce. Nine tenths of Japanese trade consisted in moving rice from places where there was a surplus to places where there was a deficiency of that staple, and in moving it to and from the great central and provincial granaries. Rice does not store well, does not support transit well, and is a bulky and expensive article to carry about ... Hence we can understand the eagerness with which, in the sixties, the daimios bought foreign steamers, and the immense prices they gave for them in the hope of reducing the enormous cost and loss incurred in native transport by sea or land.*"

F. V. Dickins, *The Life of Sir Harry Parkes* Vol. 2, p. 13.

8. See *The Capital of the Tycoon* Vol I. p. 263, by Sir Rutherford Alcock.

9. Joseph Heco in *The Narrative of a Japanese*, Vol II, p. 250, quotes *The Hochi* newspaper as stating that during the season of 1890 there were 44,348 cases of cholera and 30,874 deaths therefrom, in a total population of 40 million.

10. Asst. Surgeon John T. Comerford in his diary (see *Miscellanea Japonica*, 1954, by Frank Hawley) relates

that when the first battalion of English troops arrived in Yokohama in 1864 they had to live in tents and sleep on the ground. Within a month, 100 out of the total of 500 were on the sick list with dysentery.

11. *The Japan Chronicle—Jubilee Number, 1909,* p. 36 a.

12. Some years later, in 1873, the *Hiogo News* reported that apart from the Dutch sailor, the only other foreigner up to that time who had walked from Yokohama to Kobe, was the then foreign superintendent of Telegraphs, who did so for the purpose of assuring himself that his instructions concerning the construction of the new telegraph line had been properly carried out.

COBB & CO. OF YOKOHAMA

Pages 122 - 131:

For some of the information in this article, I am indebted to Mr. Alan Queale of Coolangatta, Queensland, Australia—an enthusiastic authority on all matters concerning Cobb & Co.,—and to the Alexander Turnbull Library, Wellington, New Zealand, for providing extracts from the *Otago Witness, Timaru Herald,* and other New Zealand newspapers of the eighteen-sixties, wherein were printed many extracts from the *Japan Gazette* and other Yokohama newspapers of the time. New Zealanders were then interested in coaching affairs in Yokohama because the Hoyt brothers, well known as proprietors of Cobb & Co., in Otago, had sold out in New Zealand and gone to Japan.

Owing to the lack of complete files of newspapers in libraries in Japan, and the difficulties of research in such Japanese libraries as do exist, it was found at times easier to secure desired information concerning Yokohama from New Zealand institutions than from libraries in Japan. (See also *Tales of the Foreign Settlements* in Japan p. 318).

Some of the information in this chapter appeared in articles contributed by the author to the Sydney *Bulletin*

Notes

in Dec., 1960, and to the *Mainichi Daily News* in April, 1961.

1. Now known simply as Bourke Street.

2. A rich fund of material concerning Cobb & Co., is contained in the Lionel Lindsay Gallery and Museum in Toowoomba, Queensland.

3. *A black horse on a red ground* was the flag of Wm. Rangan & Co., which established a line of coaches linking Yokohama with Tokyo on 1st Jan. 1869, the day Tokyo was opened to international trade. (*Japan Gazette*, 16 March, 1869).

   Rangan's flag can be seen (with some variation in the colour arrangement) in some of Kuniteru's woodblock prints of Tsukiji, one of which serves as an illustration in G. Caiger's *Tell me about Tokyo*, (1939), p. 64.

4. This old print is reproduced on the dust cover of *Tales of the Foreign Settlements in Japan* by the writer, published by Charles E. Tuttle Co., Tokyo, 1958.

5. Following the attack on the British Legation (*see Shades of the Past* pp. 26, 65, 179) and similar incidents, a succession of British Line regiments were garrisoned in Yokohama from 1864-1871. France also had troops stationed in Yokohama. Both the French and the British barracks and military hospitals were located on the Bluff, because it was cooler and more suitable there than in the Settlement.

6. The Japanese were not the only ones who looked sourly on the stage coach. The English industrialist Boulton, who had travelled on them frequently in their heyday alluded to them as *"the greatest complication of unmechanical contrivances jumbled together I have ever witnessed."*

   Coaches in Japan were soon followed by other horse-drawn foreign vehicles in and around the Foreign Settlements. Later following the introduction of railways and an improvement in the *jinrikisha*, there was less need for horse-drawn vehicles and many foreigners began to dispose of such luxuries. However, as at that time there was a craze among the Japanese for imitating Western fashions, the owners had little difficulty in finding buyers. In the *Japan Daily Herald* of March, 1877, there were advertisements in the "For Sale" column for an English built phaeton, an American buggy, an English brougham, a London-made landau, and "a Tokio-made brougham lined with leather."

7.   See *Retrospect of Coaching in Australia*, by William Lees, Brisbane 1917.

8.   See *Old Coaching Days in Otago and Southland*, by E. M. Lovell-Smith, Christchurch, N.Z. 1931.

9.   The *Japan Overland Mail* of 27 June, 1868, in reporting the arrival of the "Albion" in Yokohama, stated: *"It would also appear that the gold mines in Sadow (Sado) have been represented in Australia as being in easy reach of Yokohama; four-wheeled carriages for conveyance of passengers thither form part of the Albion's cargo."* Evidently those who imported the horse-drawn carriages did not realise that Sado was an island.

10.   Hoyt Bros. were the owners of a small wooden paddle-steamer "City of Yedo" which conducted a daily passenger and packet service between Yokohama and Tokyo, leaving Yokohama in the morning and returning from Tokyo in the evening. In those days many of the steamers operating in Japan were in a poor condition, and accidents arising from the boilers bursting were not infrequent. On 1st August, 1870, the boilers of the "City of Yedo" blew up whilst she was tied to the pier at Tsukiji. Over 70 persons, Europeans and Japanese, were killed instantly or died later from injuries received.

11.   Typescript in the Alexander Turnbull Library, Wellington, N.Z. on *Early Shipping in New Zealand* by C. F. Turner.

12.   *The Otago Witness* of 25 Dec., 1869, quoted from a letter received from Yokohama under date of 8th Oct., 1869: *"The Hoyts will commence running their coaches next month to Yeddo. I hear they have sent to Australia for drivers."*

    ("Yeddo" was the manner in which many foreigners spelled Yedo or Edo, the old Tokugawa capital, which was re-named Tokyo in 1868).

Notes

13. Following the loss of revenue arising from the introduction of the postal system and the railways, and the severe competition from other coaching companies, both foreign and Japanese, Cobb & Co., concentrated more on carriage building and on their livery stable service. However, other coach services to Tokyo continued until around 1886, by which time, according to the *Japan Weekly Mail* of 3 July, 1886, many of the vehicles were in a *"scandalous condition . . . nothing better than skeletons of timber and rags . . . dragged by animals that are a disgrace to humanity, and only kept from the knackers for this purpose."*

14. Some of the romance which we like to associate with the coaching days disappears on reading the description of a trip to Tokyo in the early days published in the *Japan Weekly Mail* of 12 July, 1884, in a series entitled "Echoes from the Past," although the writer was probably making comparisons with the coaches of England and the Continent.

    The coach was described as little better than a partially *"covered wagon, which vehicle in humorous disregard of honourable associations was called a stagecoach . . . The driver winded a horn proclaiming departure after the best English fashion."* It was drawn by *"a pitiful pair of bare-boned ponies."* The dozen passengers had to *"get out and walk on steep ascents"* at which places *"the Caucasians were civilly requested to descend while the Japanese were peremptorily ordered out, and assisted if necessary by muscular propulsion. . . ."*

    A stop for refreshments was made at Black-Eyed Susan's, during which it was not unusual for some of the foreign passengers to maul the lady in question. (For more concerning Black-Eyed Susan see *Shades of the Past* pp. 89-93).

15. The earliest directory in which we have been able to trace his name is *Hongkong Daily Press Directory,* 1869, where he is shown as being a saddler in C. Adds' Livery Stables in Yokohama.

16. One *bu (ichi-bu)* was a silver coin in circulation

before the Yen. The usual spelling adopted by most of the early foreigners was *boo* (singular) and *boos* (plural) but in some early books *bu* (singular) (plural *bus*) will be found. At first it had a value equal to 20 pence or nearly a quarter of a U.S. $ but following the minting of inferior coins there was much confusion regarding the *bu* coinage, and several rates of exchange were quoted depending on whether for old or new issues.

With the introduction of Yen and Sen currency, the *bu* was withdrawn. It was then considered equal to 25 *sen* or a quarter of a Yen.

17. Before Japan established a postal system, many captains of overseas vessels trading with Japan used to supplement their income by bringing in mail for firms and individuals, but often they would delay the handing over of such letters as long as possible, in case they contained any commercial intelligence that might upset the market and interfere with their own private trading.

18. A detailed specification of these nine stamps is to be found in *Bambi Book* No. 21, 1959, a philatelic publication in Japanese by Asahi Shimbun-sha, Tokyo.

THE ENERGETIC REV. M. BUCKWORTH BAILEY

Pages 132 - 139:

1. J. R. Black in *Young Japan*, 1880, relates that:
   "*On the 18th October, 1863, the English Episcopal Church, under the name of Christ Church, was opened for Divine service, which had hitherto been held, first in the private parlour of the British Consul's residence, and subsequently in the Court room of H.B.M's Consulate. The new edifice was 46 feet long by 30 feet broad, and was calculated to seat from 300 to 350 persons. Its cost was about $2,800 (£700).*"

2. See *Tales of the Foreign Settlements in Japan* pp.222-224.

3. When telegraphs were introduced into Japan, the Government ordered many of the old trees that lined the

Tokaido, and other of the great highways, to be cut down so as to make way for the telegraph poles, although in some places it was thought that was done more out of spite for the old Tokugawa regime which had been responsible for the planting of those fine trees.

It was also said that in some few places trees were cut down by the villagers in order to better show off the modern telegraph poles which passed through their village, but generally at first the country people viewed the poles with disfavour.

"The country people disliked having the wires cross their rice fields, for they said the evil spirits prevent the crops from growing ... At first the ignorant farmers used to cut the wires and throw stones at the glass insulators on the poles; they would also watch the wires for hours to see the messages go by, but at last they ceased to trouble their heads about it, and let the telegraph alone."

See, E. Warren Clark in *Life & Adventures in Japan*, 1878.

HORSE RACING IN THE EARLY DAYS

Pages 140 - 152:

1. There were several bowling alleys in Nagasaki, Yokohama, and Kobe, within a year or so of each port being opened.

2. J. R. Black – *Young Japan* Vol. 1, p. 147.

3. Archives of British Consulate, Nagasaki.

4. The U.S.S. "Oneida" was wellknown in the treaty ports of Japan during early days of the Foreign Settlements. The crew members participated in many of the social activities until the vessel tragically sank, after coming into collision with the ss "Bombay," as is described in *Shades of the Past* pp. 129-139.

5. A popular translation of *harakiri*, among some writers of those early days, was "happy despatch," although the

actual translation is "belly-cutting." A popular misspelling, *harikari*, which originated over ninety years ago, still persists in some quarters.

THE REMARKABLE MR. SMITH

Pages 153 - 159:

1. See Note 7 on "Musings on a Centenary."

2. See "Realms of Silver," London, 1954, p. 72.

3. See *Japan Weekly Mail*, 14 Dec., 1878.

4. This figure is given by W. E. Griffis *(The Empire of the Rising Sun)* who was himself a *yatoi* (salaried foreigner) employed by the Japanese Government. The term *yatoi* was considered by many of the foreign experts in the employ of the Japanese Government to be a disparaging term which belittled the work they were doing. Even the *Japan Weekly Mail,* a paper which tended to defend the Japanese viewpoint, complained on 30 July, 1892:

   "... *All persons in the service of the Government who do not possess official rank are yatoi. There are Japanese yatoi in every Department ... No method exists of officially describing those persons' position except to call them yatoi ... a term very often resented by foreigners as a rudeness ... Japanese reply that ... as no foreigner can possess official rank in Japan ... nothing remains but to call him yatoi ... The results are that foreigners who in their own countries would have honourable positions, have official titles or enjoy literary or scientific distinctions abroad, men of age and high attainments, are in Japan reduced to the level of the lowest semi-official in a Department. . ."*

5. In the United States Consular Court at Yokohama on 11 Jan., 1873, before Mr. Consul Shepard. — See *Japan Weekly Mail,* 24 Jan., 1873.

6. See *Japan Weekly Mail,* 26 Aug., 1876.

Notes

TRAVELS TO OSAKA

Pages 160 - 167:

1. Those letter carriers, who carried important despatches, usually travelled in pairs in case one should meet with an accident. The letters were either carried over the shoulder in a carefully secured packet, or tied to a bamboo stick.

    Express letter carriers were relieved at short stages, and by travelling day and night were able to cover the distance from Yedo to Nagasaki—about 850 miles—in nine days.

2. The difficulties of travel in Japan of about a century ago were described by Sir H. Parkes, British Minister, in a despatch, dated Yedo, 21 April, 1870, to the Earl of Clarendon:-

    "Japan, unlike China, does not possess navigable rivers; the rate of travelling averages only twenty miles a day, and provinces that are separated by 400 to 500 miles are at nearly a month's distance from each other. The two capitals of Yedo and Kioto, though connected by the best line of road in the country, are at a fortnight's distance apart."

3. From *The Capital of the Tycoon*, by Sir Rutherford Alcock.

4. See Note 3 on "Cobb & Co., of Yokohama."

5. See earlier chapter, "Cobb & Co., of Yokohama."

6. *The Hiogo News*, 26 Nov., 1868.

7. See *The Hiogo News*, 3 Nov., 1869, and 8 Jan., 1870.

8. *Jinrikisha*, literally man-power-vehicle, was contracted to rikisha, and later Anglicised to ricksha or rickshaw. An American Baptist missionary, named Jonathan Goble, claimed to having invented the *jinrikisha*, and in Nov., 1878, shortly after a tax had been levied on all such vehicles plying in Tokyo, he unsuccessfully made application that a portion of the tax should be relegated to him for use in building a school for the blind. Whilst Goble appears to have introduced the vehicle into Japan, he did

Notes

not invent it. Similar contraptions are described in European books and are depicted in illustrations produced over a period of several centuries before Goble introduced his wheeled chair into Japan.

9. With the introduction of horse-drawn carriages, especially in some of the larger cities where a craze had developed for all things foreign, the jinrikisha-men suffered severe competition. The Kyoto Hack Carriage Company, for example, which commenced business in 1889 was a great success. The fare was 2 sen for about two thirds of a mile, at which rate the carriages were well patronised, whilst the jinrikisha-men were half idle. During the first two weeks of business the gross receipts of the Kyoto Hack Carriage Company amounted to Yen 12,000. (*Japan Weekly Mail*, 2 Feb. 1889).

10. *Japan Weekly Mail, 22* May, 1874, quoting from *The Hiogo News.*

11. Imperial Japanese Government Railway report quoted in *Japan Weekly Mail*, 3 Oct., 1874.

12. *Osaka Nippo* quoted in *Japan Weekly Mail*, 5 Aug., 1873.

13. During 1962 there were more than 11,400 deaths from traffic accidents in Japan.

THE DAUNTLESS MR. McLEOD

Pages 168 - 177:

1. Korea (derived from "Korai," the ancient name of a portion of the peninsula) is also known as Chosen meaning the "Land of the Morning Calm." Before Japan took over the country, some people described it facetiously as "The Land of the Morning Calm and the Afternoon Repose." After the Pacific War, when Korea regained her freedom, some American troops stationed there dubbed it "Korea, the land of the morning calm, the afternoon demonstration, and the night soil."

272

Notes

2. According to the inscription in the book it was "published for the Author party at C. Levy and the Sei Shi Bunsha Co., Yokohama and engraved in Tokyo." C. Levy was the proprietor and manager of *L'Echo du Japon*, a French newspaper published at No. 183 Settlement, Yokohama. The existence of this French newspaper in Yokohama was made possible by the large number of French troops, who were then stationed there, and by the comparatively large French community in those days.

3. Other works by N. McLeod were entitled *Japan and the Lost Tribes of Israel, Map and Chart of Korea, Tourists Map and Chart of Japan*.

4. Ponto-cho is the street running between Sanjo Bridge and Shijo Bridge along the west bank of the Kamogawa. The popularity of the Ponto-cho geisha quarter rivals the Gion quarter on the other side of the river.

5. Horses were a common sight throughout Japan until 1939 when they were mobilised and many were sent to China to serve in the transport services of the Japanese Army in the war against China. None came back. Their place has since largely been taken by the three-wheeled motor vehicles or *bata-bata*, so named, when first introduced, from the noise they made. The number of horses in Japan in 1936 was estimated at 1,400,000. Today the figure has dwindled to 540,000, and owing to mechanized farming methods the number is steadily decreasing.

   1939 was not the first occasion on which large numbers of Japanese horses were shipped to China. Much earlier in 1860 the British Government sent an agent to Japan to purchase horses, bullocks, and fodder for the British Army forces in China.

   Later foreign horses were imported into Japan for use by the bodyguard of the British and French Ministers. Japanese horses were too small and too evil-tempered for that purpose. In 1867 twenty-five Arab horses were sent to Japan as a present to the Shogun by Napoleon III of France. From then onwards, many horses were imported for racing and breeding purposes to improve the native stock.

Notes

6. According to McLeod the widths of the nostrils were:

Bronze Daibutsu at Kamakura	.. ..	2'3"
Bronze Daibutsu at Nara	.. .. ..	3'0"
Wooden bust of Daibutsu at Kyoto	. ..	6'6"

The measurements given by McLeod for the Daibutsu at Kyoto are wrong. The width of the nose is about 5'. The Kyoto Daibutsu was described by Terry in his excellent *Guide to Japan*, 1928, as "a gilded monstrosity not worth looking at, occupies a tawdry shed." Since then all the gilding has disappeared, but by selling some of the land the temple authorities have been able to replace the tawdry shed with a cheap building, but the Daibutsu remains as a wretchedly ugly bust, lacking all artistic merit. The surroundings bear witness that the old gods are dying among the crumbling temples of Kyoto.

7. There are many references in the literature of those days to the low prices prevailing in Japan. For example E. Warren Clark in *Life and Adventures in Japan*, 1878, when describing a trip to Mount Fuji, wrote: *"We took dinner at a wayside hotel where we had good accommodation and an hour's rest, and on taking leave our host presented his bill to the fabulous extent of 2 cents and a half."*

Even some years later, prices of entertainment in Japan were still very cheap, according to European standards, as may be judged from the following itemised account, cited by E. R. Scidmore in *Jinrikisha Days in Japan*, 1891, for a party of seven at a Yokohama theatre, including food which as customary was served in the theatre box. No admission charge was made for the two family servants who attended on them.

Admission (including theatre box) for 7 persons	¥2.58
Hire of chairs and mats	.50
Messenger hire	.10
Tea and sweets for 7 persons	.30
Persimmons, figs and grapes for 7 persons .	.30
Eels and rice, etc., " " " .	3.50
Tea-house fee	1.00
Gratuities	.30
Total for 7 persons	¥8.58

The total cost of the outing for 7 persons was then equivalent to about US$ 6.50 or about 26 shillings.

8. Reproduced from Murdoch's *History of Japan*, Vol 3, p. 699.

9. Dr. Engelbert Kaempfer, a German physician attached to the Dutch East India Company's branch on Deshima in Nagasaki harbour during 1690–1693, was one of the most remarkable chroniclers of all time. In spite of the secrecy, in which the Japanese veiled their country, he left in five volumes a most detailed picture of Japan of those days. He covered the history, geography, manners, customs, art, and religious beliefs of what was then a little-known island empire, a most remarkable achievement considering that all the Japanese with whom the Dutch came into contact were bound under oath not to disclose anything concerning the domestic affairs of the country, its religion, its politics or its history. He also gave an intimate and detailed account of life in the little Dutch community on Deshima. See "Shades of the Past" pp. 37-50.

10. The following is from *The Japan Mail*, 10 Feb., 1874; *"On Wednesday evening last, Mr. McLeod gave his lecture upon the 'Identity of the Mikado, Miya and Kuge Sama etc. with the Ten Lost Tribes of Israel.' He attracted but a small audience, and did not even contrive to keep them together above a few minutes. First one went away, then another, then another, until soon four only of the faithful remained to discuss Mr. McLeod's contention of the presence of the Unicorn in the Court of the Mikado!"*

THE DISAPPOINTED REV. WILTON HACK

Pages 178 - 183:

1. Under date of 27 Nov. 1857, Townsend Harris noted in his journal that the Prince of Shinano had informed him that out of every one hundred children born in Japan

not more than thirty reached the age of twenty years.

The historian W. E. Griffis in *Dux Christus*, 1904, wrote: "*Those who know only the Japan of a certain school of writers from Sir Edwin Arnold to Lafcadio Hearn can never believe in the awful physical condition of the lowest classes in the Japan of 1870 and before. A stalwart imagination is necessary to picture to the mind the rottenness and foulness of the diseased humanity, then visible daily in the highways and villages, and that streamed past Dr. Hepburn everyday in his dispensary.*"

Infanticide and abortion were also factors which checked any increase in population. The former, known as *mabiki*—also used in describing the thinning out of seedlings in a row of vegetables—became so prevalent in the country districts, during periods of famine and plague in the Tokugawa era, that in 1767 it was prohibited by official edict. (see *Japan* by Sir George B. Sansom).

In the eighteen-seventies the moats of many castles were being filled in to make way for the growing towns, and for the new roads which were being constructed to carry the increased traffic and the telegraph lines. In commenting on these developments the *Japan Daily Herald* in Jan. 1874 stated: "A favorite use to which these moats were put has long been known as places where unwanted newborn female babies could be disposed of, despite the efforts of the authorities to prevent the crimes."

2. *The South Australian Register,* 7 Sept. 1876.

3. Archives of The Public Library of South Australia.

4. At about this time the Government of Queensland was seeking to keep the Chinese out, because of their "*gambling propensities and immoralities.*"

5. Some twenty-two years later there was another occasion on which Japanese immigration into the Northern Territory was suggested, but by then the South Australian Government was opposed to the idea. In 1898, the South Australian Government learned from the British Ambassador in Tokyo, Sir Ernest Satow, that

J. L. Parsons (who at that time was acting as Japanese consul in Adelaide but formerly had been the Government Resident in the Northern Territory) was *"in Tokio endeavouring to negotiate with Japanese capitalists the sale of lands situated on the banks of the Victoria River in the Northern Territory and to induce them to send thither a large body of Japanese settlers."*

This proposal was a private one by Parsons. The South Australian Government requested the British Colonial Office to inform the Japanese Government of its opposition to the scheme.—See *South Australian Parliamentary Paper* No. 37 of 1898.

6. Archives of The Public Library of South Australia.

7. See Supplement to the *South Australian Register*, 6 Sept. 1877, also *Japan Daily Herald*, 22 June, 1877, quoting from *Rising Sun & Nagasaki Press*.

8. See Supplement to the *South Australian Register*, 6 Sept. 1877.

9. Archives of British Consulate, Nagasaki.

THOSE VERY QUEER JAPANESE

Pages 184 - 194:

1. During the eighteen-eighties European dresses became fashionable among Japanese ladies wishing to ape the Empress, who at that time adopted European dress for certain occasions. Then, as always in Japan, there was a reaction and for several decades Japanese women were rarely seen in foreign dress. Except for a few who had lived abroad, most Japanese women dressed in kimono. Forty years or so ago there were very few Japanese department stores with foreign dress sections; there were no speciality stores selling Western style dresses, nor were there any dressmaking establishments or ladies tailors, other than the few to be found in the treaty ports or in the capital.

    For Japanese women to commence dressing in Western style was in the nature of a hazardous jump in the dark. It was therefore understandable that before venturing outside in foreign dress, they generally first experimented, about the house, with an *appapa*, which was the Japanese term for a "Mother Hubbard." That garment had been invented by missionaries in the South Seas and had been introduced by them to the natives of Pacific isles to hide their nakedness—a charm and feature of the native's existence of which some were greatly proud and much enjoyed.

An official Japanese Government report of thirty years ago on some of her Pacific mandated islands or rather possessions, described the Mother Hubbard as *"a garment resembling the night gown worn by Western ladies."* Because there is likely to be some dispute as to the accuracy of the official Japanese Government definition, and in any case for the benefit of those single gentlemen who may not be acquainted with such garments, it should be explained that a Mother Hubbard really resembled a sack, often drawn in at the neck with strings, and which fell in copious folds to the toes. Almost invariably it was made in large sizes, sometimes large enough to accommodate a baby elephant. That, however, was intentional, because it was designed to disprove that women had figures. In short it was a feminine garment as seductive as a large potato sack.

2. The letter carriers and couriers—postmen in loin cloths --ran at a swinging trot, carrying a packet of letters at the end of a bamboo stick, and were capable of covering distances up to 40 or more miles in a day.

3. Thirty years later fashions had changed. The pendulum had swung to the other extreme, as it is prone to do in Japan, and the Japanese, like so many people in the West at that time, were rather sensitive about anything suggestive of nudity—outside of home circles. And so it came about, in 1893, that the Japanese Government raised an objection to a mural in the Chicago World Fair which depicted a *jinrikisha* man clothed only in a "breech cloth and sandals." They wanted a *haori* and pants added.

But again the pendulum has swung back to the other

extreme. A few spangles and a pair of shoes are now considered adequate clothing for some show girls in Japan.

4. This was one of the several ways in which the foreign residents and tourists of a hundred years ago spelled the Daibutsu of Kamakura. There are two tombstones in the Yokohama Foreign Cemetery erected to the memory of Major Baldwin and Lieut. Bird who were *"Cruelly assassinated by Japanese at Kamakura, Nov. 21, 1864, when returning from Dieboots to Yokohama."* (See Shades of the Past p. 98).

5. E. B. De Fonblanque writing of a visit made to Yokohama in 1860 said: *"The bronzes exposed for sale at Yokohama (sic) are principally modern, but now and then an old and valuable piece may be found."* From *Nippon and Pecheli*, 1862.

Henry Adams writing from Japan in 1886 (*Letters from Japan*, Kenkyusha Series, 1960), said *"Japan has been cleaned out."*

These are typical of many, many lamentations that Japan had already been stripped of her best works of art as early as eighty or ninety years ago.

6. The word "Bund" derived from the Hindustani word *bandh*, meaning an embankment or dyke, was commonly used in the Foreign Settlements to designate the road running along the waterfront.

The choicest land lots in the Yokohama Settlement were located along the Bund. After the great earthquake and fire of 1st Sept. 1923, the debris from the burnt out city of Yokohama was dumped into the sea, along the Bund, to form a park. The Bund in Yokohama then became an inland road.

7. Those were the days of beards, waxed moustaches, and high neck-choking collars, all of which, if we believe what some of those travel authors wrote, must have made quite an impression with the Japanese "mousume." The latter word was generally the nearest those travel authors got to reproducing the word *musume* (daughter) —which they incorrectly used when referring to any young woman—respectable or otherwise.

Notes

8. Most tourists are bent upon a geisha party, but most come away with the impression that it was not worth the cost. Many would agree with what Henry Adams wrote in 1886, in a letter to John Hay, when he described a geisha party:

> *"No words can give you an idea of their drollness. I am lost in astonishment at this flower of eastern culture. I cannot quite say that it is like an imaginary theatre in a nursery of seven-year-old girls, or that it is absolutely and disgustingly proper, because all my Japanese friends got drunk . . . and some of the singing women were highly trained; but for an exhibition of mechanical childishness, I have seen nothing to equal it...."*

> *Henry Adams' Letters from Japan,*
> Kenkyusha, Tokyo, 1960.

9. A licenced brothel in Yokohama which achieved fame by seeking foreign patronage, and thereby was mentioned by Rudyard Kipling in his "MacAndrew's Hymn":

> *Judge not, O Lord, my steps aside in Gay Street in in Hongkong!*

> *Blot out the wastrel hours of mine in sin when I abode—*

> *Jane Harrigan's an' Number Nine, The Reddicks an' Grant Road.*

It was destroyed by fire in the great earthquake of 1st. Sept. 1923. See also chapter "Yokohama, the Wild West of the Far East."

10. *"A new native profession has sprung up in Yokohama, that of 'cicerone.' The influx of Japanese pilgrims who visit the Settlement on their way to or from the sacred mountain (Mount Fuji) athirst for news and credulous of aught, created the demand..."* Japan Herald, April, 1873.

11. Originally an Anglo-Indian word derived from Malay —*godong*—but commonly used throughout the Far East, and particularly in Japan, instead of warehouse.

> *"The tea firing is done in tea-firing godowns . . . half-naked perspiring men and women bending above the great kettles and allowing the rain of sweat*

Notes

> *invoked by the high temperature (120° F) to fall therein, upon the tea. One is apt to eschew tea for a while,"* from Terry's Guide to the Japanese Empire, (1928).

12. W. E. Griffis—"Dux Christus," 1904.

13. *"It's a shame so few Japanese women now wear the kimono. There's nothing more attractive than the back of a woman's neck as revealed by a kimono,"* said Charlie Chaplin, with twinkling eyes, at a press interview in Tokyo, on 18 July, 1961.

14. With the introduction of *pama* (a contraction of "permanent waves") and henna dyes, red headed Japanese women are now quite common—as common in fact as Japanese men with Roman noses. However, if the Japanese, or at least many of those in the theatrical world and in show business, are not satisfied with the shape of their nose and choose to change it, that is their business. All that we shall therefore do is to explain the process. At first the offending nose was built up with wax, but as the wax had a tendency to slip and so in time produced noses of really remarkable shapes, *niku* (meaning flesh or meat) was then used instead of wax. The flesh was taken from the rump of the person whose nose was to be re-modelled—a case, as it were, of from base to base!

  According to the *Asahi Evening News* of 9 Aug., 1962, the advances made in plastics have now produced near perfect noses. "Plastic surgery on noses in Japan is second only to surgery on eyelids. An estimated 500 doctors practice plastic surgery in Japan."

15. Commodore Perry and others would have us believe that they were scandalised at the scenes in the public baths where the sexes mingled, unconscious of their nudity, but not so Laurence Oliphant, then secretary to Lord Elgin who came to Japan a few years after Perry. He rather enjoyed passing the public bathhouses, because the bathers would pour out of the bath and crowd the doorways to get a view of the strange foreigner who was passing by.

281

Notes

THE WILD OATS OF THE GRAND DUKE ALEXANDER

Pages 195 - 201:

1. From *Sketches of Life in Japan* by Major H. Knollys, London, 1887.

2. *The Japan Weekly Mail*, 29 Jan., 1881, reported:
   "Twelve Russian war vessels are for the moment stationed in Nagasaki, seven or eight in Yokohama, and four in Kobe. The Russian admiral has just cashed a bill in Nagasaki for 800,000 dollars ... for the purchase of coal."

3. See *Madame Chrysanthème* by Pierre Loti, the pen name of Lieut L. M. Julien Viaud, an officer on the French war vessel "Triomphante" which was laid up in Nagasaki harbour during the summer of 1885, during which time Viaud set up housekeeping on shore with a Japanese girl.

   Recently on coming across B. H. Chamberlain's comment that *"the volume can in nowise be recommended either to misses or to missionaries"* we re-read it to see if there was anything we had missed, but found it to be as dull as most other naughty books of the nineteenth century.

   Puccini's "Madame Butterfly" was first performed in 1904.

   For further details see "Mesdames Chrysanthemum and Butterfly" in *Shades of the Past*.

4. *Terry's Guide to the Japanese Empire*, 1928—the most readable of all guides—described the Maruyama quarter:
   "The pretentious and imposing Yoshiwara on Maruyama presents a curious and instructive spectacle after nightfall. The utmost order prevails, and the district is as safe as any other part of the port. In line with the custom prevailing in certain other cities, the sloe-eyed, statuesque houris of Nagasaki do not always sit in slatted cages facing the thoroughfare, but at the side, flanking the entrance of the establishment; to see them one must be sufficiently interested to advance a few paces inward from the street. Many of the houses are three-storied, with quaint balconies and species of hanging loggias.

282

> *When these are decorated with paper lanterns, when
> throaty voiced geisha sing the native contralto songs
> the plaintive twanging of the samisen, the swish of
> silken kimonos and the soft pit-pat of tabi-shod feet
> are wafted out through the fragrant twilight, the
> effect is strikingly Oriental...."*

Many foreigners incorrectly use the word *Yoshiwara*
as a synonym for *licenced quarters*, whereas it was the
name of a particular licenced quarters in Tokyo.

The geisha quarters still exist in Nagasaki and elsewhere in Japan, but not the licenced quarters. Licenced
prostitution was abolished by law in 1957, as the cul-
mination of nation-wide drives, conducted on and off
over a period of 80 years, against the powerful interests, political and otherwise, which had been striving to
maintain the old licenced prostitution system, because
of the immense profits it had yielded them.

5. See *Once a Grand Duke* by Alexander Grand Duke of
   Russia, New York, 1932.

6. An officer of the Sailors Regiment of the Imperial
   Guard, appointed to H.I.M.S. "Rynda."

7. The Grand Duke, when writing his memoirs, seems to
   have imagined that he was the first close representative
   of European royalty to be received by the Japanese Emperor, but in that he was about twenty years late; at
   least a dozen or so others had preceded him.

   The first member of a European royal family to visit
   Japan was the Duke of Edinburgh in 1869. As a guest
   of the Mikado—as the Emperor was then known in the
   Western world—he was accommodated in the summer
   palace at Hama-go-ten and accorded treatment and courtesies such as would have been bestowed on the highest
   in the land. For example, when his procession moved
   along the streets on the occasion of a visit to the Mikado,
   the upper windows of all the houses on the line of route
   were sealed with strips of paper, so that no one could
   look down upon one whom the Emperor chose to honour.

   The arrival of some foreign princes presented special
   problems. There was the case of Prince Henry of Prus-
   sia, who as an officer on a German warship in Kobe
   went hunting in the hills behind Nishinomiya with some

German residents. The Prince was seen by the local policeman firing at a bird near a temple, and was thereupon arrested and jailed. After the exchange of a flurry of telegrams at the highest level, the identity of the Prince was established and he was released. The unfortunate Governor of Osaka had to tender apologies and resign.

8. *"The House of Romanoff in the persons of the Grand Dukes, has steadily evaded the call of duty during the war. These titled magnates, adorned with resplendent uniforms ablaze with decorations won on the soft carpets of St. Petersburg, have incurred—doubtless without their knowledge—the derision of soldiers of all the armies of the world."*

The War in the Far East, by The Military Correspondent of *The Times,* John Murray, London, 1905.

DEMON TILES

Pages 202 - 206:

1. The Hongkong & Shanghai Banking Corp. was the first foreign bank to establish a branch in Kobe. That was in 1870 at No. 80 Kyo-machi. About 1872, it appears to have moved next door to No. 81, and later to No. 2 on the Bund.

2. *Joss,* is from the Portuguese *dios,* and means idol, god, or luck. It is a common word frequently used in that most wonderful gibberish known as pidgin English. "Pidgin" was said to be the resultant of the Chinese attempt to pronounce "business."

   A "joss-pidgin-man" was therefore a god-business-man or a clergyman.

Notes

CHASING THE HOPE DIAMOND

Pages 207 - 216:

1. Mr. Winston's press-agents and others were constantly grinding out stories of the bad luck the diamond had brought to previous owners. It was all good publicity particularly as the diamond was not for sale. They told of how Marie Antoinette had worn it and had later lost her head; or how illness and death came to Solomon Habib, an Armenian diamond merchant, who handled the gem; and of how bad luck came to Mrs. Evalyn Walsh McLean, the then No. 1 American hostess, who had a famed gem collection quite apart from the Hope Diamond. They told of a succession of tragic deaths in Mrs. McLean's family after she had purchased the diamond, and of the ill luck which came upon her in the form of Gaston Means. That crook, and onetime detective, had extracted over $100,000 from the generous but gullible lady, on the pretext of paying for the return of the Lindberg baby. It was only when Means tried for an additional $35,000 that Mrs. McLean "whistled for the cops, who eventually put Means away for 15 years." Such was the manner in which the *Saturday Evening Post* described the misfortunes which came to those associated with the Hope Diamond.

    After Mrs. McLean's death, Harry Winston bought her famed gem collection, including the Hope Diamond with all its legends.

2. Author of *The Rise & Fall of the Japanese Empire*, London, 1951, and other books.

3. See "The Carew Case" in *Shades of the Past*.

MUSINGS ON A CENTENARY

Pages 217 - 228:

1. Apart from the arrival of Australian prisoners-of-war during the war, and the Australian Occupation Forces after the cessation of hostilities, this was the largest party of Australians, up to that date, to arrive in Japan

285

at one time. The number has since been exceeded by larger groups of Australian tourists.

2. Under favourable weather conditions, Mount Fuji may be seen by tourists approaching Yokohama by ship, or from some of the Yokohama hills, for example from the Foreign Cemetery on the Bluff. It may also be seen from some of the tall buildings along the plaza facing the moat of the Imperial Palace in Tokyo, or from the train en route from Tokyo to Osaka or vice versa. However, as it is often enveloped in mist, many visitors to Japan never see it.

3. As Japanese dressed in Kimono are rarely seen in the streets these days, many tourists now visit theatres where old style plays are being performed in order to see Japanese native dress. On the other hand many patronize modern revues or cabarets where the girls wear foreign clothing or none at all. With the greater prosperity now being enjoyed by the people of Japan, kimono are again being purchased by the women, but generally only for use on special occasions, or by those who wish to make an impression on visiting foreigners.

4. Since then "Waltzing Matilda" has become one of the most popular songs on TV, although it is doubtful just what the average Japanese can make out of such words as "birrabong," when it is sung in English!

5. The touts of Japan's shady life would as usual have been among those gathered on the wharf, and others would have been waiting elsewhere ashore, at strategic points, to intercept all males unaccompanied by ladies. Those touts had been displaying an aggressiveness which was making it dangerous for foreigners to move about in certain places. In Aug. 1959, following an international incident in Tokyo, which arose out of their aggressive touting of an Austrian journalist, who was on a visit to Japan sponsored by the Japanese Foreign Ministry, the police took steps to clear the touts from around the principal tourist hotels.

6. The Acting-Consul who kept the diary was Dr. Frederick G. Myburgh, a physician at first attached to the

British Consular Service in the capacity of a Dutch interpreter. He carried out his duties so effectively that he was soon promoted to vice-consul and later consul. When the port of Kobe was opened on 1 Jan. 1868, he was appointed the first British Consul for Hyogo and Osaka, but within three weeks he died from an illness—generally fatal in those days—which to-day would be known as appendicitis. He was buried in the early Ono Cemetery in Kobe, which in 1952 was moved into the mountains at Shuhogahara, behind Futatabi.

7. The Mexican silver dollar was introduced into China in 1854.

Japan had no currency of a well determined value when trade was opened in 1859; consequently foreign traders brought in Mexican dollars which circulated in the Foreign Settlements together with other silver coins of about the same weight and value. The Japanese had turned out silver coins, but those coins did not replace the Mexican $, because they were not acknowledged by foreigners as legal tender. In 1875, a Japanese "Trade Dollar, 420 grains, 900 fine" (so imprinted in English) was minted, which circulated alongside Mexican dollars. A few years later the "Trade Dollars" were replaced by silver "One Yen" pieces, 416 grains, 900 fine, which were accepted at par with the Mexican Dollars. The expression "Dollar", meaning either the new Yen local currency or Mexican Dollars, thereafter continued to be used in the Foreign Settlements for many years. After the beginning of this century the word Yen came into general use. In post-war years, the dollar is often spoken about, but, where used, it invariably means the U.S. $.

The Mexican $ (and of course the yen) originally of about the same value as the U.S. Silver $, was worth about 5/-, but thereafter it steadily declined following the persistent fall in the price of silver. After Japan adopted the gold standard in 1897 the yen was equivalent to about 2/- or about 50¢ U.S. Pre-war in 1941 it was officially quoted at about 22¢ U.S. or around 14d, but on the open market transactions took place at less than half the official rate. In 1962, the yen is worth a little more than ¼¢ or about four for a penny.

The importance of silver as a monetary basis has been declining for years. However the demand for it in this new age of photography, rockets, and space exploration has been increasing to such a degree that by Sept., 1962, the price of silver on the London market had reached the record figure of 100d an ounce, and was still advancing.

8. It is a fact that the old Japanese system of reckoning—before the people became historically minded and before commercial practices required something more accurate—was an "inclusive" system, and particularly was that so in calculations of due dates for religious services for the dead. On certain anniversary days—of which there were a great number—Buddhist services for the dead were conducted. Under the old "inclusive" system of reckoning, the third Buddhist anniversary service, for example, was conducted on what was actually the second anniversary.

The observance of a great number of anniversaries for the dead, became unduly costly and inconvenient, especially in large families. It was therefore not unusual for a number of anniversaries to be lumped together. This was considered permissible provided the services were held ahead of the due date and not after, the idea being that the spirits of the dead could not be kept waiting beyond the due dates.

To advance this explanation for holding an historical centenary of an international happening ahead of the due date—when pressed for an explanation—was a stratagem which did not impress those who knew of the political reasons behind the so-called "centenary" celebration.

9. See article entitled "The American Clipper Ship 'Lady Pierce'," reproduced from *China Mail*, which appeared in London *Times* and New York *Times*, Oct. 1854.

10. Quoted by R. Hildreth in *Japan and the Japanese*, Boston, 1860, pp. 534-5 as appearing in a copy of an address presented to Burrows by the Japanese.

11. *Ibid.*

12. See *Shades of the Past* pp. 54, 81, 179.

Notes

13. In their dealings with Burrows the Japanese authorities made frequent references to the "Emperor." Actually the Emperor was hidden away in Kyoto, leading a life of aimless inactivity, whilst the Tokugawa Shogunate was attempting to represent to the world that their Shogun in Yedo was the Emperor of Japan.
See *Shades of the Past*, p. 88.

14. See article "The American Clipper Ship 'Lady Pierce'," reproduced in London *Times* and New York *Times*, Oct. 1854.

15. *Ibid.*

16. The Japanese newspapers of 1959 carried condemnatory reports of several ill-mannered members of the Diet, who had purloined as souvenirs, sake cups and dishes, when leaving the Imperial wedding banquet at the Palace, on the occasion of the Crown Prince's wedding. Such a happening would have been unthinkable in the years preceding the war, but similar displays of bad manners did occur in the confused period immediately after the Restoration in 1868, when some boorish samurai from the provinces of Satsuma and Choshu were occupying positions of power in Tokyo. Cutlery and even full bottles of champagne were souvenired from Imperial banquets in those days.

> *The sermon, Mr. Bowdler, was bad
> enough, but the appendix was abo-
> minable.*

RULES AND REGULATIONS FOR THE PEACE,
ORDER AND GOOD GOVERNMENT OF
BRITISH SUBJECTS WITHIN
THE DOMINIONS OF THE TYCOON OF JAPAN

Whereas by an Order in Council providing for the
exercise of Consular Jurisdiction over British Subjects in Japan under 6 and 7 Victoria, Chapter 24,
dated the 23rd of January, 1860, power is given to
the Consul General and Consuls or Persons duly
authorized in such capacities in the dominions of
the Tycoon of Japan in the port, place or district in
which they may severally reside, to make rules and
regulations for the peace, order and good government of Her Majesty's subjects being within the
dominions of the aforesaid Tycoon, and for the observance of the Stipulations of any Treaty or Regulations appended thereto, made between Her Majesty, Her heirs, successors and the Tycoon of Japan.

Be it known that I, Rutherford Alcock, Her Majesty's Envoy Extraordinary, Minister Plenipotentiary
and Consul General in Japan, in consideration of
divers reasons affecting the peace, security and good
government of Her Majesty's subjects in Japan, and
also in consideration of divers other good and
weighty reasons, do hereby make the following Rules
and Regulations, to wit:

1. That British subjects shall not ride or drive

on any public road or highway in Japan in such a furious or careless manner as to endanger the persons being in any such public road or highway, nor ride or drive in any street of any town or village at a pace beyond that of a walk.

2. That all British subjects in passing along roads and streets in Japan shall, whether walking, riding or driving, observe the following rules of the road; that is to say, in meeting any person, cortège, procession or vehicle, they shall take and keep the left hand side of the road, and on overtaking and wishing to pass on before any such person, cortège, procession or vehicle, they shall leave the left hand side, and if practicable without collision, but not otherwise, they shall pass on the right side of the road.

3. That the discharge of firearms, whether by night or day in any place in Japan, except in such places and within such limits as shall be designated for the purpose by the Japanese Authorities in concurrence with Her Majesty's Consul, is hereby prohibited.

4. That no British subject shall go out in pursuit of game within the limits of the port of Kanagawa absolutely, or at any Port or other place, save under the authority and sanction of the Consul in writing.

5. That no British subject shall intrude into any private grounds without the invitation or leave of the owners, or into any battery, arsenal or other establishment of any Japanese not ordinarily open to the public.

6. That no British subject shall on any pretence

assault or offer any violence to any Japanese official or functionary.

7. That no British subject shall persist in any act of violence or outrage after he shall have been warned to desist therefrom, or in case any such British subject shall refuse or neglect immediately on being charged with the commission of any offence, to deliver a card bearing the stamp and seal of Her Majesty's Consul showing his identity, he shall be liable to arrest by any Japanese official duly empowered according to the Japanese law and by a Consul's warrant or licence.

8. That no British subjects shall in excursions within the limits assigned to each port, take up their residence in the towns or villages; nor without express permission granted in writing by the Consul, sleep during a night at any place or places away from the Foreign location at the Port where they are domiciled.

9. That every British subject who shall act contrary to any or either of the Rules and Regulations aforesaid shall be liable for each and every offence to pay a fine of $200, or to be imprisoned for one month.

10. That no British subject shall permit any Chinese in his employ to ride anywhere in Japan, except in immediate personal attendance on his master in travelling for a lengthened journey, and then not within a town or village; and that in case any such Chinese shall so ride with the permission of his master, the master shall be liable to pay a fine for every such offence of $200, or to be imprisoned.

Given under my hand and seal of office at Yeddo within the dominions of the Tycoon of Japan on the 19th day of November, 1861.

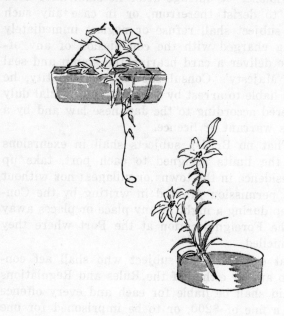

CHRONOLOGICAL
TABLE
INCIDENTAL
TO ARTICLES IN
THIS BOOK

1542	Portuguese arrived in Japan, following which Christianity was introduced.
1600	Dutch ship "de Liefde" arrived in Japan (Will Adams as pilot).
1609	Dutch commenced to trade with Japan.
1613	English East India Company's trading post opened at Hirado.
1614	Proclamation issued suppressing Christianity.
1622	Great martyrdoms of Christians at Nagasaki.
1623	English closed trading post and left Japan.
1636	Japanese forbidden to leave Japan.
1637	Shogun Iyemitsu decided to close Japan to the Western World.
1638	Seclusion policy proclaimed in Japan.
1639	Portuguese expelled from Japan.
1641	Dutch trading post confined to Deshima.
1690	Dr. Kaempfer arrived at Deshima.
1788	First English whaler arrived in Japan waters.
1792	Catherine II of Russia attempted to establish relations with Japan.
	Lieut Laxman landed at Hakodate.
1799	American ship "Eliza" arrived in Nagasaki.
1812	Captain Golownin and other Russians in captivity in Japan.
1848	Ranald MacDonald landed in Japan.
1849	Ranald MacDonald left Japan.

Chronological Table

July 1853	Commodore Perry's "black ships" arrived in Yedo Bay.
Feb./Mar. 1854	Commodore Perry returned and signed a treaty of peace and amity with Japan.
July 1854	Silas E. Burrows arrived in Japan on his clipper ship "Lady Pierce."
Oct. 1854	British signed similar treaty.
Aug. 1856	Townsend Harris first U.S. Consul General, landed at Shimoda.
July 1858	Townsend Harris signed treaty of amity and commerce with Japan.
July 1858	Lord Elgin arrived in Japan.
Aug. 1858	Anglo-Japanese treaty of commerce and friendship signed.
June 1859	Rutherford Alcock arrived as Britain's first Minister to Japan.
July 1859	Yokohama, Nagasaki, and Hakodate opened to foreign trade.
1860	First recorded ascent of Fuji by a foreigner.
1860	Japanese Mission to U.S.A.
July 1861	Japanese *ronin* attack British Legation in Yedo.
1862	First horse race meeting in Yokohama.
1863	Christ Church, Yokohama, opened.
1866	Great fire in Yokohama Foreign Settlement.
1 Jan. 1868	Hyogo and Osaka opened.
1868	Restoration of Emperor to power, and overthrow of Tokugawa Shogunate.
Nov. 1868	The Emperor left Kyoto and entered Yedo, which thereafter became known as "Tokyo" —the eastern capital.
25 Dec. 1868	First horse-race meeting in Kobe.
1870	The Sutherland stamps in use around this time.
1871	All classes of Japanese permitted to ride on horseback and enjoy privileges previously reserved for samurai class.
1877	Japanese Government rejects suggestions for Japanese emigration to Northern Territory of Australia.
1885	Pierre Loti came to Nagasaki.

1886–8   Grand Duke Alexander lived ashore at Nagasaki.

1899   Extraterritoriality came to an end.

1902   Lady Hope of Hope Diamond fame lived in Yokohama.

Aug. 1945   Occupation troops entered Japan.

May 1958   Yokohama City officially celebrated the so-called centenary of opening of port.

1 July 1959   Actual centenary of opening of Yokohama.

ABOUT THE AUTHOR

H. S. Williams was born in Melbourne, Australia, in 1898. He was headed for a scientific career, at first as a junior analyst in the Commonwealth Laboratory of Australia, then as a medical student at the Melbourne University. He was already seriously interested in the Japanese language and history as a hobby, and at the end of his third year in medicine he came to Japan on a holiday.

On arrival in Japan in 1919, an advertisement in the former *Japan Advertiser* caught his attention, and by replying to it he hoped to have the opportunity of seeing inside one of the hongs in Japan of which he had read so much. He later went for an interview, confident in the belief that he would not be engaged. To his great dismay he found that he was hired as an assistant in the old Scottish hong of Findlay Richardson & Co., Ltd. He thereupon temporarily postponed his return to Australia, but eventually decided to give up his career and make his future in Japan.

Later Williams became managing director of the silk firm of Cooper Findlay & Co., Ltd.

In 1941 he left Japan and enlisted in the Australian Army. He attained the rank of major and saw service in Africa, the Pacific, and Burma. He arrived back in Japan a few weeks after the surrender as a member of the Occupation Forces, and remained in the Australian Army in Japan until 1949 when he resumed his business career.

H. S. Williams is now managing director of A. Cameron & Co., Ltd. and was sole Trustee of the famous James Estate at Shioya near Kobe, which however he recently sold to Japanese interests.

In 1953, he commenced writing historical articles for various publications in Japan and abroad. He is recognized as an authority on the Foreign Settlements in Japan and is the author of two other books dealing with those days: *Tales of the Foreign Settlements in Japan* and *Shades of the Past or Indiscreet Tales of Japan.*

299

INDEX

"I proposed to bring a bill into Parliament to deprive an author who publishes a book without an index of the privilege of copyright, and, moreover, to subject him for his offence to a pecuniary penalty.
Lord Campbell—*Lives of Chief Justices* Vol 3, Pref.

Index

302

Index

Index

Index

Index

Index

Index

Other TUT BOOKS available:

TWO CENTURIES OF COSTUME IN AMERICA
by *Alice Morse Earle*

TYPHOON! TYPHOON! An Illustrated Haiku Sequence by *Lucile M. Bogue*

UNBEATEN TRACKS IN JAPAN: An Account of Travels in the Interior Including Visits to the Aborigines of Yezo and the Shrine of Nikko by *Isabella L. Bird*

ZILCH! The Marine Corps' Most Guarded Secret by *Roy Delgado*

Please order from your bookstore or write directly to:

CHARLES E. TUTTLE CO., INC.
Suido 1-chome, 2–6, Bunkyo-ku, Tokyo 112

or:

CHARLES E. TUTTLE CO., INC.
Rutland, Vermont 05701 U.S.A.